SHAKESPEARE SURVEY

SHAKESPEARE SURVEY

AN ANNUAL SURVEY OF
SHAKESPEARIAN STUDY & PRODUCTION

3

EDITED BY
ALLARDYCE NICOLL

Issued under the Sponsorship of

THE UNIVERSITY OF BIRMINGHAM
THE UNIVERSITY OF MANCHESTER
THE SHAKESPEARE MEMORIAL THEATRE
THE SHAKESPEARE BIRTHPLACE TRUST

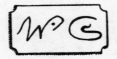

CAMBRIDGE
AT THE UNIVERSITY PRESS
1970

Published by the Syndics of the Cambridge University Press
Bentley House, 200 Euston Road, London N.W. 1
American Branch: 32 East 57th Street, New York, N.Y. 10022

ISBN 0 521 06416 3

First published 1950
Reprinted 1966 1970

Printed in Great Britain
at the University Printing House, Cambridge
(Brooke Crutchley, University Printer)

PREFACE

In accordance with the principle outlined in the Preface to the first volume of *Shakespeare Survey* —that the 'core' of each volume should consist of a general survey designed to indicate what the past fifty years have contributed to a particular aspect of Shakespearian study—the present volume has as its core a consideration of Shakespeare the man and the writer. "Studies in the Life of Shakespeare since 1900" reviews the biographical work that has been accomplished during this century, while "Shakespeare's Reading" deals with the poet engaged in his task of fashioning into plays what he has found among his books. Related to these two articles are a reproduction of Shakespeare's deposition in the Mountjoy case, a re-examination of the latest theories regarding the chronological order of his plays and a study of the possible influence of certain civil disturbances on the conception of *Coriolanus*.

In the survey of the Shakespearian collections in the British Museum appears the second of the articles devoted to accounts of libraries important because of their riches in this field, while "Shakespeare and Denmark" continues the series of contributions designed to give information concerning twentieth-century Shakespearian activities in diverse countries.

No volume of *Shakespeare Survey*, of course, could or should be without two other main sections—the one dealing with criticism, the other with the theatre. In this issue the former is represented by essays on the structural pattern of the tragedies and on *Measure for Measure*, the latter by a series of contributions devoted both to the stage of Shakespeare's time and to current productions.

It is gratifying to reflect that, apart from the reports of our Correspondents, *Shakespeare Survey* has the privilege of presenting here, alongside articles by British and American authors, essays from contributors in Bulgaria, Germany, Belgium and Denmark.

CONTRIBUTORS

M. St Clare Byrne
Lecturer in the History of Theatrical Art, Royal Academy of Dramatic Art

Robert de Smet
Dramatic Critic, Brussels

Una Ellis-Fermor
Hildred Carlile Professor of English, University of London, Bedford College

F. C. Francis
Keeper, Department of Printed Books, British Museum

Alf Henriques
Senior Master, Aurehöj State Grammar School, Denmark

C. Walter Hodges
Illustrator and Stage Designer

Clifford Leech
Senior Lecturer in English, University of Durham

James G. McManaway
Deputy Director, The Folger Shakespeare Library, Washington, U.S.A.

Marco Mincoff
Professor of English, University of Sofia, Bulgaria

J. M. Nosworthy
Lecturer in English, University of Wales, University College, Aberystwyth

E. C. Pettet
Lecturer in English, Goldsmith's College, University of London

Kurt Raeck
Intendant, Renaissance-Theater, Berlin

Charles J. Sisson
Lord Northcliffe Professor of Modern English Literature, University of London, University College

F. P. Wilson
Merton Professor of English, University of Oxford

vi

CONTENTS

Notes are placed at the end of each contribution

LIST OF ILLUSTRATIONS

[*Note*: The line-drawings in the article by C. WALTER HODGES are from original sketches by the author.]

STUDIES IN THE LIFE AND ENVIRONMENT OF SHAKESPEARE SINCE 1900

BY

CHARLES J. SISSON

It would be instructive to relate the history of Shakespearian biography to that of biography in general, from its beginnings in Ben Jonson's *Conversations* or the prefatory verses of the First Folio, on to the first formal *Life* prefaced by Rowe to his edition of 1709, and so to the foundations of modern documented study in Malone's *Life* and *History of the Stage* in their latest form in the *Variorum* of 1821. Certain main trends of development are plainly observable.

The collection of oral evidence or of tradition is superseded by the collection of facts resting upon documents, and the man Shakespeare is recorded in the setting of the London theatre-world with which in his life he was mostly concerned. From the history of the stage it was a short step to the study of the Elizabethan world in which Shakespeare lived, in London or in Stratford-upon-Avon, to complete the setting for the picture of his life. These two trends have been illuminated in some of the principal monuments of the study of Shakespeare's life and environment, as in Halliwell-Phillipps's *Outline of the Life of Shakespeare* (final edition of 1887) or Sir Edmund Chambers's *William Shakespeare, A Study of Facts and Problems* (1930), and in *Shakespeare's England: An Account of the Life and Manners of his Age* (1916). The renewed interest in the study of original documents was shown early in the present century by their collection in D. H. Lambert's *Cartæ Shakespeareanæ* (1904) and again in C. F. Tucker Brooke's *Shakespeare of Stratford* (1926).

But Shakespeare's own writings are also documents which cannot fail to furnish material for biographical interpretation, criticism merging into biography. It was Malone again who first attempted a chronology of the plays of Shakespeare, to fix what are, from one point of view at least, the most significant dates of his life. A third trend of development is the exploitation of this material as a reflection of the spiritual and intellectual life of the poet. German scholars fastened upon this aspect of the subject early in the nineteenth century, and created the philosopher-poet at the opposite pole from Pope's journeyman of the theatre. From this emerged also the picture of a soul in its famous Four Periods, which we owe mainly to Dowden's *Shakespeare: A Critical Study of his Mind and Art* (1875), and which prevails invulnerable to criticism as orthodox faith, supported on the Continent by such books as Brandes's *William Shakespeare* (1898).

Our material may therefore be grouped with some convenience under three headings, in the order of their importance within our present field of study, Documentary Study, Study of Environment, and Creative Biography, though there will inevitably be some overlapping and doubtful classification.

DOCUMENTARY STUDY

Betterton's famous pilgrimage to Stratford to gather material for Rowe's *Life* set an example for later biographers. Much is recorded by Malone, and a great deal of new information, supported by publication of the original documents, is presented in the various collections of Halliwell-Phillipps.

The foundation of the Shakespeare Birthplace Committee at Stratford in 1847, leading to the Birthplace Trust of 1866, established by Act of Parliament in 1891, has had important developments for scholarship. A library and repository of local archives grew, from 1863 onwards, of increasing volume and importance for Shakespearian study. Much is owed to its librarians. F. C. Wellstood's *Catalogue of the Books, Manuscripts, &c. in Shakespeare's Birthplace* appeared in 1925. Original records have been made available by the labours of R. Savage in *The Parish Registers of Stratford-on-Avon* (1897–1905) and *Minutes and Accounts of the Corporation of Stratford-on-Avon* (1921–30). The consequent exploration of Stratford archives, spreading out into Warwickshire, has been a feature of the present century. Sir Sidney Lee's *Stratford-on-Avon* (1907: originally issued in 1885) set the starting point for later research. Mrs C. C. Stopes and E. I. Fripp published a number of books, miscellanies of information, from 1901 to 1930. To Fripp's *Shakespeare Studies* (1930) we owe an account of John Brownsword, schoolmaster at Stratford in Shakespeare's boyhood. E. A. B. Barnard's *New Links with Shakespeare* (1930) brought fresh documentary material, and E. Vine Hall's two series of *Testamentary Papers* (1933) collected contemporary Stratford wills. Much of the manuscript material now accumulated in the Birthplace Library, however, still remains unexplored.

A variety of explanations has been offered of a period of Shakespeare's life during which no records are available, all resting upon the theory that Shakespeare left Stratford about 1587 for London, though his presence there is not on record until Greene's attack in 1592. It is argued that he was a schoolmaster in a Catholic family, or in an ordinary school, or was in a lawyer's office, or was picked up by a travelling company. A. C. Acheson's *Lost Years of Shakespeare* (1920) makes him a member of Pembroke's Company in 1591, an intimate of Southampton and an enemy of John Florio. Such theories—and there is no end to them—have as a rule little more foundation than the old stories of Shakespeare's excellence as a butcher's boy, or as a horse-holder in London. A more serious case is made out by O. L. Baker, in *Shakespeare's Warwickshire and the Unknown Years* (1938), for the belief that Shakespeare was a player in a travelling company, perhaps for a time in the household of a Lancashire gentleman, Alexander Hoghton, on the evidence of a will. What is beginning to emerge is the reasonable belief that his career as actor and dramatist began at an earlier date than was previously accepted, and scholars are now beginning to date his first plays as early as in 1588. Recent biographical and critical work is apt to look with suspicion upon the simple story which presents Shakespeare leaving Stratford for London in the eighties and retiring from London to Stratford in the second decade of the next century, in favour of the more natural and probable picture of the man dividing his time between the two centres of his interests throughout his life. The Stratford records are consistent with such a view.

A second hunting-ground for facts, the records in the great London repositories, had already yielded fruit in the eighteenth century, when Joseph Greene in 1747 discovered Shakespeare's will, which is preserved in Somerset House, the Principal Probate Registry. This Registry, with the Public Record Office, the Guildhall, and the Parish Registers of London churches, received increasing attention as the nineteenth century progressed. Much information was gained on stage-history, and consequently on Shakespeare's relations with his fellow-actors, and on the conditions of his literary work. Most of this would come more precisely under a survey of studies in the stage. But a remarkable discovery of direct biographical significance was made at the Public Record Office by C. W. Wallace of Nebraska in 1910, who was able to devote some years to intensive exploration of legal records. Among uncalendared bundles of Court of Requests papers he found a suit in which Shakespeare appeared as a witness in a matrimonial case in 1612, and was described as a gentleman of Stratford-upon-Avon (see Plates II and III). The evidence further relates that in 1604 he lodged with the family concerned, London French folk, in Silver Street, Cripplegate. What is perhaps more important is his signature appended to the record of his own evidence, the only certain piece of his writing apart from other already known signatures, and the only signature written freely and naturally, without impediment from illness or from the cramped space of labels on conveyancing documents.

The significance of this discovery became apparent when a great palaeographer, Sir Edward Maunde Thompson, made the signature a capital factor in his study *Shakespeare's Handwriting*, published in 1916. The application of this study to a manuscript play preserved at the British Museum, together with historical, bibliographical and literary analyses, resulted in a notable book, *Shakespeare's Hand in the Play of 'Sir Thomas More'* (1923), in which Thompson, A. W. Pollard, W. W. Greg, J. D. Wilson, and R. W. Chambers collaborated, adducing evidence that the Three Pages of Addition D in the manuscript were Shakespeare's holograph. The book led to much discussion, but the theory has on the whole received increasing assent, despite such criticism as it has received from Germany, as by L. L. Schücking, and from America, as by S. A. Tannenbaum. Both books contain valuable collotype facsimiles of the signatures and of the pages of the *More* manuscript. The whole of the manuscript was reproduced in a volume of J. S. Farmer's *Tudor Facsimile Texts*, unsatisfactorily owing to its condition. There has been much support for the further attribution to Shakespeare of Addition III in the same play, as by R. C. Bald in 1931 and in 1949 (see *Shakespeare Survey*, II).

C. W. Wallace also discovered Chancery proceedings of 1615 which showed Shakespeare concerned in the title-deeds of the Blackfriars Gatehouse in London, which was his property, in the last year of his life. These documents were additional to others bearing upon the property, known to Malone. The harvest may appear slight for so much labour, but the search is tempting, and Wallace had a notable successor in J. L. Hotson, a researcher of great diligence and high competence in record science as in scholarship. He undertook an examination of the records, among others, of the Court of Common Pleas and of Queen's Bench, with results which were published in two books, *Shakespeare versus Shallow* (1931), and *I, William Shakespeare* (1938). From the former we learn of petitions for surety of the peace in 1596 in which Shakespeare was concerned, from which Hotson argues that the poet was then living in Southwark, that William Gardiner, a well-known Surrey Justice of the Peace of ill-repute, may be identified as Shakespeare's butt in Justice Shallow, and that Shakespeare's company may then have been associated with Francis Langley at the Swan Theatre in Paris Garden. His conclusions, however, have met with resistance, as from T. W. Baldwin and J. E. Hannigan. In Hotson's later book, we learn much of interest concerning Thomas Russell, an overseer of Shakespeare's will, and other contemporaries. Hotson had already been able to identify the Walter Johnson who attested the Blackfriars Deed signed by Shakespeare as the Host of the Mermaid Inn (*Atlantic Monthly*, 1933). It is regrettable that much of the work of Wallace and Hotson was published in a form not easily accessible to scholars, in popular magazines.[1]

The war made further research of this nature impracticable, but it will doubtless attract other workers in more settled times. It may be doubted whether much information is likely to be gained with direct bearing upon Shakespeare, but it is probable enough that more general exploration, not focused upon the poet in person, will yet throw a fuller light upon his life both at Stratford and in London. The still unexplored jungle is extensive enough. An interesting discovery was made known in the Fourth Report of the Historical Manuscripts Commission upon the Rutland Manuscripts, in 1905. Payments of 43 shillings were made to Shakespeare and to Burbage for the provision of an *impresa* for a Tournament at Belvoir Castle in 1613, by the Earl of Rutland, a patron of the theatre. The payment is recorded in his steward's account-book there. The *impresa* itself has not survived.

There have been various attempts to add to the number of authentic signatures of Shakespeare by the discovery of books bearing his name in writing. There is little support for the signature in the Bodleian copy of Ovid's *Metamorphoses* (1502), but that in the British Museum copy of Florio's *Montaigne* (1603) is accepted by E. K. Chambers, though not by E. M. Thompson. A serious claim is made for a signature 'W. Shakspere' in a copy of William Lambard's *Archaionomia* (1568) purchased for the Folger Library in 1938. J. Q. Adams, in an article in the *Bulletin of the John Rylands Library*, XXVII (1943), maintained the authenticity of the signature. The signature is obscured by the ornament on the title-page over which it is written, and is best examined as an offset on the verso through a looking-glass. The excellent photograph here reproduced (see Plate I B) is thus made from the offset. A number of marked variations from any known signature or from normal Secretary hand causes doubts, after examination of the original, fortified by expert opinion of the reproduction, not least in respect of the *h* and of the style in general. It might perhaps even suggest a *memoriter* imitation of the Mortgage signature. The claim is, however, supported by the recency of the revelation of the signature in the process of ironing, as also by the reference to Shakespeare (written in later) as resident in Westminster.

The claim was made in the same journal in 1940 by Alan Keen on behalf of a copy of the 1550 issue of Hall's *Chronicle* that its numerous marginalia were annotations by Shakespeare, and that we see him here at work upon three of his English history plays. (The claim is modified in letters to the *Times Literary Supplement* in 1947.) Among other doubts, it has been pointed out that one of the plays, *Henry V*, certainly rests upon the 1587 Holinshed, and not on Hall. Clara Longworth-Chambrun claimed in 1938, in her book *Shakespeare Rediscovered*, that a copy of the 1587 Holinshed in private hands bore marks and writing by Shakespeare, and was his own copy. It has not, however, been submitted to expert opinion.

An elaborate work on *The Shakespeare Documents* by B. R. Lewis in 1941, unsatisfactory as it was in many respects, had the merit of placing at the disposal of scholars a collection of facsimiles of the more important documents in chronological order, to set alongside the meticulous transcripts to be found in E. K. Chambers's *William Shakespeare*. One of the most valuable services made to scholarship in the present century is, indeed, the ample provision of dependable collotype facsimiles of biographical and literary documents.

The twentieth century has been unable to add to our knowledge in respect of the iconography of Shakespeare. The Stratford bust by Jansen continues to receive assaults, of course, though no evidence has been adduced against the essential authenticity, even if not done from life. Mrs Stopes was able to give further details concerning the repair of the monument in the eighteenth century. The engraving by Droeshout in the First Folio has a similar claim, but no more, to authenticity. No other representations have any such claim, though attempts have been made from time to time to establish them, as recently for a portrait in private hands, formerly known to Halliwell-Phillipps. M. H. Spielmann's monograph, *Shakespeare's Portraiture* (1924), is the fullest treatment of the question, and is on the whole unchallenged, except by uninformed opinion.

STUDY OF ENVIRONMENT

The study of the setting for Shakespeare's life and work offers a limitless field beyond the scope of definition. It would be difficult to exclude almost any aspect of Elizabethan and Jacobean scholarship from its share in the illumination of his life or his writings. This became evident in a notable book published in the centenary year of 1916, *Shakespeare's England*, in which the thread of illustrations from Shakespeare ran through an Elizabethan encyclopaedia of knowledge. The vast amount of recent work on the history of the London and provincial stages, again, or upon the drama in general, all has indirect bearing upon Shakespeare. Of this, a separate survey must take account. But there are certain regions of knowledge which have been explored of late with a more especial reference to Shakespeare, to very significant purpose.

E. A. Plimpton made a good start in 1933 with his book *The Education of Shakespeare* on the educational horizon of Shakespeare's outlook. This was vastly developed by two voluminous and important works of T. W. Baldwin. *William Shakspere's Petty School* (1943) deals amply with the process and substance of his elementary schooling, literary and religious, in great detail, and concludes further that Shakespeare's own religion was orthodox Protestantism, a conclusion arrived at in a different approach by Cumberland Clark (*Shakespeare and the Supernatural*, 1933). The opposite view has been stated again from time to time, as by I. J. Semper in the *Catholic World* (February 1943), who suggests that between 1585 and 1592 Shakespeare was a domestic teacher in some Catholic family, to set against A. Gray's theory of his ushership in the family of Sir Henry Goodere (1926). The general trend of evidence adduced in recent years leads to the belief that John Shakespeare was a Catholic recusant. This particular debate is always clouded by the terms Protestant and Catholic, which should perhaps be replaced for this period by conformist and recusant as a truer basis for argument. T. W. Baldwin's further contribution in this field, *William Shakspere's Small Latine & Lesse Greeke* (2 vols., 1944), dealt at large with the grammar school, with the later stages of educational development, and the influences of classical training in grammar and rhetoric in the Elizabethan world, and suggests reasons for considering the theory that Aubrey put forward, of Shakespeare's early period of schoolmastering. But the chief conclusion is to set the level and significance of Shakespeare's grammar-school literary education higher than would before have been agreed.

The question of Shakespeare's own reading, so closely connected with these matters, has received much attention ever since Richard Farmer's *Essay on the Learning of Shakespeare* (1767). The early years of the century showed the main lines of interest in two books, H. R. D. Anders's *Shakespeare's Books* and J. C. Collins's essay "Shakespeare as a Classical Scholar" in *Studies in Shakespeare*, the latter pressing against Farmer's view the internal evidence for Shakespeare's first-hand knowledge of his Latin and even Greek authorities. The general trend of subsequent study has indicated the reasonable belief that Shakespeare was no classical scholar in the narrow sense, but was far from being dependent upon translations at any rate for his Latin poets. Attempts to prove first-hand knowledge of Plato or of Attic tragedy have not brought conviction. But there has been no serious scholarly support for the view that another author must be sought for Shakespeare's poems and plays, arguing from the premise that they require a writer of higher social status or of university education, though the output of books maintaining this view, in favour of Bacon or Derby or other claimants, continues apace. The mythology, thought, and literature of the classical world was part of the air Shakespeare breathed, with all intelligent Elizabethans. So too of the great French and Italian writers. And the evidence is adequate that he gave close study, not only to the *Metamorphoses* of Ovid, but also to North's *Plutarch*, to Florio's *Montaigne*, to Holinshed, and to a considerable group of other books which can be listed. The list of his books has been enlarged occasionally, as, for example, by Thomas P. Harrison Jr., who adduces evidence to show that he used the 1572 *Secret of Secrets* (*J. Q. Adams Memorial Studies*, 1948), and by Hardin Craig, who demonstrates that he used Wilson's *Arte of Rhetorique* (*Studies in Philology*, 1931). Sir Israel Gollancz's *The Shakespeare Classics* (1907–13) reproduced some part of his library of books, in continuation of earlier work giving extracts from Holinshed or Plutarch, and many studies have been published illustrating Shakespeare's manifest reading of, *inter alia*, Montaigne or Elyot. A. Quiller-Couch's *Shakespeare's Workmanship* illustrated the process of his reading and craftmanship. What emerges beyond reasonable doubt is the picture of a hard-reading man of letters engaged upon poetry and the drama, exploring literature for subjects and material to his taste or suitable for the demands of his company.

A man does not, however, nourish his mind on books alone. It has been a notable feature of twentieth-century literary studies in general that literature has been increasingly interpreted in terms of its intellectual and historical background, and that a number of books have sought to construct the main constituent elements in the atmosphere breathed by men of letters, and by their readers or their audiences, in each century, as also of the forces of change and disruption in systems of thought to which Shakespeare for one could not fail to be submitted, being 'for all time', no doubt, but being certainly 'of his age' none the less.

The two volumes of *Shakespeare's England* (1916) gave an encyclopaedic account of the life and thought of the age, with an ample supply of illustrations from contemporary sources, each chapter from the pen of an authority upon his subject. It was planned by Sir Walter Raleigh, and brought to completion by Sir Sidney Lee and C. T. Onions, and is an indispensable book of reference for students of Shakespeare, as well as an absorbing book in its own right as a picture of Elizabethan life. A delightful book by D. H. Madden, *The Diary of Master William Silence* (1897 and 1907), re-created the intimate life of the countryside and its sports, with some direct bearings upon Shakespeare's own memories reflected in his plays. F. P. Wilson's *The Plague in Shakespeare's London* (1927) illuminates an aspect of life of importance to Shakespeare and to his theatre for very practical reasons. The general features of Elizabethan life were illustrated in lively works by J. D. Wilson and M. St Clare Byrne. And a valiant enterprise of G. B. Harrison produced a series of *Elizabethan Journals* (1928–33), which covered each year from 1591 to 1603, in a form resembling a personal diary of daily matters of importance, derived from a far-reaching study of contemporary printed books, memoirs, and State Papers. The journal records also the publication of books and the performances of plays, matters of significance to all sharing in the intellectual life of London, not least to Shakespeare the poet and dramatist. J. E. Neale's *Queen Elizabeth* has provided the necessary historical background, hitherto lacking, in an authoritative modern study of the reign, and of the institutions of importance to her subjects.

One of the principal desiderata in this connexion is a full and clear account, resting upon first-hand knowledge of procedure and proceedings, with illustrations and examples, of the principal Courts of Law in Elizabethan England. The account given in *Shakespeare's England* is in many respects misleading and erroneous, not least with regard to Star Chamber. The separate treatments of each Court in the publications of the Selden Society do not meet the need. Such knowledge was, in fact, part and parcel of Shakespeare's mind and experience.

The general outlook of the Elizabethan intellectual world, on the other hand, has received much attention of late. The main trend of scholarship has been away from the simpler view which represents Shakespeare as the man of the Renaissance in the sense that a dividing line exists between the Renaissance and the Middle Ages, and in the direction of a view that presents continuity in a stream of thought merging the medieval world in the modern world. W. W. Lawrence, in his remarkable *Shakespeare's Problem Comedies* (1931), could take it as an accepted view that medieval England was implicit in Elizabethan England, and in Shakespeare's mind, and could rail safely at the notion of a Chinese Wall dividing the one from the other. The foundations of the Elizabethan world of thought were studied in the light of this fundamental truth by a number of philosophic scholars to great effect. B. Willey's *The Seventeenth Century Background* (1934) perhaps led the way. Hardin Craig's *The Enchanted Glass* (1936) covers a vast field of thought in the Elizabethan mind in its compressed and pregnant mastery of the subject. T. Spencer followed with *Shakespeare and the Nature of Man* (1942). E. M. W. Tillyard's *The Elizabethan World Picture* (1943), with its successor applying its main conceptions, *Shakespeare's History Plays* (1944), set out luminously the cosmic philosophy which was part of Shakespeare's being, and which affects the interpretation of his writings. The medieval bases of this world-picture appear plainly, in a geocentric world, in which the Chain of Being governs macrocosmos and microcosmos in a hierarchy of law and order.

Other writers emphasize the importance of this theme, and illustrate the significance of the chief disintegrators of medieval thought in the transition to the modern world, Copernicus in the heavens hitherto dominated by Ptolemy, Machiavelli in state-craft and political thought, and Montaigne in ethical thought, with wide implications. Alfred Harbage's *As They Liked It* (1947) is important for the study of Shakespeare's moral thought, and D. C. Allen's *Star-Crossed Renaissance* (1941) deals thoroughly with astrology.

A factor of special importance in the background of Shakespeare's literary and dramatic work has been much considered of late, the audience for which Shakespeare catered in the theatres performing his plays. The subject opened up by A. C. Bradley's essay in *Oxford Lectures on Poetry* (1909), and by C. J. Sisson's *Le Goût Public et le Théâtre Elisabéthain* (1922), was developed by A. Harbage in his *Shakespeare's Audience* (1941), and by H. S. Bennett in his British Academy Lecture of 1944. We have moved far away from the traditional view of an audience of groundlings resisting the art and poetry of a great dramatist. "The Elizabethans were trained listeners", wrote Bennett, and adduced sermons as examples of their listening. The universal study of rhetoric, and delight in it, is reflected in the poetry and drama of the time, as in Shakespeare's own education and evident tastes, and in colloquial English of the time.

The sum and substance of this work, and of a great deal more on various aspects of these matters, is that Shakespeare now appears both to biographer and to critic as moving in a world of thought as of fact both infinitely more fully realized and understood than before, as living and having his being in an English landscape set in a country that has been intensively explored and set on record. There is little excuse left for the exercise of entirely free imagination that ignores the immense accumulation of facts and knowledge within which imagination must properly be bounded.

CREATIVE BIOGRAPHY

There is obviously a certain awkwardness in subsuming under the same section of this survey a biography by Sir Sidney Lee and one by, say, Frank Harris. But it is clear that no formal biography can confine itself to a statement of facts and to logical deductions from facts. All biography worth the name is bound to be interpretative, and in a measure creative in that sense. The difference lies in the scholarly conscience of the biographer, whether interpretation shall be limited by certainty of knowledge, or whether our Shakespeare shall be created anew by the pallid glow of intuition after the image of the biographer. We have had a great deal of both during the present century, both in England and abroad.

Among what we might call orthodox biographies, Sidney Lee's *Life of Shakespeare*, which first appeared in 1898, was revised and enlarged in 1925. Of this *Life* it might be said that it eschewed most completely any intrusion by the biographer upon the facts recorded. But the very self-denial of the biographer had its defects. To dismiss the *Sonnets*, for example, as a series of *pastiches*, with no relation to the thoughts and feelings of their writer, could not fail to evoke protest and resistance. On the Continent, on the other hand, the *Lives* of Brandes, translated into English in 1898, and of Brandl (1922), gave full play to the imagination of their authors, who assumed that Shakespeare's writings offered clues in all directions to his readers concerned above all with his spiritual biography. *A Life of William Shakespeare* (1923) by J. Q. Adams, a distinguished American scholar, sought to preserve the equilibrium of facts and interpretation (though to describe Stratford as a hamlet is apt to lead into errors of importance). But even E. K. Chambers, in his *William Shakespeare, A Study of Facts and Problems* (1930), the title of which proclaims the deliberate objectivity of his approach, cannot escape from the inevitable attempt to explain certain facts, for example, the state of the text of *Timon of Athens*, as symptoms of a state of mind, or as evidence of experiences, forming part of a biography. It is well-nigh impossible to deny some scope at least to that intellectual curiosity which can only be satisfied by imagination. Frank guessing on these lines is perhaps on the whole better than a series of such suggestions, in which the biographer protects himself by a guarded 'it is not impossible' or 'some have thought', as those which are a feature of Sidney Lee's *Life*.

Two more recent books, both notable, point the moral in their titles that it is vain to attempt to separate historical fact from the writings of a poet, which are also facts in their own right, in the records of a great life. P. Alexander's *Shakespeare's Life and Art* (1938) and Hazelton Spencer's *Art and Life of William Shakespeare* (1939) represent perhaps in their order of words the comparative bias of the biographers in their syntheses of these capital factors, the latter being more subject to the influence of Dowden's powerful suggestion. The extreme of resistance to the theory of Shakespeare's life as itself a drama reflected directly in his plays was expressed in

C. J. Sisson's British Academy Lecture, *The Mythical Sorrows of Shakespeare* (1934). So also R. W. Chambers's lecture of 1937, *The Jacobean Shakespeare*, scouted the concept of a Shakespeare driven to pessimism in a new and pessimistic era. A brilliant essay leading far in the opposite sense, independent of Dowden, and backed by the whole panoply of scholarship, was J. D. Wilson's *The Essential Shakespeare* (1932) in which Lascelles Abercrombie's *Plea for the Liberty of Interpreting* before the British Academy (1930) was obeyed to the full. The pendulum, swinging from pole to pole, from Lee to Brandes, is gradually settling to rest in the centre, and few would now either accept the full lyrical interpretation of the plays, or deny to them their reflection of the growth and the increasing maturity of a poet's mind through which experience was transmuted into art as in a crucible.

A considerable group of books remains, in which more freedom is given to imagination and to individual interpretation of the evidence offered by the plays, in the attempt to reconstruct the life or character of Shakespeare. They vary from critical biographical adventures to creative work in the form of a dráma, or of novels like Frayne Williams's *Mr Shakespeare of the Globe* (1941), in which an intolerable deal of imaginative sack moistens the dry half-pennyworth of factual bread to make a meal for readers hardened to the menu of the film, or the more scholarly and more truly creative novel by John Brophy, *Gentleman of Stratford* (1939). An earlier novel by Clara Longworth-Chambrun appeared in French in 1934 as *Mon Grand Ami Shakespeare, Souvenirs de John Lacy*, and in English in 1935 as *My Shakespeare, Rise!* G. B. Shaw's play, *The Dark Lady of the Sonnets* (1910), had successfully exploited the theatrical possibilities of fictional biography, resting upon a popular romantic interpretation of the *Sonnets*, not without some scholarly support. Other plays on the commercial stage have introduced Shakespeare into their dramatis personae. It has been estimated by M. H. Spielmann in 1922 that sixty-nine plays, in six languages, had already been written presenting Shakespeare on the stage, since 1800.

A great number of attempts have been made, from all levels of scholarship and understanding, to assess or re-create Shakespeare the Man, a title often used for such studies, in article or book, ranging from the impressive lecture of that great Shakespearian A. C. Bradley (1910) to the rhapsody in book-form of the journalist F. Harris's *The Man Shakespeare* (1909) which sought to give such satisfaction to curiosity concerning Shakespeare as may only be justified from close personal knowledge supported by intimate documentation in private letters. More intelligible attempts have been made to re-create the internal and spiritual biography of Shakespeare from the study of his writings. *The Voyage to Illyria* (1937), by K. Muir and S. O'Loughlin, sought for evidence of his experience in his imagery and in his use of his sources, a method which is obviously uncertain and personal in application. A recent book, *The Real Shakespeare: A Counterblast to Commentators*, by W. Bliss (1947), reproving such speculations, falls into its own private pit of other speculations. Ivor Brown's *Shakespeare* (1949), while resting upon hard and generous reading, exploits 'internal evidence' to the full in the search for his own conception of the man, and has many ingenious suggestions to offer, such as the identification of 'Anne Whateley of Temple Grafton' as a rival to Ann Hathaway, losing Shakespeare as a husband only by one day. But such variations of name are common in similar documents in Elizabethan archives, e.g. 'Anne Elsnor' for 'Anne Elsdon' in another marriage licence.

At the other extreme, we have scholars at work pursuing clues in documentary fact linked up with clues from the writings of Shakespeare in the search for elucidation of his personal interests and career. In Clara Longworth-Chambrun's voluminous work it is difficult to separate knowledge from free interpretation and even fancy, as in her account of the relations between Shakespeare and Sir Thomas Lucy in *Shakespeare Rediscovered* (1937), which appear as a side-issue in Shakespeare's life of intimacy in Catholic circles. *A Study of 'Love's Labour's Lost'* by Frances A. Yates (1936), a work of serious scholarship, drives to their utmost limit the clues suggested by this play and by contemporary history, and by the phrase occurring in the play, 'the school of night', to which so much attention has been paid in recent years, ever since A. Acheson, in *Shakespeare and the Rival Poet* (1903), argued for the existence of an organization known as 'The School of Night', for Chapman's *Shadow of Night* as a poem of this School, and for *Love's Labour's Lost* as a satire upon it. From this Miss Yates proceeded, led by J. D. Wilson's edition of the play (1923), to a full structure representing Shakespeare as an intimate of the Southampton circle, a friend of John Eliot and enemy of Florio (who was satirized as Holofernes according to Clara Longworth-Chambrun in 1921 in her *Giovanni Florio*), a Catholic schoolmaster in Southampton's household, and the mouthpiece of criticism by the Essex-Southampton group against the Raleigh group, against the School of Atheism or of Night which included Raleigh, Chapman, Henry Percy, Stanley, Sir George Carey, Marlowe and Harriot. It may be questioned whether such work should not have been recorded in an earlier section of this survey, but the extent of surmise involved, and the uncertainty of the premises of the argument, not least of the phrase 'the school of night' as it is used in this play, suggest to a majority of scholars that the theory, stated as biographical fact, rests more upon construction than upon reconstruction. The general attitude towards this fascinating subject is that *Love's Labour's Lost* is certainly topical in so far that it reflects the interests of polite society at the time, but that further conclusions are doubtful. A poem of 1594, *Willobie his Avisa*, has been carefully studied, as by G. B. Harrison in his edition of 1926, with the conclusion that it was written against Southampton and his circle, including Shakespeare, as a reply to *Lucrece*, written as an attack upon Raleigh. A further conclusion was that Henry Willoughby's 'familiar friend W. S.' was William Shakespeare, and that his amour with a Dark Lady is involved in the story. The evidence, tenuous as it is, gained some support from further clues furnished by J. L. Hotson in 1937. But it may well be asked whether the description of 'W. S.' as an 'old player' in 1594 could properly apply to Shakespeare, then some thirty years of age.

The *Sonnets* too, closely linked up with these speculations, have been subjected to biographical exegesis, with the help of surmise and imagination. They have been described, for over a hundred years, as 'Autobiographical Poems', and Gerald Massey could write in 1872 of *The Secret Drama of Shakespeare's Sonnets*. Edition after edition has rearranged the sonnets to suit this or that version of the story involved. The Dark Lady and the Rival Poet concerned have set minds roving at large over the known Elizabethan world, with Mary Fitton, Mrs Davenant, and Willoughby's 'Avisa' as favourites for the one claim, and Drayton and Chapman for the other, in a long series of books to which the present century has added many. In the Fair Youth, Southampton and Essex claim the suffrages of J. A. Fort and Lord Alfred Douglas respectively. The game goes on merrily, and Miss Barbara Mackenzie in 1946, in *Shakespeare's Sonnets: Their Relation to his Life*, offered material for a novel, if not the novel itself, improving on A. Acheson's *Shakespeare's Sonnet Story* (1922).

Warnings in plenty, on the other hand, have been given against pressing too far the topical or autobiographical interpretation of the plays or the poems, upon which so many inventions or guesses are based. O. J. Campbell's *Comicall Satyre and Shakespeare's Troilus and Cressida* (1938) and *Shakespeare's Satire* (1943) urge upon us the conception rather of an artist engaged deliberately upon art-forms, and not swayed by personal experience, thus cutting at the root the luxuriant growth of imaginative biographical interpretation. Indeed, in the general movement of thought to-day, the conception of Shakespeare as artist bids fair to obliterate the 'native wood-notes wild' which attract sentimental idolatry and romance, or the journeyman of the stage oblivious to art.

The extreme of such free speculation, unimpeded by common sense as by exact knowledge, is the unhappy ambition to replace the life of William Shakespeare as author of his own works by the life of some other improbable and impossible writer, whether Bacon, Fulke Greville, the Earl of Oxford, or the Earl of Derby, as urged in intricate argument, resting upon imaginary allusions or cyphers, in an endless series of books, by a succession of writers such as Percy Allen or Abel Lefranc, to cite two names of higher repute than most, in the present century. J. M. Robertson took the trouble to dismiss one branch of the heresy in his conclusive *The Baconian Heresy: A Confutation* (1913).

CONCLUSION

The sum-total of the fruits of half a century of study thus surveyed can seem disappointing only to the ill-informed, even when we consider the labour expended, the army of students, and the sea of publications, which so impressed C. H. Herford in his excellent sketch of *Recent Shakespearian Investigation* in 1923. The further knowledge gained is of the highest importance, though the fresh certainties achieved are few in number. The Requests suit, with its signature above all, is of capital significance even apart from the signature. J. L. Hotson's researches into Shakespeare's relations with Thomas Russell opened up a circle of friends and acquaintances such as before could only be guessed at. And the Rutland *impresa* illuminates the position of both Shakespeare and Burbage in polite society.

More could hardly be hoped for, after the enthusiastic and competent pursuit of information in previous centuries. The fact is, of course, that we know far more about Shakespeare than could reasonably be expected by those who are aware of the paucity of our knowledge of other Elizabethan dramatists. And it is well to realize that what we have learned that is new is in accordance with what has long been known, new knowledge fortifying old. The work of Chambers, Wallace, and Hotson amplifies and consolidates what Malone and Halliwell-Phillipps knew long ago, and bears out the records of contemporary opinion. There is no conflict, no dissonance. The Stratford Man, and the London Dramatist and Poet, are plainly one and the same, sharing the one person and the one life.

The man 'civil in his demeanour' that Chettle, his contemporary and fellow-dramatist, knew personally, is the same man who appears in the pages of the Court of Requests. There Wallace found the story of a man at home and trusted in the house of the French Huguenot family of Mountjoy in Silver Street, the man to whom they turned for help in family affairs and who gave that help, forwarding Mary Mountjoy's marriage with Stephen Belott, her father's apprentice, at the request of her mother. And in later years he spoke kindly of Stephen, when there was a family split on Mary's dowry, and even when father and apprentice alike were criticized by their own church and colony. He 'was a very honest fellow', and 'was a very good and industrious servant', said William Shakespeare.

So also we can look with new eyes upon the tributes in verse paid to Shakespeare in the First Folio when we are given good reason to know, as we are by Hotson, that Ben Jonson was not the only panegyrist who was a personal friend of Shakespeare, that Leonard Digges was stepson of the overseer of his will, Thomas Russell, and that James Mabbe was the friend of Digges. It would seem that Shakespeare moved in the right circles in Elizabethan society after all, and was at home with Oxford dons among others.

The mass of instruction added, on the other hand, to enlarge our indirect acquaintance with the material needed for a life of Shakespeare, is very considerable, whether it be in relation to the conditions under which he lived and worked as actor, dramatist, and poet, or to the background of his thought and his art in the intellectual atmosphere of his day. It is perhaps in the exploration, definition and illumination of this background that the last fifty years have contributed most to the increase of the knowledge desired. For it is, after all, the poet and dramatist who is the principal object of our interest. The joyful fact is that there appears to be, from all the knowledge gained, the completest harmony and congruency between the man as we know him, in his individual being and social relations, with the writer and thinker; a man and an artist at home alike in the world into which he was born and in the medium of the art which he practised.

A capital fact added to our total of knowledge is the high probability of Shakespeare's contribution to the play of *Sir Thomas More*, and of the existence in the British Museum of three pages of dramatic manuscript in his own writing, written in the very heat of composition, straight from the anvil of his genius, a picture of the poet more faithful and more illuminating than any existing image by painter or sculptor.

It may well be that the principal advance which we owe to the present century concerning Shakespeare is the realization that his is above all the record of the life of a man of letters, a conscious artist moved by a literary ambition which was the directing force, and the mainspring, of his actions. Upon this conclusion all the best in interpretation of his life and work in recent years has converged. And it is, after all, but a reaffirmation of much of the earliest contemporary evidence that we possess, which was clouded for so long by the misunderstandings of later centuries.

NOTE

1. The present article was written and in proof before the appearance of Leslie Hotson's *Shakespeare's Sonnets Dated*, in which several articles originally contributed to magazines have been reprinted.

SHAKESPEARE'S DEPOSITION IN THE BELOTT-MOUNTJOY SUIT

[The Belott-Mountjoy Suit was discovered by C. W. Wallace, *Nebraska University Studies*, x (1910), 263; for transcripts of various parts of the documents, see E. K. Chambers, *William Shakespeare*, II (1930), 90–5.]

The following transcript of Shakespeare's deposition, reproduced in Plates II and III, has been made by Arthur Brown and checked by Charles J. Sisson. Square brackets denote deletions in the manuscript; pointed brackets denote mutilations in the manuscript (with the number of letters missing, when determinable, indicated by dots within the brackets); half-square brackets denote interlineations.

William Shakespeare of Stratford vpon Avon in the Countye of Warwicke gen*tleman* of the age of xlviii yeres or thereaboutₑ sworne and *ex*amined the daye and yere abouesaid deposethe & sayethe

1. To the first Interrogatory this deponent sayethe he knowethe the *partyes plaintiff* and deffendt and hathe ⌜know⟨..⟩⌝ them bothe as he now remembrethe for the space of tenne yeres or thereaboutₑ/

2. To the second Interr this deponent sayeth he ⌜did⌝ knowe the compl*ainant* when he was servant wᵗʰ the deffendant, and that duringe the tyme of his the complainantₑ service wᵗʰ the said deffendt [he] he the said Compl*ainant* to this deponentₑ knowledge did well and honestly behaue him selfe, but to this deponentₑ remembrance he hath not heard the deffendt confesse that he had gott any great proffitt and comodytye by the [said] service of the said compl*ainant*, but this depont saithe he verely thinkethe that the said compl*ainant* was A very good and industrious servant in the said service And more he canott depose to the said Interr*ogatory*/

3. To the third Interro*gatory* this deponent sayethe that it did evydentlye appeare that the said defft did all the tyme of the said complainantₑ service wᵗʰ him beare and shew great good will and affecceon towardₑ the said compl*ainant*, And that he hathe ⌜hard⌝ the defft and his wyefe diuerse and sundry tymes saye and reporte that the said compl*ainant* was a very honest fellowe: And ⌜this depont sayethe⌝ that the said deffendant did make A mocion vnto the compl*ainant* of marriadge wᵗʰ the said Mary in the bill mencioned beinge the said deffendantₑ sole chyld and daughter and willinglye offerred to perform the same yf the said Compl*ainant* shold seeme to be content and well like thereof: And further this deponent sayethe that the said deffendantₑ wyeffe did sollicitt and entreat this deponent to moue and perswade the said Compl*ainant* to effect the said marriadge and accordingly this deponent did moue and perswade the compl*ainant* therunto: And more to this Interrogatye he cannott depose/

4. To the ffourth Interro*gatory* this deponent sayth that the defend*ant* promissed to giue the said Compl*ainant* A porcion [of monney and goodₑ] in marriad⟨..⟩ wᵗʰ Marye his daughter:/ but what certayne ⌜porcion⌝ [some] he Remembethe not/ nor when to be payed [yf any some weare promissed,] nor knoweth that the defend*ant* promissed the [defendt w] *plaintiff* twoe hundered poundₑ wᵗʰ his daughter Marye at the tyme of his decease./ But sayth that the *plaintiff* was dwellinge wᵗʰ the defend*ant* in his house And they had Amongeste them selues manye Conferences about there marriadge wᶜʰ⟨   ⟩ was Consumated and Solempnized. And more he cann⟨   ⟩¹

5. To the vᵗʰ Interro*gatory* this Deponent sayth he can saye noth⟨...⟩ touching any parte or poynte of the same Interro*gatory* for he knoweth not what Implementₑ and necessaries of houshould stuffe the def*endant* gaue the *plaintiff* in marriadge wᵗʰ his daughter Marye./   William Shak*per*

¹ What appears to be a *t* is a descender from the damaged line above. Sir Hilary Jenkinson, who examined the document with us, confirmed this reading.

SHAKESPEARE'S READING[1]

BY

F. P. WILSON

John Selden is reported to have said: "No man is the wiser for his learning: it may administer matter to work in, or objects to work upon, but wit and wisdom are born with a man." For two and a half centuries we have been asking how far learning administered matter for Shakespeare's wit and wisdom to work in or objects for them to work upon. If a friend had put to Shakespeare the Second Outlaw's question "Have you the tongues?", would he have answered, with Valentine, "My youthful travail therein made me happy"?

Soon after his death two poets wrote about Shakespeare in terms that suggest that his learning, that is, his knowledge of Greek and Latin, was scanty. One of them said that he had "small Latin, and less Greek": the other praised him as Fancy's child, warbling "his native wood-notes wild". But Jonson and Milton are among the most learned scholar-poets this country has produced; and if we test Shakespeare, as perhaps they were testing him, by their own severe standards of scholarship, then indeed we must say he had not even the "edging or trimming of a scholar".

In the eighteenth century two extreme points of view were expressed. On the one hand, critics like John Upton and Zachary Gray, bent on making Shakespeare 'polite', found him learned in both the tongues and traced to classical originals many a passage of natural description and many a moral sentiment. On the other hand, Richard Farmer, a man deeply read in Elizabethan literature, traced to many a forgotten English book the learning which the dramatist was supposed to have taken direct from the classics and went so far as to state that he "remembered perhaps enough of his *school-boy* learning to put the *Hig, hag, hog*, into the mouth of Sir Hugh Evans; and might pick up in the Writers of the time, or the course of his conversation, a familiar phrase or two of French or Italian: but his *Studies* were most demonstratively confined to *Nature* and *his own Language*".

To-day, our estimate of Shakespeare's learning will not be pitched so high as Upton's, yet neither will it be pitched so low as Farmer's. We shall say he had "small Latin and *no* Greek"; but that his Latin, small indeed in comparison with Jonson's, was yet sufficient to make him not wholly dependent upon translation. We shall say with the actor Will Beeston that he "understood Latin pretty well" and mean by that much what Jonson meant by 'small Latin'. That he read Ovid as well as Golding's Ovid, some Seneca and Virgil as well as English Seneca and Virgil is, I think, proved. Nor is it in the least unlikely. He lived in an age that respected learning, an age that built its educational system upon the belief that in the classics alone, the sacred writings excepted, was to be found "the best that is known and thought in the world". Consequently some knowledge of Latin was possessed by all who had had a grammar-school education. To find a writer wholly ignorant of Latin we have to descend as low in the literary hierarchy as John Taylor, the Water Poet, who acknowledged that his 'scholarship' was but 'scullership' and that in Latin he proceeded only from 'possum' to 'posset'. So far as his attainments in learning go, Shakespeare may be likened to another popular dramatist. No university wit and schooled we do not know where, Thomas Dekker could yet read Latin with some facility. He could and did translate sentences from the Church Fathers from that popular and long-lived anthology *Flores Doctorum* assembled by a thirteenth-century Irishman, Thomas Hibernicus; and he could describe the terrors of hell in words borrowed from Sebastian Barradas's vast commentary on the four Gospels, a work which has not been translated into English, and (it seems safe to say) never will be. Shakespeare could have done as much, if he had cared.

On these matters there is general agreement. Few who have read through T. W. Baldwin's treatise on *William Shakspere's Small Latine & Lesse Greeke* will have the strength to deny that Shakespeare acquired the grammar-school training of his day in grammar, logic, and rhetoric; that he could and did read in the originals some Terence and Plautus, some Ovid and Virgil; that possessing a reading knowledge of Latin all those short-cuts to learning in florilegia and compendia were at his service if he cared to avail himself of them; and that he read Latin not in the spirit of a scholar but of a poet. But granted that Shakespeare could read Latin, is there any evidence that he had access to any modern tongue other than his own? Here, I think, there is no general agreement. The evidence that he read Italian depends solely upon the fact that no English versions are known of some of the tales from which he took his plots. For *Cymbeline* did he turn to the *Decameron*, for *Othello* to Cinthio, and for *Measure for Measure* to Cinthio's *novella* and play as well as to George Whetstone's rendering of Cinthio? That an Englishman who can read Latin can make out the sense of an Italian *novella* has been proved experimentally again and again, but that Shakespeare read at all easily and widely in Italian literature—in Petrarch, Ariosto, and Tasso as well as in the writers of *novelle*—has not, I think, been proved. And as doubtful is the extent of his reading in French literature.

Let me illustrate the difficulty of coming to a decision by examining Shakespeare's alleged debt to Boccaccio. We know that Chaucer took the story of patient Griselda not from the *Decameron* but from Petrarch's Latin version of the last tale in the *Decameron*; and we argue that he did not know the *Decameron*, or at any rate possess a manuscript of it, because if he had he would most surely have made use of it. The evidence that Shakespeare had read the *Decameron* rests upon the resemblance between the wager-plot in *Cymbeline* and Boccaccio's tale of the four Italian merchants. If he knew the *Decameron*, it might be argued, it is odd that he did not give more evidence of it. But are we so certain that he knew even this one tale of Boccaccio's? That it could not have been his sole source has been proved. The stage-direction to the wager-scene in *Cymbeline* is sufficient to show this: "*Enter Philario, Iachimo, a Frenchman, a Dutchman, and a Spaniard.*" When Posthumus Leonatus joins them, representatives of five nations are upon the stage. To characterize the qualities of different nations was a common rhetorical device. Thomas Wilson recommends it in his *Art of Rhetoric* under 'Descriptio', and gives as an example: "The Englishman for feeding and changing of apparel: the Dutchman for drinking: the Frenchman for pride and inconstance: the Spaniard for nimbleness of body, and much disdain: the Italian for great wit and policy: the Scots for boldness: and the Boeme for stubbornness." Shakespeare followed example in more than one passing reference in his plays, and in *Cymbeline* itself the 'wit and policy' of the Italian (in the bad senses of those words) is referred to by Imogen and Iachimo. In *Henry V* Shakespeare passed from rhetoric to drama when he created representatives of the four peoples of these islands, with the Welshman Fluellen so greatly outshining the rest. A Jacobean audience, then, identifying upon the stage (as perhaps they could from the appearance and costume of the actors) an Italian (Iachimo), a Frenchman, a Dutchman and a Spaniard, might well expect some sharp satirical observations on national character. They were given nothing of the kind. The Italian and the Frenchman are necessary to the action, but the Dutchman and the Spaniard are mutes and hang loose upon the play as unnecessary encumbrances.

What has happened? It is not often that an examination of Shakespeare's sources convicts him of taking over recalcitrant material which he does not bend to his dramatic intention. Some critics, it is true, have argued that *Hamlet* provides an example. Those who find that Bradley's *Hamlet* is better than Shakespeare's "in the sense that...it hangs together with a more irresistible logic", or those who believe that *Hamlet* is "full of some stuff that the writer could not drag to light, contemplate, or manipulate into art" will speak of Shakespeare's failure, or partial failure, to modify or transmute the old traditional story which he knew from the lost play of *Hamlet* and other sources;[2] and some see in Hamlet's comments over the body of Polonius incongruous relics of that Amleth who dismembered the body of the courtier he had slain and threw it to the pigs. That Shakespeare in *Hamlet* found his materials intractable and failed to impose upon them the subtle meanings of a new design will not be universally agreed; but here in *Cymbeline*, in these fossil characters of the Dutchman and the Spaniard, are clear vestiges of some unassimilated source. That source could not have been Boccaccio, for there the company is all Italian. There was, however, another treatment of this widely popular wager-theme, translated into English from the Dutch early in the sixteenth century and popular enough to go through at least three editions by 1560; and there sure enough, in *Frederick of Jennen*,[3] the company is said to come from 'divers countries', Spain, France, Florence and Genoa. *Frederick of Jennen* is a crude thing to put beside the choice Italian of Boccaccio, but in this detail and in a few others it is closer to *Cymbeline*; and editors have no longer the right to say that Shakespeare's sole source in this play was Boccaccio.[4]

Did Shakespeare then turn both to Boccaccio and to *Frederick of Jennen* or some similar analogue? Or was there some one work, now lost, in which he could have found all that he borrowed? It is here that conjecture raises its head, and with it rises the ghost of a lost play. I confess to feeling some impatience with those critics who, at a loss for a Shakespearian source, invent a hypothetical play. As Hamlet found, it is so difficult to test the honesty of a ghost. Belief upon belief is false heraldry, and false scholarship too. Yet I am not sure I am right to be impatient. That many printed books of that age have been lost I do not believe, but that many plays have been lost is certain. So serious are the losses that the historian of Elizabethan drama—especially of our drama in the sixteenth century, before the habit of reading plays had become popular—must often feel himself to be in the position of a man fitting together a jigsaw, most of the pieces of which are missing. Some sort of picture emerges, but is it the true picture? For example, how much of our dramatic history would need to be rewritten if those "two prose Books" were to turn up which were acted at the Bel Savage Inn in London before 1579? They were acted some years before Lyly turned dramatist, yet Stephen Gosson could not have chosen apter words if he had been describing the prose comedies of Lyly, "where you shall find never a word without wit, never a line without pith, never a letter placed in vain".[5] If by some happy chance the account-books of Shakespeare's company were to come to light, how many titles of lost plays might they reveal? We may argue that our losses are not so severe as for the companies which Philip Henslowe financed, because the Chamberlain-King's company was more stable and its plays worthier the reading. Yet we have lost much, and many a play which Shakespeare saw upon the stage, and perhaps acted in, has gone beyond recovery. What honey did he extract from that hive of activity, the Elizabethan stage, especially in his early years when he was finding himself? Here is a part of his reading and seeing and hearing where we cannot follow him, or can follow only imperfectly. Yet if I am told that his imagination may have taken impetus from some quite inferior play on a theme which he was contemplating, a play so inferior to his own as *The True Chronicle History of King Leir*, I cannot think that I am being told anything that is improbable.

But when all has been said of Shakespeare's knowledge and use of the tongues, the fact remains that what he read he read for the most part in English. Dryden said that "he needed not the spectacles of books to read Nature; he looked inwards and found her there". We shall do well to remember the context in which these words are placed. Dryden, himself a scholar-poet, was answering those critics who accused Shakespeare of wanting learning, that is, a knowledge of the classics, and was praising Shakespeare on the ground that they were not necessary to him. He is not saying that Shakespeare was indifferent to the world of books. I find it impossible to believe in a Shakespeare who was not at some time in his life an avid reader. Did he never put his head into the shop of his fellow-townsman Richard Field except to sell him *Venus and Adonis* or maybe to correct the proofs of that poem and *Lucrece*? As he walked through Paul's Churchyard, did he avert his eyes from the advertisements of new books plastered on every post? To read some critics we might suppose so. It has been pointed out that while a whole library of Jonson's books has survived with his name and motto inscribed upon them, of Shakespeare's books there survive only a few more or less doubtful specimens. What does this prove? That Shakespeare was a modest man, perhaps, who did not write his name in books. Or that he read not for scholarship and erudition but to keep himself level with life. He too was *tanquam explorator*, though not in the same books and not in the same way.

Certainly he was no plodding reader. If Shakespeare is to be identified with any character in *Love's Labour's Lost* it is with Berowne, and Berowne says:

> Small have continual plodders ever won,
> Save base authority from others' books.

But the King of Navarre's answer will do for Shakespeare and Berowne: "How well he's read, to reason against reading!" One supposes him to have been a rapid reader who could tear the heart out of a book as quickly as any man. It is to be observed how little use he made in his plays of some of the books that he looked at. We catch him dipping into that spirited piece of anti-Catholic propaganda, Samuel Harsnett's *Declaration of egregious Popish Impostures*, and coming up with the names of Edgar's fiends—Flibbertigibbet and the rest—and a few phrases. He remembers from Sir William Segar's *Book of Honour and Arms* the first and second causes for a trial of arms and builds them into the character of Don Armado. When *The Tempest* was kindling in his mind, he remembered from Richard Eden's *History of Travel* the great devil of the Patagonian giants, and made him Setebos, the god of Caliban's dam; remembered also, so Malone suggested, some names for his characters, Alonso, Gonzalo, Ferdinand, and others.

These were books to be tasted, and we know such books were among Shakespeare's books (when we know it at all) only from the 'orts' and fragments that he used. But there are "some few to be chewed and digested". So a contemporary of Shakespeare's with whom he is sometimes confused. There was the Bible, and North's Plutarch, and Hall and Holinshed. The evidence suggests that when a theme took possession of his mind, especially a theme with a long tradition behind it, he read widely—not laboriously, but with a darting intelligence, which quickened his invention. When the theme of Macbeth took possession of him, he read Holinshed on Macbeth, but turned back also, twenty folio pages earlier, to the reign of King Duff, and there read the story of Donwald in whom the King had a 'special trust', of the King's visit to Donwald's castle, of how Donwald "though he abhorred the act greatly in heart, yet through instigation of his wife" contrived the King's death, of his pangs of conscience, his dreadful end, and the monstrous sights observed in nature after this monstrous deed, horses eating their own flesh, the sun continually covered with clouds, "a sparhawk also strangled by an owl". Three pages later he read how a brave husbandman and his two sons defended a walled lane against the Danes with such bravery that they turned defeat into victory, stored it away in his retentive memory, and with careful husbandry made use of it in *Cymbeline*. If we may believe Wilfrid Perrett, who published in 1904 the best account that we have of the story of King Lear from Geoffrey of Monmouth to Shakespeare, Shakespeare consulted not only Holinshed on Lear, and Spenser, and the old play, but also *The Mirror for Magistrates* and Camden's *Remains* and even the original version in Geoffrey of Monmouth's Latin. And we have to add that at some moment of time, as he was meditating on these materials, they coalesced with Sidney's story in the *Arcadia* of the Paphlagonian unkind king.

Are these the speculations of scholars creating Shakespeare in their own image? They sound very like it. Yet recent critics make even more startling claims for one of his plays. Not indeed for all. Shakespeare knew when to stop, even if his critics do not. North's Plutarch was sufficient for his Roman plays, Lodge's *Rosalynde* for *As You Like It*, Hall and Holinshed for *Richard III*. But the historical background for *Richard II*, they tell us, did not come merely from Hall and Holinshed. The play depends also for incident and interpretation of character upon Froissart, two versions of a French chronicle on the death of Richard, a metrical history also in French, an anonymous play *Thomas of Woodstock*, and Daniel's *Civil Wars*. It sounds incredible, so incredible that J. Dover Wilson falls back upon the hypothesis of a lost play written by an historical scholar which would have given Shakespeare just those episodes and hints which he could not have found in the English books. But another able writer on the sources of *Richard II*, M. W. Black, observes with courageous logic that copies of the French works could have been borrowed in London from John Stow and John Dee—Holinshed tells us that—and argues that for a rapid reader, gifted in the art of skipping, the preparatory reading was not so formidable after all. And if Shakespeare prepared himself more thoroughly for this play than for any other play in the canon, he did so, says Black, "because he was enthralled with the story and because he was laying the foundation for a great cycle of history plays".[6]

So far, I have spoken almost exclusively of those works which gave him hints for plot and character. But what of the reflection in his plays of the political and moral beliefs of his time? What of that concern with order and disorder in the state, in society and in the mind of man, which Shakespeare shared with all thinking contemporaries and which is present in his plays more constantly and more powerfully than in those of any other dramatist? Was he, like Corin in *As You Like It*, a 'natural philosopher'? Did he absorb the culture of his age merely from the circumambient air? True it is that he was one who observed men and manners in court and city, town and country, church and tavern, and no man who writes on Shakespeare's reading should forget that the "ample sovereignty of eye and ear" gave him more than books can. Yet when we remember that he was profoundly concerned with the problem of good and evil, that most of the books published in his England were concerned with religion and morality, can we resist the conclusion that he was a reader of some of these? But which? The Bible, of course, which he knew as few men know it to-day, which he knew as intimately and naturally as if it had come to him by instinct. But which other books? When we ask this question of his contemporaries we can usually give a certain answer. We can track Jonson and Chapman, Marston and Webster everywhere in the snow of the moralists. Long before Charles Crawford provided the evidence John Addington Symonds guessed that Webster kept a commonplace-book. The contents of this commonplace-book he wove laboriously, though often skilfully, into the texture of his dialogue, and the verbal resemblances are so close that we cannot be in doubt.[7] But when Shakespeare is giving new life to some old commonplace we can never be sure in whose snow we are to track him. It is the rarest thing to find him borrowing from a book that is not his immediate source in words so close that they will convince a sceptic. When I have mentioned the opening of Prospero's speech, "Ye elves of hills, brooks, standing lakes, and groves", which comes from Golding's Ovid, and Gonzalo's description of an imaginary commonwealth, which comes from Montaigne's essay on 'Cannibals' as translated by Florio, I have mentioned two strikingly exceptional examples. How remarkable it is that the question whether Shakespeare owed much or anything to Montaigne or to Florio's translation is still unsettled. Some say that he owed much; others hold that the parallels which have been adduced could have come to Shakespeare from other writers, or are the commonplaces of all time, or are opinions which seem to us singular but were then widespread. The great Montaigne scholar, Pierre Villey, came to the conclusion that if Montaigne had never written his essays, nothing warrants us in supposing that except for one brief passage in *The Tempest* a single word would have been changed in the plays of Shakespeare.[8] Does this mean he was no reader? Or rather that his commonplace-book was his memory and he the very Midas of poets, transmuting all he touched?

Let me take as an example one thought and one image. And let the thought be Hamlet's "there is nothing either good or bad, but thinking makes it so". Had he been reading William Baldwin's *Treatise of Moral Philosophy* (1567) where it is attributed to Plato: "Nothing unto a man is miserable, [but] if he so think it: for all Fortune is good to him, that constantly with patience suffereth it"?[9] Or Jerome Cardan's *De Consolatione*: "A man is nothing but his mind: if the mind be discontented, the man is all disquiet though all the rest be well, and if the mind be contented though all the rest misdo it foreseeth little"?[10] Or had Shakespeare in mind Spenser's "It is the mind that maketh good or ill"? Or, to come yet closer to *Hamlet* in wording and in date, had he been reading that anthology of *sententiae* published by Nicholas Ling in 1597, *Politeuphuia, Wit's Commonwealth*: "There is nothing grievous if the thought make it not"?[11]

And let the image be that one which came to his mind more than once when he was writing of the chaos and anarchy which follow violation of 'degree'. It is in the famous speech on 'degree' in *Troilus and Cressida*, in a scene in *Sir Thomas More*, in *Coriolanus*, in this speech of

Albany's when his eyes are at last opened to the cruelty of Goneril and Regan to their king and father:

> If that the heavens do not their visible spirits
> Send quickly down to tame these vile offences,
> It will come,
> Humanity must perforce prey on itself,
> Like monsters of the deep.

Go back a hundred years and more to the morality-play *Everyman*, and we find these words put into the mouth of God:

> For and I leave the people thus alone
> In their life and wicked tempests,
> Verily they will become much worse than beasts;
> For now one would by envy another up eat.

Go back nearly a hundred years again to *The Pride of Life*, where a bishop complains that men have ceased to fear God, truth has gone to ground, the rich are ruthless, and men

> farit as fiscis in a pol
> The gret eteit the smal.

But this proverbial image is much older than *The Pride of Life*. We can trace it back to the Fathers. But as John Poynet does this for us in a book which Shakespeare could have read, let me quote his words. In this passage from *A Short Treatise of Politic Power* (1556) Poynet is writing about the necessity of order and degree in the state and of what disasters follow when these are not observed:

The Ethnics...saw that without politic power and autority, mankind could not be preserved, nor the world continued. The rich would oppress the poor, and the poor seek the destruction of the rich, to have that he had: the mighty would destroy the weak, and as *Theodoretus* saith, the great fish eat up the small, and the weak seek revenge on the mighty: and so one seeking the other's destruction, all at length should be undone and come to destruction.

Shall we then say that this thought and this image were suggested by any one of the passages I have quoted? I would rather say they were suggested by none, yet were suggested by all. Somehow, like all thinking men in his day, he acquainted himself with that vast body of reflection upon the nature of man and man's place in society and in the universe which his age inherited in great part from the ancient and medieval worlds. And when the moment came, thought and image rose from the pool of his memory to receive its appropriate language and rhythm. We who are cut off for the most part from that great tradition in which Shakespeare was bred can realize only with difficulty how many thoughts and even images came to his audience with the pleasure not so much of discovery as of recognition, proverbial maxims and moral sentiments, not newer than the familiar stories which he took over for his plots. And yet, for his earliest audiences too, there was discovery, even when there was recognition; for what was old had become new. Always there was the power of "dressing old words new"; always the power of bodying forth dramatic theme and idea in characters at once particular and general; always the power of bringing whatever concerns the needs, high and low, of the natural man into the order of a great design.

NOTES

1. A paper read at the Fourth Annual Shakespeare Conference, Stratford-upon-Avon, on 12 August 1949.

2. Cf. A. J. A. Waldock, *Hamlet* (1931), p. 49; T. S. Eliot, *The Sacred Wood* (1920), p. 91.

3. Apparently an error for *Jenuen*, Genoa. The tale has been edited by J. Raith, *Aus Schrifttum und Sprache der Angelsachsen*, Band 4 (1936).

4. Cf. H. R. D. Anders, *Shakespeare's Books* (1904), p. 63, and especially W. F. Thrall, "*Cymbeline*, Boccaccio, and the Wager Story in England", *Studies in Philology* (1931), pp. 639–51.

5. *The School of Abuse*, ed. Arber, p. 40.

6. *Joseph Quincy Adams: Memorial Studies* (1948), pp. 199–216.

7. To cite an example which escaped F. L. Lucas's notice, the Cardinal's speech (*The Duchess of Malfi*, v, v):

> "When I look into the Fishponds, in my Garden,
> Methinks I see a thing, arm'd with a Rake
> That seems to strike at me"

was suggested, as A. H. Bullen pointed out (*Gentleman's Magazine*, 1906, p. 78), by Julius Capitolinus, *Life of the Emperor Pertinax*. See also L. Lavater, *Of Ghosts*, ed. J. Dover Wilson and May Yardley (1929), p. 61.

8. *Revue d'Histoire littéraire de la France* (1917), pp. 357–93.

9. Cited by T. W. Baldwin, *William Shakspere's Small Latine & Lesse Greeke*, II, 353. But the passage had already appeared in Sir Thomas Elyot's *Of the Knowledge which Maketh a Wise Man* (1533), sig. M 3ᵛ.

10. Translated by T. Bedingfield (1573); cited by Hardin Craig, "Hamlet's Book", *Huntington Library Bulletin*, VI (1934), 29.

11. P. 59 *b*. Where Ling took it from, I do not know.

RECENT STUDIES IN SHAKESPEARE'S CHRONOLOGY

BY

JAMES G. McMANAWAY

Shakespeare's first formal editor, Nicholas Rowe, was mildly interested in the problem of chronology, but lacked the equipment and the intellectual curiosity to solve it. "It would be without a doubt", he wrote in 1709, "a pleasure to any man, curious in things of this kind, to see and know what was the first essay of a fancy like Shakespeare's. Perhaps we are not to look for his beginnings, like those of other writers, among their least perfect writings, art had so little, and nature so large a share in what he did, that, for aught I know, the performances of his youth, as they were the most vigorous, and had the most fire and strength of imagination in them, were the best." To which Dr Johnson wisely replied in 1765 that "Shakespeare, however favoured by nature, could impart only what he had learned; and as he must increase his ideas, like other mortals, by gradual acquisition, he, like them, grew wiser as he grew older, could display life better, as he knew it more, and could instruct with more efficacy, as he was himself more amply instructed". The concept of Shakespeare as an original genius who wrote by the mere light of nature would never have plagued the critics, had they heeded the words of Ben Jonson in the First Folio:

> Yet must I not give Nature all: Thy Art,
>   My gentle Shakespeare, must enjoy a part.
> For though the Poets matter, Nature be,
>   His Art doth give the fashion. And, that he,
> Who casts to write a living line, must sweat,
>   (Such as thine are) and strike the second heat
> Upon the Muses anvile: turne the same,
>   (And himselfe with it) that he thinks to frame;
> Or for the lawrell, he may gaine a scorne,
>   For a good Poet's made, as well as borne.
> And such wert thou.

And so the students of the development of Shakespeare's art have from Malone's day laboured to piece together the fragments of Shakespeare's biography, to detect his every reference to contemporary events and his every borrowing or imitation or travesty, and to isolate and date each allusion to his works and each book or pamphlet that shows his influence. The results of such investigations were admirably and succinctly stated by Sir Edmund Chambers in 1930 in the appropriate chapters of *William Shakespeare: A Study of Facts and Problems*, and it is my purpose to bring together the significant contributions which scholars have made in the two succeeding decades. The plays will for convenience be treated in the order in which Chambers lists them in his chronological table, with his dates supplied in parentheses. The poems will follow.

1 *HENRY VI* ('1591–2'). Charles F. Denny[1] argues that the author of the original version of the play used Hall as a source, placed the emphasis on foreign wars, and featured Bedford as well as Talbot. The archaic style of the Talbot death scenes and Joan's colloquy with the fiends, both derived from Hall, are proof to Denny that this version was the *harey the vj*, marked 'ne' by Henslowe when it was acted by Strange's men at the Rose on 3 March 1592. The reviser gave more attention to domestic troubles, relied principally on Holinshed as a source, and enhanced the exploits of Talbot at the expense of Bedford, who is almost forgotten. C. A. Greer[2] agrees with Denny and earlier commentators that one purpose of the revision was to integrate the play with 2 and 3 *Henry VI* and urges that for metrical reasons the incident of Talbot's titles, the Temple Garden scene, and the York-Mortimer scene must have been written shortly after the completion of *Richard III*. Three-fifths of the play are, he thinks, based on Hall and Holinshed, but the remainder has no chronicle source and must have been derived from an early play, probably Henslowe's *harey the vj*.

The irregularities in the act divisions[3] and in the title of Winchester (see Greer: 'Revision') may have resulted either from collaboration or revision; they lead W. W. Greg[4] to say that "we seem to come nearer Wilson's 'continuous copy' in this than in any other play".

Both Peter Alexander[5] and Hazelton Spencer[6] argue that the inequalities of style are not necessary proof of composite authorship, for great unevenness is to be expected in the early writings of a genius. Probably we should date the first version 1589 or 1590, with a revision about 1594 or 1595, or even as late as 1598.

2 and 3 *HENRY VI* ('1590–1'). There is little disposition now to reject Tyrwhitt's interpretation of Robert Greene's deathbed attack on Shakespeare as an "upstart crow beautified with our feathers" as proof that Shakespeare wrote 2 and 3 *Henry VI*, or Thomas Kenny's long neglected argument based thereon (*The Life and Genius of Shakespeare*, 1864) that *The Firste Parte of the Contention of the Twoo Famous Houses of York and Lancaster* and *The True Tragedie of Richard Duke of York* are stolen and surreptitious quartos. Chambers had access to Alexander's first publications on the subject in time to revise his opinions and assign the now accepted dates of 1590–1 to the plays.

RICHARD III ('1592–3'). The textual discrepancies between Q1 and F1 that have led some critics to postulate two Shakespearian versions of *Richard III* have been satisfactorily explained by D. L. Patrick[7] and his reviewers as the result of a sort of communal effort of memorial reconstruction of the text which was printed as Q1. Lewis F. Mott[8] considers that when Shakespeare applied the title, 'Earl of Derby', unhistorically to the Lord Stanley who crowned Henry VII on Bosworth Field, he was attempting to emphasize the traditional loyalty of the Stanleys at a time when Ferdinando Stanley, Lord Strange, created Earl of Derby on 25 September 1593, was under suspicion because of the treachery of his father, Sir William Stanley. Late in 1593, the Earl repudiated his claims to the throne and turned his father's emissary, Hesketh, over to the authorities. R. A. Law[9] agrees that the play was written next after 3 *Henry VI*, i.e. 1592 or 1593.

COMEDY OF ERRORS ('1592–3'). In *The Comedy of Errors* we encounter as many problems as in 1 *Henry VI*. Greg (*Editorial Problem*, pp. 140–1) rejects the complicated textual hypothesis of Dover Wilson's New Cambridge edition (1922) in favour of the simpler and, to me, much more reasonable theory that the play was printed from Shakespeare's foul sheets. He notes that the stage directions indicate the play was not written for the public stage and recalls that the earliest recorded performance was at Gray's Inn on 28 December 1594. Chambers' date of 1592–3 is inacceptable to T. W. Baldwin[10] because he thinks that Shakespeare witnessed the execution of William Hartley, seminary priest, in Finsbury Fields, near the Theatre and Curtain, on 5 October 1588 and shortly after utilized his impressions of the event in the Egeon story of *The Comedy of Errors*. In his later study, Baldwin states his reasons for believing that in this play Shakespeare first attained to mastery of five-act structure, and that it was composed for Strange's men not much before Christmas 1589, after he had toured with Leicester's men in 1588. He supposes a revision before the performance at Court in 1598. Alexander (*Life and Art*, pp. 67–9) interprets the pun on the French heir (III, ii) as referring to the years between 1584, when Anjou died, and 1589, the date of Henry III's death, since at that time Henry of Navarre ceased being the heir and became king. It seems to me entirely possible that Shakespeare could have recalled the circumstances of Hartley's death as late as 1592 or 1593, and I find it difficult to believe that the gentlemen of Gray's Inn would have entertained their guests on a grand night in 1594 with a play staled by five years on the public stage.

TITUS ANDRONICUS ('1593–4'). Problems of authorship, as well as of revision, make the dating of *Titus Andronicus* difficult. It may be exclusively Shakespeare's, as Spencer (*Art and Life*, pp. 206–13) believes, who identifies the play with *Titus and Vespasian* of 1592 and dates it 1589. The internal evidence of style leads J. Q. Adams to the opinion that the play could not have been written long before 1592.[11] Alexander (*Life and Art*, pp. 74–7) considers it a Pembroke play, written before that company went on tour in 1592–3. Dover Wilson[12] attributes to Shakespeare only a reviser's part in the play, which was written by George Peele in 1593 for Strange's men to use while on tour, was augmented by him upon their return to London, and revised by Shakespeare in time for performance at the Rose on 23 January 1594. T. M. Parrott's review[13] accepts Peele as the original author but argues that the play precedes his *Honour of the Garter* and probably was written before 1592, when it was alluded to in *A Knack to Know a Knave*. Wilson contributes to the dating of the play a list of close parallels with *Lucrece*, which was just then (1593) in process of composition and was printed in 1594. If the play was written as early as 1589, it must have been re-worked by Shakespeare in 1593–4.

TAMING OF THE SHREW ('1593–4'). This play has sometimes been identified with the *Love's Labour's Won* in Meres' list of 1598. Its history is entangled with that of *The Taming of A Shrew*, which was first printed in 1594, and which some consider a Bad Quarto of *The Shrew*. T. M. Parrott[14] accepts *A Shrew* as the source, dates it late in 1589 or 1590 because it has no borrowings from *The Jew of Malta*, and attributes it to Samuel Rowley and an unidentified youthful collaborator with an academic background. Shakespeare's rewriting took place, he believes, about 1595–6. Hardin Craig[15] revives with modifications the suggestion of Ten Brink that *A Shrew* and *The Shrew* are respectively a Bad Quarto and a thoroughgoing revision of a lost play of 1589 or earlier. Greg (*Editorial Problem*, pp. 73–4) considers *A Shrew* to be a derivative but not a reported text—"all the writer had to go upon was a fairly full synopsis of F. together with a few recollections or perhaps reported fragments of the dialogue". The Folio text was, he thinks, printed from an imperfectly normalized stage transcript, but this differs from Shakespeare's original text by the loss of the Christopher Sly framework in the latter part of the play. There seems to be no adequate reason for changing the dates assigned by Chambers.

TWO GENTLEMEN OF VERONA ('1594–5'). There is general agreement that *Two Gentlemen* is the earliest of the romantic comedies and possibly one of the first plays written at the outset of the career of the Chamberlain's men early in the season of 1594–5. T. W. Baldwin[16] notes the borrowing from Brooke's *Romeus* of the adage that a nail drives out a nail, traces its use in this play, *Romeo*, and *Lucrece*, and argues that the three works were written in the order named. The evidence is not weighty, but since it would not necessarily push the date of *Two Gentlemen* back more than one year, it may be valid. It is safe to date *Two Gentlemen* about 1594.

LOVE'S LABOUR'S LOST ('1594–5'). Most of the textual difficulties in *Love's Labour's Lost* which earlier editors explained as the result of numerous revisions are disposed of by Greg's observation (*Editorial Problem*, p. 127) that the Quarto text was printed from Shakespeare's foul sheets. Janet Spens[17] theorizes that in its original form the play had only two pairs of lovers and that the introduction of Dumaine and Rosaline produced complications. She postulates a revision between October 1593 and April 1594, the purpose of which was to enhance the importance of Berowne—to be played by Essex—at a private performance at which Southampton had the role of King. Rupert Taylor[18] emphasizes the indebtedness of the play to the Gray's Inn Revels of 1594 for the Muscovite Mask and to the Nashe-Harvey quarrel of 1592–6 and notes the use of the *Venus and Adonis* stanza. He prefers to date the play in the middle of 1596. According to Frances A. Yates,[19] no version could have existed earlier than 1593, when *Pierces Supererogation* and Eliot's *Ortho-epia Gallica* were published, and any revision must have taken place after the Gray's Inn Revels and the writing of Northumberland's 'essay' on love and the pursuit of learning. She prefers, however, to consider the play as having been written in one piece in 1595, with the possibility of minor changes for a late revival. The possibility of an earlier date is suggested by Fred Sorensen,[20] who describes the account in Holinshed of a Russian masque presented before Henry VIII in 1510, in which there were Russian costumes and also blackamoors. He suggests that all the necessary information could have been got from Hakluyt's *Principal Navigations* (1589), which contains a description of Russia and Russian costume, and from Holinshed. Though many topical allusions to Florio, Nashe, Harvey and others have been pointed out, it is unsafe, as E. A. Strathmann[21] has shown, to treat *Love's Labour's Lost* as an attack upon the Raleigh Group or The School of Night. Baldwin (*Five-Act Structure*) insists upon a date between August 1588 and August 1589. It appears wiser, as yet, to retain the more conservative date, 1594–5.

ROMEO AND JULIET ('1594–5'). Baldwin (*Five-Act Structure*) thinks that the construction of the plot indicates *Romeo* follows closely after *Two Gentlemen*; he confirms a date of 1591 by reference to the earthquake of 1580, to Marlowe's supposed imitation of *Romeo and Juliet's* "Gallop apace, ye fiery-footed steeds" in *Edward II*, and to the treatment of the adage that a nail drives out a nail. The later date is preferred by John W. Draper,[22] who finds astrological references that date the play in July 1596. Allusions to the expedition against Cadiz in 1596 are noted by R. W. Babcock, S. A. Tannenbaum and E. P. Kuhl.[23] But Sidney Thomas[24] argues for 1595 on the basis of the reference to "the terrible Earthquake the first of March the same yeare [1584]" in William Covell's *Polimanteia* (1595), a work probably known to Shakespeare because of its praise of "Lucrecia Sweet Shakespeare". Unless the play was written and performed only a few times just before the plague closed London theatres in 1592, it is difficult to understand why there are no allusions to it earlier than 1598. There is no question of Q 1 (1597) representing an early version and Q 2 (1599) a revision, for Greg (*Editorial Problem*, p. 61) has shown that Q 2 was printed in the main from Shakespeare's foul papers, and H. R. Hoppe[25] that Q 1 is printed from the report of performances of a text like that in Q 2. Either 1595 or 1596 would be an acceptable date.

RICHARD II ('1595–6'). The indebtedness of *Richard II*, v, iv to Daniel's *Civil Wars* (III, 57 ff.), entered in the Stationers' Register on 11 October 1594 and published in 1595, sets one limit for the play—see Dover Wilson's edition,[26] which corrects a long-standing misinterpretation of the evidence. The other is supplied by Chambers' (*William Shakespeare*, II, 320–1) discovery of the record of a performance at the house of Sir Edward Hoby on 9 December 1595. Thus the dating of the play is unusually easy and accurate. Shakespeare's supposed dependence on a lost play about *Richard II* is strongly attacked in M. W. Black's[27] study of the sources and A. P. Rossiter's edition of the anonymous play, *Woodstock*.[28]

A MIDSUMMER-NIGHT'S DREAM ('1595–6'). The appropriateness of this play for a wedding celebration has led to the formulation of hypotheses that it was composed as early as 1591 and as late as 1600, and at least seven different marriages have been suggested. Chambers favours the wedding of Thomas Berkley and Elizabeth Carey at Blackfriars on 19 February 1596. Much depends on the allusion to the weather at II, i, 81–117, which has seemed to describe equally the summers of 1594, 1595, and 1596. An examination of contemporary records induces in Sidney Thomas[29] a belief that the passage gives only a partially accurate description of the weather in 1594; it does not fit 1595 at all; but it describes perfectly the conditions of 1596. He suggests that the occasion may have been the double wedding of the daughters of the Earl of Worcester on 8 November 1596.

KING JOHN ('1596–7'). From the time of Pope, it has been suggested that Shakespeare was in some fashion concerned in the authorship of *The Troublesome Reign of King John* (Q. 1591). Alexander (*Life and Art*, pp. 85–6) finds it difficult to understand how the old play should be "so well digested in the scenes as to permit Shakespeare to follow it nearly scene by scene" but yet should "show so little corresponding modesty or cunning in its writing as to appear like a tissue of borrowed and only half-assimilated phrases from *Henry VI*, *Richard III*, as well as *King John* itself". And Dover Wilson[30] is so much impressed by the fact that Shakespeare reveals no independent knowledge of the Chronicles in his *Life and Death of King John* as to suggest that Shakespeare's first version of the play antedates his earliest acquaintance with Hall and Holinshed. The imitation of *John*, II, i, 137–8, which has no counterpart in *Troublesome Reign*, in *The Spanish Tragedy*, I, ii, 170–2 (first noted by Steevens), he can explain only by changing the date of Kyd's play to 1590, and supposing that *King John* was written by Shakespeare in the same year and for the same company. This pushes the date of *Troublesome Reign* back to 1588 or 1589. About 1594 Shakespeare, he thinks, revised his play. On the grounds that many passages are "more mature, more flexible in their rhythms" than anything else Shakespeare wrote up to 1594, and that the allusions which he had previously cited point to a later date, G. B. Harrison[31] suggests 1596.

THE MERCHANT OF VENICE ('1596–7'). Earlier notions about the manuscript used in the printing of Q 1 (1600) of this play have been displaced by the belief that the printer's copy was Shakespeare's foul sheets (see Greg, *Editorial Problem*, pp. 123–4); if this be so, many of the difficulties that vexed Dover Wilson are easily explained without recourse to his complicated textual theories. No discoveries have been made that would affect the conventional dating.

1 and 2 *HENRY IV* ('1597–8'). F. G. Fleay (*Biographical Chronicle of the English Drama*, II, 181), J. Q. Adams (*Life of Shakespeare*, p. 513), and Chambers have independently expressed the opinion that shortly after 1 *Henry IV* was first acted an edition was authorized in order to satisfy the affronted parties that 'Oldcastle' had been changed to 'Falstaff'. Since the First Quarto of 1 *Henry IV* appeared in 1598 (see Stationers' Register, 25 February 1598), the play must have been written in 1597. The arguments of Dover Wilson[32] and E. M. W. Tillyard[33] that from the outset Shakespeare planned a trilogy (1 and 2 *Henry IV* and *Henry V*) have been ably controverted by M. A. Shaaber.[34] If he is correct, the Cobhams could not have taken offence at once, for enough time must be allowed after the first performance of 1 *Henry IV* for a sequel to be called for and for Shakespeare to have written at least part of 2 *Henry IV* with the name 'Oldcastle' (*Old.* stands for *Fal.* as late as I, ii, 137 in the Quarto of 1600; see Collier's edition, 1842). It is likely that Part 2 was not completed before 25 February 1598, for if the sequel had been performed before the publication of Part 1, the title-page of the earlier play would have distinguished between the two parts (first suggested by Malone in 1778). An earlier date for Part 1 is advocated by Leslie Hotson,[35] who, having set 23 April 1597 as the date of the first performance of *Merry Wives*, has to push 1 and 2 *Henry IV* back to the season of 1596–7. A suggestion by Henry N. Paul is quoted by S. B. Hemingway[36] to the effect that Shakespeare was interrupted in the composition of Part 2 at IV, iii by the Queen's order to write a play showing the fat knight in love. This he did in two weeks, so that *Merry Wives* might be performed at Windsor in entertainment of the Knights of the Garter; and since Lord Cobham had objected to the name 'Oldcastle', he selected 'Falstaff' to replace it for the reason that in 1 *Henry VI* he had shown how Sir John Fastolfe was deprived of his Garter. Thereafter, Falstaff was used in all the plays. Late in 1597 or early in 1598 is the date for Part 2 most acceptable to M. A. Shaaber.[37]

MUCH ADO ABOUT NOTHING ('1598–9'). The attempt to explain discrepancies in the text by assuming a source play or an earlier version by Shakespeare himself has been advocated by Wilson[38] and seems to have at least the partial approval of Hardin Craig.[39] It is objected to by Allison Gaw,[40] and, in my opinion, is nullified by Greg's explanation (*Editorial Problem*, p. 122) that Q. was printed from Shakespeare's foul papers that lacked final revision. No reasons have been found for changing the dating in Chambers.

HENRY V ('1598–9'). The allusion to Essex dates the play as in Chambers.[41] The decision to kill Falstaff led, as Wilson and Duthie point out, to the introduction of new matter at II, i and iii; III, ii, 63 ff., and IV, i, 34 and to the alteration of certain other passages. Another interpolation is identified by J. H. Walter,[42] who believes that Falstaff was extirpated at the behest of the Master of Revels out of deference to Lord Cobham and not because Kempe was unavailable to play the part.

JULIUS CAESAR ('1599–1600'). No change in dating has been proposed, but Dover Wilson[43] finds additional support for Tyrwhitt's suggestion that Shakespeare or someone else modified the text before the printing of the Folio.

AS YOU LIKE IT ('1599–1600'). *As You Like It* is not named by Meres in 1598, and it is entered in the Stationers' Register on 4 August 1600; so the determination of the date of composition is almost as simple as for *Julius Caesar*.

TWELFTH NIGHT ('1599–1600'). Commentators since 1930 have tended to change the date to 1601 or 1602. Wilson[44] collects the evidence supplied by Richmond Noble, Violet Wilson, and others, and adding new details about Sir Anthony Shirley's trip to Persia argues for an initial performance at the Middle Temple on 2 February 1602, in which a singing boy played Viola, and a revival in 1606, when it became necessary to give the songs to Robert Armin as Feste and make consequent adjustments in the text, including the introduction of Fabian.

HAMLET ('1600–1'). Sir Edmund Chambers may be permitted to introduce the survey of recent scholarship on the date of *Hamlet* with his acceptance of 1601 as the earliest possible date of composition.[45] This is the date supported by Wilson in his edition of the play,[46] which makes full use of Henry David Gray's discussion[47] of the intimate relation of the play to the War of the Theatres and to the almost certain closing of the playhouses at the time of Essex's rebellion. Contributory evidence is supplied by Leo Kirschbaum,[48] who finds that since Harvey uses the historical present elsewhere his reference to Essex's commendation of *Hamlet* need not have been written before the Earl's execution in 1601.

The problem of the authorship of the old *Hamlet* which is referred to in 1589 and of the *Hamlet* that seems to have been performed by Shakespeare's Company in 1596 is complicated, and the evidence tenuous, and it is hardly possible to consider the voluminous literature of the subject. It may be worth noting that Alexander (*Life and Art*, p. 154) is not unwilling to suggest that Shakespeare and not Kyd wrote the *Ur-Hamlet*. R. A. Law's[49] analysis of the fable indicates that no other hand than Shakespeare's need *necessarily* have contributed to the story. J. Q. Adams[50] is prepared to believe that Shakespeare may well have tinkered with the play in 1596, and Wilson is of the same opinion.

MERRY WIVES OF WINDSOR ('1600–1'). One of the few items of new biographical material about Shakespeare in recent years has been related to the dating of *Merry Wives* by its discoverer, Leslie Hotson.[51] In 1596 and 1597, Shakespeare was involved in a dispute with a certain William Wayte, nephew of an unscrupulous Justice of the Peace in Surrey named William Gardiner, whose first marriage (with Frances Lucy) entitled him to show her arms with his—and the silver cup which was purchased for Bermondsey Church out of the proceeds of his estate displays the white luces. Hotson thinks that Shakespeare satirized Gardiner, who died in late November 1597, in the person of Shallow in *Merry Wives* and *2 Henry IV* and that *Merry Wives* was performed on 23 April 1597 before the Knights of the Garter at Windsor. While Alexander (*Life and Art*, p. 125) and A. W. Pollard[52] accept the date, others reject it outright or, as Greg,[53] find the date and the suggested occasion attractive but doubt that Shakespeare would have dared to offer an intolerable insult to the Court by using the name of Brook again.[54] Both

Greg and Pollard deride the notion that Gardiner is satirized in the person of Justice Shallow. A different turn is given to the discussion by J. E. V. Crofts,[55] who attempts to connect the play with the rivalry between Essex and the Howards and with an incident late in 1597. This explanation is ingenious but improbable. Reference has already been made (p. 27) to the alternative of H. N. Paul in the discussion of 2 *Henry IV*. Until new evidence is discovered, it seems best to admit that many of the questions about *Merry Wives* are unanswerable. Inasmuch as there were both private and public performances, it is likely that many alterations were made in the text to introduce or remove topical hits. The process may have continued for a period of years, beginning as early as 1597 (but if so, why did Meres fail to name the play in 1598?) and continuing as late as 1601.

TROILUS AND CRESSIDA ('1601–2'). Alexander's suggestion that *Troilus* was written for performance at one of the Inns of Court is generally accepted. O. J. Campbell[56] cites supporting evidence in the legal terminology of the play but rejects the opinions of Dover Wilson (*The Essential Shakespeare*, pp. 218 ff.) that a warning was intended for Essex. Spencer (*Art and Life*, p. 284) believes the play must have been written earlier than *Poetaster* (1601), because its Latinized diction is just the kind of thing Jonson was ridiculing. One specific attempt has been made to identify the law court at which *Troilus* was first performed—by Leslie Hotson,[57] who thinks there was a close link between Shakespeare and the Warwickshire men at Middle Temple and, interpreting "Loue's Labour's Won" to mean "Loue's Sorrow Is Gained", identifies *Troilus* with the play of that name in Meres' list and suggests a performance on one of the 'grand days' in early 1598. The allusion of Marston (of the Middle Temple) in *Histriomastix* (1599) is contributory evidence. The later limit of the play is fixed by the entry in the Stationers' Register on 7 February 1603.

ALL'S WELL THAT ENDS WELL ('1603–4'). The presence of two styles in this play has led many to the conclusion that it is a reworking (with an alternative title) of the *Loue's Labour's Won* mentioned by Meres. Craig, for example (*Interpretation*, p. 224), believes parts of it go back to the period of *Love's Labour's Lost* while the rest was written after 1600, in the mood of *Measure for Measure*. Greg's description of the text (*Editorial Problem*, p. 146) raises the question whether the Folio text was printed from an incomplete or uncompleted author's manuscript, supplemented by his 'plot' or scenario and the efforts of a literary editor. These speculations do not affect the date, which is probably 1602–4.

MEASURE FOR MEASURE ('1604–5'). There is little disagreement with a date of 1604, since the play was performed at Court on 26 December of that year. What Wilson in his edition interprets as signs of numerous revisions, with expanding and curtailing of the text, Greg (*Editorial Problem*, p. 146) thinks may have been produced in a careless transcript by Ralph Crane "from foul papers that had been a great deal altered".

OTHELLO ('1604–5'). *Othello* was performed at Court on 1 November 1604. An earlier limit is suggested by Alfred Hart,[58] who finds an allusion in 1 *Honest Whore*, for the writing of which Henslowe paid £5 between 1 January and 14 March 1604. He points out, also, that the Bad Quarto of *Hamlet* (1603) borrows phrases from it.

KING LEAR ('1605–6'). Though G. B. Harrison [59] finds interesting resemblances between a passage in *Lear* and a news pamphlet of February 1606 dealing with eclipses and other prodigies reported from Carlstadt in Croatia and thus dates the play between February and December of 1606, Greg [60] makes a better case for composition and performance of the play in 1605, with the old *Leir* (Q 1, 1605) being published because of the popularity of *King Lear*.

MACBETH ('1605–6'). In his edition,[61] Wilson tosses caution to the winds by suggesting, as J. M. Robertson (*Literary Detection*, 1931) had done before, that the play was written next after *Hamlet*, about 1601 or 1602, and performed at Edinburgh, whither Shakespeare had fled after the revolt of Essex. Most writers are more conservative, dating it the summer of 1606. H. N. Paul [62] finds striking new evidence for believing that the first performance was on 7 August 1606 at Hampton Court before King James and King Christian of Denmark.

ANTONY AND CLEOPATRA ('1606–7'). There has been no attempt to alter the dates accepted by Chambers.

CORIOLANUS ('1607–8'). Evidence, other than stylistic, is scant. G. B. Harrison [63] contributes one new item: an allusion to Hugh Middleton's project for bringing clean water into London, work on which began in February 1609. Since this was a common topic of conversation, the play may have been written shortly before or just after this date.

TIMON OF ATHENS ('1607–8'). Lacking objective evidence, commentators agree on a date between 1605 and 1608.

PERICLES ('1608–9'). In *Pericles* we meet again the possibilities of revision and of composite authorship. A play of this name was seen by Giustinian between 5 January 1606 and 23 November 1608, and a play was entered for publication on 20 May 1608. The production seems to have caused the reprinting in 1607 of Twine's *Patterne of Paynfull Adventures*. In 1608 appeared George Wilkins' prose version of the story, based almost certainly upon performances of Shakespeare's *Pericles* and filled out with matter from Twine.[64] There is disagreement about the authorship of the earliest dramatic version and about the possibility of two revisions of it (the second to meet Jonson's criticisms) by Shakespeare, but general agreement that Wilkins had no hand in the play.[65]

CYMBELINE ('1609–10'). The case remains as presented by Chambers.

WINTER'S TALE ('1610–11'). Again the case remains as stated by Chambers.

TEMPEST ('1611–12'). Nothing has been discovered that would affect the accepted dating.

HENRY VIII ('1612–13'). The date of *Henry VIII* is readily fixed by the burning of the Globe on 29 June 1613 at, probably, the first performance.

TWO NOBLE KINSMEN ('1612–13'). As in the case of *Henry VIII*, current research deals with the problem of divided authorship, the date of composition having long been fixed within narrow limits.

SIR THOMAS MORE ('undetermined'). In his study of the play R. C. Bald [66] evaluates the scholarly discussions of recent years and points out a major difficulty: finding a time at which Shakespeare might be working in collaboration with a number of Henslowe's playwrights and yet writing the kind of poetry found in the passages in hand 'D'. Such a time, he suggests, came about 1600, when the records show that Henslowe was paying for few new plays and when his hirelings might be expected to seek employment elsewhere.

SONNETS. According to H. E. Rollins,[67] most scholars date the *Sonnets* between 1593 and 1599. Chambers,[68] however, prefers 1595–1600, because of new evidence that links Shakespeare to plans for a marriage between William Herbert and Elizabeth Carey; he notes also an entry in S.R. on 3 January 1600 of "Amours by J.D. with certen oy[r] sonnetes by W.S.", a book otherwise unknown and perhaps never printed. In the belief that the "mortal Moone" of 107, the "pyra-myds" of 123, and "the childe of state" of 124 are the "Moone of huge and mighty shippes" of the Armada, the Egyptian obelisks re-erected by Pius V, and Henri III of France, Hotson (*Shakespeare's Sonnets Dated*, pp. 1–36) dates these sonnets 1589. I think he is right about 107 and 123 and possibly about 124. But I cannot agree that the first 126 sonnets were written by 1589 until a satisfactory 'Mr W. H.' is produced.

VENUS AND ADONIS ('1592'). No dissent, except by literalists; in 1592 nothing of his had appeared in print.

LUCRECE ('1593–4'). No dissent.

THE PHOENIX AND TURTLE ('1601'). No dissent.

The absence of revolutionary changes in the chronology may make it appear that we have but a dusty answer for our pains. Several developments are, however, worthy of further comment. First, little reliance nowadays is put upon metrical tests. In the only general study, H. D. Gray[69] uses percentages based upon the average of the figures given by Neilson and Thorndike of double endings, run-on lines, and speeches ending within the line, and discovers that few of the plays are far from where we should expect them. *Merchant* seems later than *Julius Caesar* and *Henry V*, but still precedes *Much Ado*; *Shrew* yields uniform figures, but *Love's Labour's Lost* can be divided into early and later work.

Second, thanks to the study and interpretation of the evidence afforded by theatrical docu-ments by R. B. McKerrow and, chiefly, W. W. Greg, we now have a much better understanding of the manuscripts from which many of Shakespeare's plays were printed and are saved from much of the speculation about collaboration and multiple revisions that vitiated earlier discussions of text and chronology.

Third, there is the growing acceptance of the theory that from 1594 until his retirement, while Shakespeare was continuously and successfully connected with one major theatrical company, the plays which he wrote and completed for the public stage were tinkered with only to introduce or delete topical allusions, if only because changes in the script made trouble for the actors. (*Macbeth* is a special case, and such plays as *Merry Wives* and *Troilus*, which were intended for private performance, fall into a separate category.)

Shakespeare's attitude towards the plays written before he joined Strange's men in 1594 appears to have been different. The frequency with which plays that had belonged to the Queen's men, for example, were rewritten by Shakespeare at the height of his powers suggests that A. W. Pollard may have been very near the truth in his hypothesis that Shakespeare was with this company in 1588 and 1589.[70] New information about these years is greatly to be wished, not only from the kind of study by which Baldwin is pushing back the dates of the early plays, but through intensive studies of *The Troublesome Reign*, and of *Leir*—and *Hamlet*. Care should be exercised, however, to avoid the errors of A. S. Cairncross,[71] whose efforts to assign early dates to plays of Shakespeare's maturity ignores the fact of Shakespeare's artistic growth. In the early years everyone was experimenting; Shakespeare was learning from all the rest, and they from him, so that a rational chronology can be worked out for the development of Elizabethan drama. To put *Othello* and *Twelfth Night* before 1593 or 1 and 2 *Henry IV* before 1587 is not only to revive the concept of Shakespeare as an erratic 'original genius' but is to consider that he wrote in a vacuum, uninfluenced by his contemporaries and exerting no influence upon them.

NOTES

1. "The Sources of 1 *Henry VI* as an Indication of Revision", *Philological Quarterly*, XVI, 225–48.

2. "The Place of 1 *Henry VI* in the York-Lancaster Tetralogy", *PMLA*, LIII, 687–701. "Revision and Adaptation in 1 *Henry VI*", in *University of Texas Studies in English* (Austin, 1942), pp. 110–20.

3. See Peter Alexander's *Shakespeare's 'Henry VI' and 'Richard III'* (Cambridge University Press, 1929), p. 185. Alexander suggests elsewhere that Shakespeare may have written 1 *Henry VI* for the Pembroke company as early as 1587.

4. *The Editorial Problem in Shakespeare* (Oxford University Press, 1942), p. 139.

5. *Shakespeare's Life and Art* (Nisbet, 1939), p. 79.

6. *The Art and Life of William Shakespeare* (Harcourt, Brace, 1940), pp. 152–5.

7. *The Textual History of 'Richard III'* (Stanford University Press, 1936). See reviews by W. W. Greg, *The Library*, XIX, 118–20; Alice Walker, *Review of English Studies*, XIV, 468–9. See also Greg (*Editorial Problem*, p. 80) for a discussion of the 'Clock' passage, which is not in F 1.

8. "A Political Allusion in Shakespeare's *Richard III*", in *Todd Memorial Volumes* (Columbia University Press, 1930), II, 41–4.

9. "*Richard III*—A Study in Shakespeare's Composition", *PMLA*, LX, 689–96.

10. *William Shakespeare Adapts a Hanging* (Princeton University Press, 1931). See also his *William Shakspere's Five-Act Structure*...(University of Illinois Press, 1947).

11. *Shakespeare's 'Titus Andronicus'. The First Quarto 1594.* (The Folger Shakespeare Library, 1936), p. 10.

12. *Titus Andronicus* (The New Shakespeare) (Cambridge University Press, 1948).

13. *Shakespeare Association Bulletin*, XXIV, 117–23.

14. "*The Taming of a Shrew*—A New Study of an Old Play", in *Elizabethan Studies and Other Essays in Honor of George F. Reynolds* (University of Colorado Studies, II, 4) (Boulder, 1945), pp. 155–65.

15. "*The Shrew* and *A Shrew*: Possible Settlement of an Old Debate", in *Elizabethan Studies...in Honor of George F. Reynolds*, pp. 150–4.

16. *William Shakspere's Small Latine & Lesse Greeke* (University of Illinois Press, 1944), II, 345.

17. "Notes on *Love's Labour's Lost*", *Review of English Studies*, VII, 331–4.

18. *The Date of 'Love's Labour's Lost'* (Columbia University Press, 1932).

19. *A Study of 'Love's Labour's Lost'* (Cambridge University Press, 1936).

20. "The Masque of the Muscovites in *Love's Labour's Lost*", *Modern Language Notes*, L, 499–501.

21. "The Textual Evidence for 'The School of Night'", *Modern Language Notes*, LVI, 176–86.

22. "The Date of *Romeo and Juliet*", *Review of English Studies*, XXV, 55–7.

23. See *Philological Quarterly*, VIII, 407–8; IX, 72–3, 307–8.

24. "The Earthquake in *Romeo and Juliet*", *Modern Language Notes*, LXIV, 417–19.

25. *The Bad Quarto of 'Romeo and Juliet'* (Cornell University Press, 1948).

26. *King Richard II* (Cambridge University Press, 1939), pp. xxxviii ff.

27. "The Sources of Shakespeare's *Richard II*", in *Joseph Q. Adams Memorial Studies* (The Folger Shakespeare Library, 1948), pp. 199–216.

28. *Woodstock, A Moral History* (Chatto and Windus, 1946).

29. "The Bad Weather in *M.N.D.*", *Modern Language Notes*, LXIV, 319–22.

30. *King John* (Cambridge University Press, 1936), p. lv.

31. In his review of Wilson's edition, *Modern Language Review*, XXXII, 455–6; see also his "Shakespeare's Topical Significances. I: *King John*", in *Times Literary Supplement*, 13 November 1930, p. 939.

32. *The First Part of the History of Henry IV* (Cambridge University Press, 1946).

33. *Shakespeare's History Plays* (Chatto and Windus, 1944).

34. "The Unity of *Henry IV*", in *Adams Memorial Studies*, pp. 217–27.

35. *Shakespeare versus Shallow* (Little, Brown and Co., 1931), pp. 111, 130.

36. New Variorum Edition of 1 *Henry IV* (J. B. Lippincott, 1936), p. 355.

37. New Variorum Edition of 2 *Henry IV* (J. B. Lippincott, 1940), pp. 516–18.

38. *Much Ado about Nothing* (Cambridge University Press, 1923).

39. *An Interpretation of Shakespeare* (The Dryden Press, 1948), p. 121.

40. "Is Shakespeare's *Much Ado* a Revised Earlier Play?", *PMLA* L, 715–38.

41. See Dover Wilson's discussion in his edition, Cambridge University Press, 1947.

42. "'With Sir John in It'", *Modern Language Review*, XLI, 237–46.

43. "Ben Jonson and *Julius Caesar*", in *Shakespeare Survey*, II, (1949), 36–43.

44. *Twelfth Night or What You Will* (Cambridge University Press, 1930).

45. "The Date of *Hamlet*", in *Shakespearean Gleanings* (Oxford University Press, 1944), pp. 68–75.

46. *Hamlet* (Cambridge University Press, 1934; 2nd ed. 1936).

47. "The Date of *Hamlet*", *Journal of English and Germanic Philology*, XXXI, 51–61. Gray suggests that *Hamlet* was Shakespeare's 'purge' of Jonson.

48. "The Date of Shakespeare's *Hamlet*", *Studies in Philology*, XXXIV, 168–75.

49. "Belleforest, Shakespeare, and Kyd", in *Adams Memorial Studies*, pp. 279–94.

50. *Hamlet Prince of Denmark* (Houghton Mifflin Co., 1929).

51. *Shakespeare versus Shallow*; see n. 35.

52. In his review in *Library*, XII, 353–5.

53. In his review in *Modern Language Review*, XXVII, 218–21.

54. D. M. White, in "An Explanation of the Brook-Broome Question", *Philological Quarterly*, XXV, 280–3, points out that Lord Cobham died in March and that Shakespeare might have used the name deliberately. He proposes that the change to Broome was made in 1604, when the then Lord Cobham was involved in the Main Plot and Shakespeare wanted to avoid entanglement that might result from having one of his dramatis personae bear the name Brook in a play presented before the King.

55. *Shakespeare and the Post Horses* (J. W. Arrowsmith, 1937).

56. *Comicall Satyre and Shakespeare's 'Troilus and Cressida'* (Henry E. Huntington Library, 1938).

57. "*Love's Labour's Won*", in *Shakespeare's Sonnets Dated* (Hart-Davis, 1949), pp. 37–56.

58. "The Date of *Othello*", *Times Literary Supplement*, 10 October 1935, p. 631.

59. "'These Late Eclipses'", *Times Literary Supplement*, 30 November 1933, p. 856. See also pp. 878, 896, 909, and 4 January 1934, p. 12.

60. "The Date of *King Lear*, and Shakespeare's Use of Earlier Versions of the Story", *Library*, XX, 377–400.

61. *Macbeth* (Cambridge University Press, 1947).

62. "The First Performance of *Macbeth*", *Shakespeare Association Bulletin*, XXII, 149–54.

63. "A Note on *Coriolanus*", in *Adams Memorial Studies*, pp. 239–52.

64. See Hardin Craig, "*Pericles* and *The Painfull Adventures*", *Studies in Philology*, XLV, 600–5; and T. M. Parrott, "*Pericles*: The Play and the Novel", *Shakespeare Association Bulletin*, XXIII, 105–13.

65. See W. T. Hastings, "Exit George Wilkins?" *Shakespeare Association Bulletin*, XI, 67–83, and "Shakespeare's Part in *Pericles*", *op. cit.* XIV, 67–85; also Sina Spiker, "George Wilkins and the Authorship of *Pericles*", *Studies in Philology*, XXX, 551–70.

66. "*The Booke of Sir Thomas More* and its Problems", in *Shakespeare Survey*, II, 44–61.

67. New Variorum Edition of *The Sonnets* (J. B. Lippincott, 1944), II, 73.

68. "The 'Youth' of the *Sonnets*", in *Shakespearean Gleanings* (Oxford University Press, 1944), pp. 125–9.

69. "The Chronology of Shakespeare's Plays", *Modern Language Notes*, XLVI, 147–50.

70. In the Introduction to Alexander's *Shakespeare's Henry VI and Richard III*.

71. *The Problem of Hamlet: A Solution* (Macmillan, 1936).

CORIOLANUS AND THE MIDLANDS INSURRECTION OF 1607

BY

E. C. PETTET

In May 1607 a spark of revolt fell in Northamptonshire. The area, as Sir Edward Montague, one of the county members, had warned Parliament in 1604,[1] was tinder; and, blazing up, the flames ran swiftly over Northamptonshire into the adjacent counties. But, after some hesitant half-measures on the part of the local justices, the fire was rapidly and effectively beaten down. It was the old story—a doomed outburst of desperate, ill-organized peasants, so badly equipped that they were short even of spades and shovels to set about their task of laying open enclosures and filling up ditches, so poorly armed that a handful of mounted gentry, with their retainers, was enough to rout a thousand of them.[2] And the aftermath was the familiar one—executions, a Royal Commission of Inquiry, some vague promises of redress.

Most history books ignore the revolt or dismiss it in a line or two. It was, wrote E. F. Gay, "weak and ineffective".[3] Yet this same historian also states that the outbreak "had something more than the dimensions of the ordinary local riot",[4] and that there had been nothing on the same scale since the northern rebellion of 1569. Moreover, most of us, in our alarm, have a habit of magnifying any sort of civil disturbance; and, however insignificant this revolt may appear from the remote distance of three hundred and fifty years, it is reasonable to suppose that many Englishmen of the time were profoundly disturbed by it.

Quite apart from these general considerations, there were certain special features of the revolt that must have made it particularly alarming to those contemporaries who were within or on the fringe of the propertied classes. In all the major disturbances of the sixteenth century, economic and social grievances had been merged with religious and political issues; and in the 1554 and 1569 troubles economic distress hardly entered into the picture at all. The 1607 rising, on the other hand, was purely and nakedly a demand for economic redress.[5]

The primary grievance of the peasants was the old one against enclosures, whether in the open fields or the common pasture lands. Most of these enclosures had been effected in the Midlands, and it is probable that the long-standing resentment of the Midlands peasants towards the enclosing landlords had been exacerbated in the early years of James's reign by hints and rumoured promises of reform that had come to nothing. The contemporary evidence of Stow's *Annales* is quite explicit on the anti-enclosure motive of the revolt,[6] and Gay's investigation[7] confirms Stow's opinion.

Yet while the breaking down of enclosures was the chief and immediate aim of the insurgents, it seems reasonably certain that in the background there was also the fear of suffering and starvation through corn shortage. It is true that a Royal Proclamation of July 1607 alleged that "there was not so much as any necessity of famine or dearth of corn...that might stir or provoke them";[8] but though Gay is undecided whether rising corn prices furnished one of the immediate causes of the 1607 revolt, he adduces evidence for believing that shortage of corn was at least a remoter cause. There were the high prices of corn reported from the west in 1606–7, the proclamations for "the amending of the dearth of grain and other victual" in 1607–8, and the letter of William Combe to the Earl of Salisbury (June 1608) in which he mentions the dearth of corn in Warwickshire and renewed threats to resist the turning of arable land into pasture.[9] It is also notable that the 'Diggers' of Warwickshire harp on this fear of starvation in their manifesto of 1607.[10]

From all this there arose another particular characteristic of the 1607 revolt that must have worried the propertied classes. Whereas all the earlier sixteenth-century risings had been based on alliances between what Gay calls the 'gentlemen' and the 'commons', with leadership effectively in the hands of the gentry, the insurrection of 1607 was entirely a popular movement. It was instigated by the peasants, supported, if only morally and with resources, by the populace of several towns,[11] while its leaders, like that interesting figure 'Captain Pouch', were of peasant origin.

Possibly, too, there was another special feature of the insurrection that distressed the authorities. We find the rebels commonly described as 'Diggers' and 'Levellers'.[12] Now it is evident that the primary signification of these terms was a literal one, and the manifesto of "The Diggers of Warwickshire to all other Diggers" is almost pitifully innocuous[13] in its protestations of loyalty to James "our most gracious and religious king, who doth and will glory in the flourishing estate of his Commonalty".[14] Further, Stow's *Annales* testifies clearly to the orderliness of these riotous persons who "bent all their strength to level and lay open enclosures, without exercising any manner of theft or violence upon any man's person, goods or chattels".[15] Yet remembering how, not much more than a generation later, the name 'Diggers' and 'Levellers' was perpetuated by those utopian socialists and communists whose ideas so shocked the Commonwealth leaders, we may reasonably guess that some of this radical sentiment was already mixed up with the specific and public demand for a halt in enclosures. Perhaps we may even catch an echo of some of the talk of these 1607 insurgents in the opinions of the carpenter Bartholomew Stere, who, during the Oxfordshire disturbances ten years before, "intended to kill the gentlemen of that country and to take the spoil of them, affirming that the Commons long since in Spain did rise and kill all the gentlemen of Spain, and since that time have lived merrily there".[16]

Whether he was in London at the time or—as is possible—in Stratford,[17] Shakespeare would have had a particular interest in the 1607 disturbances. By now he was himself a substantial landowner, while Warwickshire was one of the disaffected areas.[18] Admittedly he would have had nothing to fear from the peasants personally, for he was not himself an encloser and may even have disapproved of the practice. But as a landowner he must have been concerned with this important agrarian problem, and though (as usual) his personal attitude eludes us, we know that he was involved in the controversy over the proposed Welcombe enclosures in 1614.[19] Further, as evidence of his probable interest in the other interrelated question of dearth and corn shortage, we remember that the Stratford Justices' Return for February 1598 had noted him as one of the chief holders of malt in the town.[20]

However, beyond these general inferences, there are good grounds for suggesting that something of the 1607 revolt is reflected in *Coriolanus*,[21] which, while exceptionally lacking in external dating-reference, is usually ascribed on grounds of style to 1607 or early 1608.

Perhaps the most striking evidence of a connexion between *Coriolanus* and the disturbances of 1607 lies in Shakespeare's treatment of the grievances of the Roman plebeians. In Plutarch the reason given for the first uprising, before the Volscian war, was the oppression of usurers, who were supported and favoured by the government.[22] After the war this particular grievance disappeared, and the trouble then was dearth, since the recent war had prevented proper cultivation of the Roman arable fields. This later distress was exploited by demagogues, who, claiming that the shortage of corn had been deliberately engineered by the nobility, also made capital out of the two unpopular senatorial proposals supported by Coriolanus: the first, that the town of Velitres, recently decimated by plague, should be colonized by the surplus Roman population, the second, that the Volscian war should be renewed in order to drain off sedition.

Now Shakespeare in his play radically alters this account of the plebeian grievances against the Senate and Coriolanus. The two proposals for the colonization of Velitres and the renewal of the war[23] he completely ignores; and probably this omission may be explained as a necessary dramatic simplification. Much more surprising, however, is his dismissal of the usury question, which he limits to the First Citizen's passing hit at the Senators who "make edicts for usury, to support usurers; repeal daily any wholesome act established against the rich, and provide more piercing statutes daily, to chain up and restrain the poor";[24] for not only is this matter of usury most prominently stressed in the early part of Plutarch's narrative: it was also a problem that had at other times deeply engaged Shakespeare's own attention.[25]

However, the most striking change occurs in Shakespeare's treatment of the dearth and corn shortage issue, which he brings into the first disturbances and underlines with a special emphasis. Barely have the mutinous Citizens caught our attention when we hear one of them shouting the question: "You are all resolved rather to die than to famish?"[26] They are rising "in hunger for bread", and Coriolanus is to be killed because then "we'll have corn at our own price".[27] When Menenius enters, his first important speech makes it clear that he understands the cause of the uprising, and if he ever did have any doubts on the matter, the First Citizen finally scatters them in his explosion against the 'fatherly' patricians: "Care for us! True, indeed! They ne'er cared for us yet: suffer us to famish, and their store-houses crammed with grain."[28] The ensuing brush between the Citizens and Coriolanus also centres on this question, and when the news of the Volscian war arrives, Coriolanus flings after the dispersing mob the gibe:

> The Volsces have much corn; take these rats thither
> To gnaw their garners.[29]

Moreover, while Shakespeare transfers the corn shortage to the opening of the play, he still keeps it as a major item of dispute in the later disturbances that break out when the Senate proposes Coriolanus as Consul. In the very first speech in which Brutus attempts to justify the plebeians' change of opinion about accepting Coriolanus he drags up the old bone of contention:

> The people cry you mock'd them, and of late,
> When corn was given them gratis, you repined;
> Scandal'd the suppliants for the people, call'd them
> Time-pleasers, flatterers, foes to nobleness.[30]

Nor can Coriolanus leave this charge alone, and he is not content till he has condemned himself in the hearing of the people with a full and explicit statement of his attitude:

> Whoever gave that counsel, to give forth
> The corn o' the storehouse gratis, as 'twas used
> Sometime in Greece....
> Though there the people had more absolute power,
> I say, they nourish'd disobedience, fed
> The ruin of the state.[31]

It is of course always possible—and sometimes sensible—to ascribe divergences between Shakespeare's plays and their sources to chance. But this particular divergence is a very marked and peculiar one: Shakespeare has reduced the grievances of the plebeians to the one matter of scarcity of corn (which he entwines with the fear of Coriolanus's absolutist temper), and he has set this grievance prominently before us in the first scene of the play, declining to follow Plutarch's account of a rising against the oppression of usury. Since the play was almost certainly written just after the 1607 revolt, and since both the problem of corn shortage and the fear of fresh disturbances persisted for some time,[32] is it not possible that Shakespeare was adapting Plutarch's story to give it the topicality of a bearing on recent events?

Nor is the theme of dearth the only element in *Coriolanus* that appears to connect the play with the 1607 revolt. There is also Menenius's parable of the belly to be considered.

This parable comes, of course, from Plutarch and merely expresses that "functional view of class organization",[33] which, generally current in Shakespeare's time, is reflected in several of his other plays. But there are certain features of the parable that call for comment. There is its length for one thing—seventy lines, or a quarter of a scene, in a singularly compact and economical play.[34] The obvious explanation of this amplitude is that Shakespeare expanded his Plutarch original because it afforded him the opportunity of saying something that he very much wanted to say; and this suggestion is strengthened by the fact that never before had he voiced the conventional political theory behind his parable with such earnestness[35] and vigorous, homely eloquence. Again, it is to be noticed that while earlier expressions of the doctrine, like those of the Archbishop of Canterbury and Ulysses,[36] are expository and general, Menenius is energetically and personally on the defensive, endeavouring to prove that the Senators and the wealthy aristocratic class they represent have an indispensable part to play in any well-ordered commonwealth.

What these features suggest is that something had given a fresh significance and sense of urgency to old ideas of political philosophy that even Shakespeare himself may have come to regard as platitudes, and that he was re-stating them, both for his own satisfaction and the good of his audience, with a sharpened sense of social consciousness. This is corroborated by a small but by no means insignificant detail. In the Folio entrance-directions for Act III, scene i, we read: "Enter Coriolanus, Menenius, *all the Gentry*...", and there are three uses of this term in the text, the first ironical:

(1)   but for our gentlemen,
             The common file....[37]

(2)
                O, he would miss it rather
Than carry it but by the suit of the gentry to him
And the desire of the nobles.[38]

(3)
                where gentry, title, wisdom,
Cannot conclude but by the yea and no
Of general ignorance.[39]

Such an importation of contemporary class labels into a Roman play might of course seem nothing more than a familiar Elizabethan anachronism. But when we observe that in an earlier play of Roman politics, *Julius Caesar*, there are no such attempts to transpose the class-system of Rome into contemporary terms, it does rather look as though Shakespeare was writing *Coriolanus* with a more conscious sense of class and class-conflict.

A similar impression is created by his treatment of the plebeians. In previous plays his attitude to the common people may be described as one of affection for the individual and good-humoured contempt for the mass. As individuals—Bottom is the essential representative here—the common people are often admirable, shrewd, good-hearted, and amusing: we regard them not very seriously, with amused tolerance, because they have a habit of making fun of one another's weaknesses and ignorance.[40] As a mass they are contemptible and often dangerous, because of their herd-irrationality, and, most of all, because of their incalculable fickleness:

          the blunt monster with uncounted heads,
   The still-discordant, wav'ring multitude.[41]

Certainly there is a good deal of this attitude in *Coriolanus*. While some of the plebeians have their moments of simple and touching good nature,[42] of humorous self-depreciation,[43] there is throughout the play the familiar representation of the mob as fickle and unstable. This is indeed the heart of Coriolanus's violent anti-democratic sentiments:

      He that will give good words to thee will flatter
      Beneath abhorring. What would you have, you curs,
      That like nor peace nor war? the one affrights you,
      The other makes you proud. He that trusts to you,
      Where he should find you lions, finds you hares;
      Where foxes, geese: you are no surer, no,
      Than is the coal of fire upon the ice,
      Or hailstone in the sun.[44]

Yet while these lines remind us of many passages in earlier plays, it is also true to say that nowhere else is the mob shown so emphatically and continuously in an unfavourable light. The common soldier—the point is underlined for us—is a coward, thinking only of spoils; the common citizen, Volscian no less than Roman, is utterly fickle and unpredictable, not merely changeable but changeable in an instant.[45] And what makes this impression so significant is that in several respects Shakespeare paints a worse picture of the common people than Plutarch does. For instance, whereas in *Coriolanus* we see the mob after the first outbreak "stealing away"[46] at the news of war, smothered with Coriolanus's abuse about the rats who go to gnaw the Volscian garners, Plutarch tells us that the plebeians behaved well after they had been pacified by Menenius.[47]

In the Volscian war, though Plutarch mentions the episode in which Coriolanus rates some common soldiers for thinking only of loot, he shows the Roman soldiers in a much more commendable light than Shakespeare does; for after the inhabitants of Corioli have come out of their city and beaten the Romans to their trenches, Coriolanus rallies his soldiers, and "there flocked about him immediately a great number of Romans".[48] Further, when Coriolanus forced the gates there were at least a few who dared to follow him. Shakespeare, on the other hand, shows us the Romans beaten to their trenches with Coriolanus cursing them for cowardice; and when Coriolanus makes his way into the city he is quite alone, while the soldiers voice their unheroic comment:

> See, they have shut him in.
> To the pot, I warrant him.[49]

Again, Shakespeare largely reduces the plebeian rejection of Coriolanus as Consul to the influence of demagogues; but in Plutarch the common people have much more solid and reasonable grounds for their action. Not only had Coriolanus prominently supported the policy of colonizing Velitres and renewing the war as a diversion; he had actually forced a band of citizens to go to Velitres. Also, Coriolanus's attitude to the corn shortage was not an old memory dragged up for the occasion, for it was at this time that the corn arrived and Coriolanus spoke so bitterly against a free distribution.

Lastly, when Coriolanus was besieging Rome, Plutarch tells us clearly that it was the people who wished to revoke Coriolanus's banishment and call him home, while the Senate, for various reasons, opposed this proposal. All this Shakespeare leaves obscure and confused.

Once more we can dismiss these changes as mere chance. But they make more sense if we regard them as, to a large extent, the natural reactions of a man of substance to a recent mob rising in his country. Whether or not Shakespeare had been shocked or alarmed by the 1607 rising is anyone's guess; but it is fairly certain that he must have been hardened and confirmed in what had always been his consistent attitude to the mob. It was one thing to regard the 'many-headed monster' as part of the dramatis personae: then one could afford to be, to some measure at least, moderate, good-humoured, judicial. But to have been faced in real life with an actual choice of loyalties—or with the contemplation of such a choice—would sharpen and bias the attitude of any writer.

Finally, there is an interesting feature of the imagery of *Coriolanus* that may point to some connexion between the play and the events of 1607. This is the number of references to country life that occur, in lines like

> Forth he goes
> Like to a harvest-man that's task'd to mow
> Or all or lose his hire;[50]

or in

> We have some old crab-trees here at home that will not
> Be grafted to your relish;[51]

or—to give a more sustained example—in Sicinius's speech:

> This, as you say, suggested
> At some time when his soaring insolence

Shall touch the people—which time shall not want,
If he be put upon't; and that's as easy
As to set dogs on sheep—will be his fire
To kindle their dry stubble.[52]

What is remarkable about these images is not so much their number (though there are at least nineteen of them) as the fact that they are found in an essentially urban and political play that is not particularly rich in imagery.

This poetic feature may have two possible bearings on the subject of this essay. It may serve to confirm Granville-Barker's suggestion,[53] arising out of the precise and full stage-directions of the play, that Shakespeare had already retired to Stratford; and this would increase, though not of course clench, the possibility that Shakespeare was in Warwickshire during the early summer rising of 1607. Further, there is the possibility that the association in Shakespeare's mind between Plutarch's story and the peasant revolt may have stimulated a spontaneous flow of country-life images; and if at first sight this appears an over-ingenious speculation, recent studies of the working of Shakespeare's poetic imagination have revealed some even more surprising and devious connexions.

NOTES

1. E. F. Gay, "The Midlands Revolt and the Inquisitions of Depopulation of 1607", *Transactions of the Royal Historical Society*, New Series, XVIII (1904), 212–13.

2. E. F. Gay, *op. cit.* note 3, p. 216.

3. *Ibid.* p. 219.

4. *Ibid.* p. 212.

5. Gay, *op. cit.* p. 196: "It was not till 1607 that resentment expressed itself unalloyed with other motives against the depopulating inclosure of the common fields, in an hitherto inadequately chronicled revolt which swept for a brief period through some of the midland counties."

6. The purpose of the revolt, writes Stow, was "only for the laying open of enclosures, the prevention of further depopulation, the increase and continuance of tillage to relieve their wives and children, and chiefly because it had been credibly reported unto them by many that of very late years there were three hundred and forty towns decayed and depopulated" (*Annales* (1631 ed.), p. 890).

7. Gay, *op. cit.* p. 214: "unappeased irritation at the depopulating inclosures was alone the foundation of the revolt."

8. Quoted by Gay, *op. cit.* note 3, p. 213.

9. See E. Fripp, *Shakespeare Man and Artist*, p. 706, where this letter is quoted: "I am overbold to acquaint your lordship with such grievances as the common people of this country...are troubled with: *videlicet*, with the dearth of corn, the prices rising to some height, caused partly by some that are well stored, by refraining to bring the same to the market out of a covetous conceit that corn will be dearer, and by engrossing of barley by maltsters, of the chief townsmen in every corporation, amongst whom the justices of the county have no intermeddling. These matters make the people arrogantly and seditiously to speak of the not reforming of conversion of arable land into pasture by enclosing."

10. "If it should please God to withdraw his blessing in not prospering the fruits of the Earth but one year (which God forbid) there would a worse and more fearful dearth happen than did in King Edward II's time, when people were forced to eat cat's and dog's flesh, and women to eat their own children." This document was printed by Halliwell-Phillipps in *The Marriage of Wit and Wisdom* (Shakespeare Society, 1846, p. 140).

11. E.g. Leicester.

12. Cf. Stow's *Annales* and the letter of the Earl of Salisbury to Sir John Manners (quoted by Gay, *op. cit.* note 3, p. 216).

13. "We, as members of the whole, do feel the smart of these encroaching Tyrants, who would grind our flesh upon the whetstone of poverty, and make our loyal hearts to faint with breathing, so that they may dwell by themselves in the midst of their herds of fat wethers" (*The Marriage of Wit and Wisdom*, p. 140).

14. *Ibid.* p. 140.

15. *Annales*, p. 890. And also the statement: "Captain Pouch kept them in good order."

16. Gay, *op. cit.* Appendix I, p. 238. Brents Stirling ("Shakespeare's Mob Scenes", *Huntington Library Quarterly*, VIII (1944–5), 213–40) shows how official counter-revolutionary propaganda deliberately branded all reformist movements with the mark of 'levelling': an attack on the bishops was an attack on property, and so on.

17. See p. 40.

18. The *Annales* tells us of 3000 rioters assembled at Hillmorton in the county.

19. See E. K. Chambers, *William Shakespeare* (Oxford, 1930), II, 141–52. E. Fripp (*op. cit.* p. 812) believes that the note-book of Thomas Greene, the Stratford town-clerk, shows us Shakespeare's opposition to these enclosures: "Sept. M[aster] Shakespeares telling J. Greene that (he) was not able to bear the enclosure of Welcombe." Fripp appears to me to argue sensibly for reading 'he' instead of 'I'. But there is only this slender piece of evidence in favour of Shakespeare's opposition.

20. E. K. Chambers, *op. cit.* II, 99–101.

21. Brents Stirling (*loc. cit.*) has already made this suggestion: "the acuteness of the enclosure problem, the resultant hunger and deprivation, and the ensuing riots...all contribute to an attitude of receptivity, to say the least, concerning such a play" (p. 225). But Stirling makes no attempt to elaborate this passing point in his essay.

22. "It fortuned there grew sedition in the city, because the Senate did favour the rich against the people, who did complain of the sore oppression of usurers, of whom they borrowed money. For those who had little were yet spoiled of what little they had by their creditors, for lack of ability to pay the usury: who offered their goods to be sold to them that would give most. And such as had nothing left, their bodies were laid hold on, and they were made their bondsmen" (W. W. Skeat, *Shakespeare's Plutarch* (1875), pp. 4–5).

23. So far as this policy is mentioned at all by Shakespeare it is transferred to the earlier rising: see I, i, 229–30.

24. *Coriolanus*, I, i, 83–7.

25. See my study of *Timon* (*Review of English Studies*, XXIII (1947), 321–36), and "*The Merchant of Venice* and the Problem of Usury" (*Essays and Studies*, XXXI (1945), 19–33).

26. I, i, 4–5.

27. Note also the parallel between the First Citizen's "the leanness that afflicts us, the object of our misery, is as an inventory to particularize their abundance" (I, i, 19–21) and a phrase in the Warwickshire Diggers' Manifesto, "there is none of them but do taste the sweetness of our wants". It is not likely that Shakespeare had read this document, but he may have been echoing what was a common sentiment among the peasants.

28. I, i, 81–3.

29. I, i, 254–5.

30. III, i, 42–5.

31. III, i, 113–18.

32. See William Combe's letter above, note 9.

33. R. H. Tawney, *Religion and the Rise of Capitalism* (London, 1938), p. 37. See also, for its bearing on this fable, Tawney's quotation (note 13, p. 258) from John of Salisbury's *Polycraticus*: "Est autem res publica, sicut Plutarcho placet, corpus quoddam quod divini muneris beneficio animatur."

34. Cf. Granville-Barker, *Prefaces to Shakespeare*, Fifth Series, p. 177: "The play contains little or no superfluous matter."

35. Observe how the First Citizen is used to bring Shakespeare's lesson home: for the moment the First Citizen is an audience projection, a means of ensuring that the listeners shall follow, mark, and digest.

36. *Henry V*, I, ii, 183–204; *Troilus and Cressida*, I, iii, 83–137.

37. I, vi, 42–3.

38. II, i, 253–5.

39. III, i, 144–6.

40. For a typical example see the asides of Dick and Smith on Cade, *2 Henry VI*, IV, ii.

41. *2 Henry IV, Induction*, ll. 18–19. In presenting this picture of the mob Shakespeare was advancing, deliberately or not, what Brents Stirling (*loc. cit.*) describes as an 'official' counter-revolutionary propaganda based on fear of the mob and fear of mob revolt.

42. See the opening of II, iii.

43. See II, iii, 19–39.

44. I, i, 171–8.

45. For an example of this compare the attitude of the Citizens at the opening of IV, vi, with their attitude at the close.

46. Stage-directions, I, i, 255.

47. "Hereupon, the city being grown again to good quiet and unity, the people immediately went to the wars, showing they had a good will to do better than ever they did, and to be very willing to obey the Magistrates in that they would command concerning the wars" (*Shakespeare's Plutarch*, pp. 6–7).

48. *Ibid.* p. 7.

49. I, iv, 47.

50. I, iii, 38–40.

51. II, i, 205–6.

52. II, i, 269–74.

53. *Prefaces to Shakespeare*, Fifth Series, p. 190: "Such evidence is, of course, no better than guesswork if you will. But *Coriolanus* speaks in this respect pretty plainly of a manuscript to be sent to London, and of a staging which the author did not expect to supervise himself."

THE SHAKESPEARE COLLECTION IN THE BRITISH MUSEUM

BY

F. C. FRANCIS

Seeing that no fewer than twenty-three early Shakespeare quartos came to the Museum with his library it is hardly fair to quote George III's remark to Fanny Burney on the subject of Shakespeare, but one is forced to conclude that his alleged attitude to the Bard was not at variance with that of his immediate forebears. For the Old Royal Library, when it came to the British Museum in 1757, had not a single Shakespeare on its shelves!

The catalogue of Sir Hans Sloane's printed books, which formed the Museum's original stock, is arranged in a way that makes it wellnigh impossible to trace the works of a particular author, but it is safe to say that the British Museum Library opened its doors to the public in 1759 almost without a single Shakespeare quarto, or folio, to its name. It owes its collection of early printed Shakespeariana largely to a few generous donors, though, in this as in many other fields, tribute should be paid to those members of the staff, in the days of the Museum's great expansion in the nineteenth century, who bought widely and intelligently.

THE GARRICK LIBRARY

The foundation of the collection was David Garrick's library of 'old English plays', which he bequeathed to the Museum in 1779. Garrick was a really considerable collector, and it is odd, considering the importance of his gift to the Museum, that the story of his collection, apart from scandalous rumours concerning its provenance, has still to be told.[1] The collection must certainly have been well known by 1757, for in July of that year an anonymous well-wisher sent Garrick the very valuable First Quarto of 1 *Henry IV*, accompanying it with a note beginning:

Sir, In my lodgings at Harwich I lately found this play. Observing it to be the first edition, I begged it of my Landlord, although incompleat, on your account....[2]

His collection was such as to attract the friendly attentions of Edward Capell, a rare event in that age of bitter rivalries. Capell in fact made the catalogue of the collection which served as the guide to its contents when it came to the Museum. George Steevens, with whom Garrick became increasingly familiar (as Capell's friendship lessened, possibly in proportion), made frequent use of these 'old plays' when preparing his edition of Shakespeare. On several occasions he borrowed them, once sending his "cart with a box and a servant to pack them carefully". In a letter written in 1773 he told Garrick, "Your collection of old plays is far from complete, though much the greatest that I know of".

Garrick's collection appears in his correspondence as something already full grown. Whether he collected it with the intention, as is sometimes alleged, of producing an edition of Shakespeare himself is uncertain. What is certain is that Steevens did not disdain his comments and criticism, and did not consider him an unworthy recipient of his critical suggestions. Garrick was generous in lending books from his library—on one occasion Steevens expresses surprise that more of the volumes had not been lost, considering the number of hands through which they passed—and he set the seal on his generosity by his bequest of his 'old plays'[3] to the British Museum, where they were forty-five years later to delight Charles Lamb who, in "the princely apartments of poor condemned Montagu House" culled "at will the flowers of some thousand dramas". There were literally about a thousand plays, when the collection was brought from Hampton on behalf of the Trustees in 1780, by the Rev. Samuel Harper, Keeper of Printed Books. They were bound in 242 volumes (243 with Capell's catalogue), in a manner which was castigated by Steevens. The plays are now mostly bound separately, though the fly-leaves of the old collective volumes, on which Capell had listed the contents of each volume, have been retained and are bound up together in one volume. Capell's catalogue, which in a manuscript note he modestly describes as "a first Essay; faulty, and uncorrected", is elegantly written, but there is no discoverable order in the entries. Fortunately it is well and accurately indexed both by titles and authors. It lists and numbers each play separately—even when part of a collected edition, as in the case of the First Folio and the Beaumont and Fletcher Folio—giving title, author, publisher, date and press-mark (see Plate IV).

Thirty-seven Shakespeare quartos came to the Museum with the collection, though only five of them were first editions. Many rarities, however, were included such as: one of three copies of the '1605' *Hamlet*, one of three copies of 1 *Henry IV* (1598), one of four copies of *Richard III* (1602), and one of five of *Romeo and Juliet* (1597). His copies of the 1619 quartos are taller and longer than those of the other quartos and leave little doubt that A. W. Pollard was right when he said that "from their uniform measurements and appearance [they were] almost certainly once bound together like those belonging to Edward Gwynne".[4] Garrick's First Folio, together with the Beaumont and Fletcher Folio, and collected editions of Dryden, Mrs Behn and Shadwell, was missing when the collection was inspected by a deputation of the Trustees in 1780. We have to regret that the Roubiliac statue of Shakespeare which once stood in Garrick's garden at Hampton, and which he also bequeathed to the Museum, could not have stood guard, in the King's library, over Garrick's own First Folio, instead of another one.

ROYAL AND OTHER COLLECTIONS

The second notable addition to the Museum's quartos came with the library of George III in 1823, which added twenty-three to the thirty-seven of the Garrick collection. These were not twenty-three 'new' quartos, but they did include the First Quarto of *Henry V*, *Troilus and Cressida*, 1609 (first issue) and a fine tall copy of the First Quarto of the *Merchant of Venice*, acquired from the Duke of Roxburghe. Several of George III's quartos came from Steevens' library and one, the 1619 *Merry Wives*, bears Capell's initials.

Considering the quality of their collections, it is a matter for great regret that neither Cracherode nor Grenville collected the quartos.[5] Their copies of the folios came to the Museum, and to Grenville the Museum owes its fine copy of the second edition of *Venus and Adonis*, one of its two copies of the first edition of *The Rape of Lucrece*, one of its three copies of the *Sonnets* and its copy of the *Poems*, one of the few with both titles and the portrait. Alfred Huth's bequest, which came to the Museum in 1910, brought not only superb manuscripts and early printed books, but also enabled the Museum to complete its 'set'—if we except the early plays written in collaboration or revised by Shakespeare—of the First Quartos. From the Huth library came the First Quartos of the *Merry Wives*, *Richard the Second* and *Richard the Third*, all these previously in the collection of George Daniel, the second with a note in his hand on the rarity of the book and a list of his Shakespeariana. The temptation to acquire from the same source a copy of the '1604' *Hamlet*, lacking in the Museum collection, was wisely resisted in favour of the fine volume of nearly seventy unique Elizabethan ballads which Huth had also acquired at the Daniel sale.

One really large purchase of Shakespearian quartos was made in 1858, when the Museum acquired from J. O. Halliwell-Phillipps, for one thousand pounds (see Fig. 1), eighteen books comprising the following (the words quoted are from Halliwell's circumstantial notes accompanying the volumes): one of the two known copies of *Hamlet*, 1603 ("this is the rare and most precious edition of the *Hamlet* of 1603, of which the only known other copy is in the collection of the Duke of Devonshire. I purchased this volume of Messrs Boone...for £120"); the 1598, 1605, 1622 and 1634 editions of *Richard III*; the four-leaf sheet E of 2 *Henry IV*, 1600 ("The present genuine copy of the original sheet is taken from a duplicate in my collection"); the 1608 and 1613 editions of 1 *Henry IV*—there are two copies of the latter, one from the Steevens collection, the other containing many variations in sheet H; the Pide Bull *Lear*—two copies, one perfect, but with the title-page mounted; the other lacking all before sig. B ("This copy should be preserved on account of its containing an extraordinary number of curious textual variations"); *Romeo and Juliet*, 1609 ("For this most rare edition...I gave Mr Daniel in exchange *The History of Tom Thumb*, 1621"); *Troilus and Cressida*, second issue; *Pericles*, 1611 ("Wants two leaves in D, unless the omission is to be ascribed to the printer the catchwords being right, it is of great literary curiosity and importance. Unique, unused by and unknown to all editors of Shakespeare"); *Pericles*, I. N. for R. B., 1630, bound by Bedford ("the binding cost me £2"); *The First Part of the Life of Sir John Oldcastle* (1600), the title in facsimile ("cut out from a volume of contemporary tracts"); finally there were *The Painfull Adventures of Pericles Prince of Tyre. Being the true history of the Play of Pericles, as it was lately presented by...John Gower*, 1608 ("one of the rarest and most important pieces connected with Shakespeare. One other copy at Zurich, but with a dedication by G. Wilkins, in a different type"), and *The True Chronicle History of King Leir* (1605), wanting C 2 and 3 which have been supplied in manuscript. As Pollard said of this accession, "few vendors have done the Museum greater service". At the David sale in 1864 the Museum acquired *Love's Labour's Lost* (1598), and the 1596 *Venus and Adonis*. Other purchases were *Richard II* (1608), bought at the Jolley sale in 1845 and *Thomas Lord Cromwell* (1602), in 1908. The Ashley library, bought in 1937, for all the discredit which now attaches to the name of its collector, Thomas J. Wise, greatly enriched the Museum collection of seventeenth-century literature including the drama. A glance at the index to his catalogue shows copies of the *Enterlude of Welth, and Helth* (1557), the *Enterlude of Johan the Euangelyst* (c. 1550), and representative collections of Beaumont and Fletcher, Brome, Chapman, Congreve, Davenant, Day, Dekker, Giles and Phineas Fletcher, Ford, Heywood, Jonson, Marston, Massinger, Nashe, Peele, Shirley, Webster and many others.

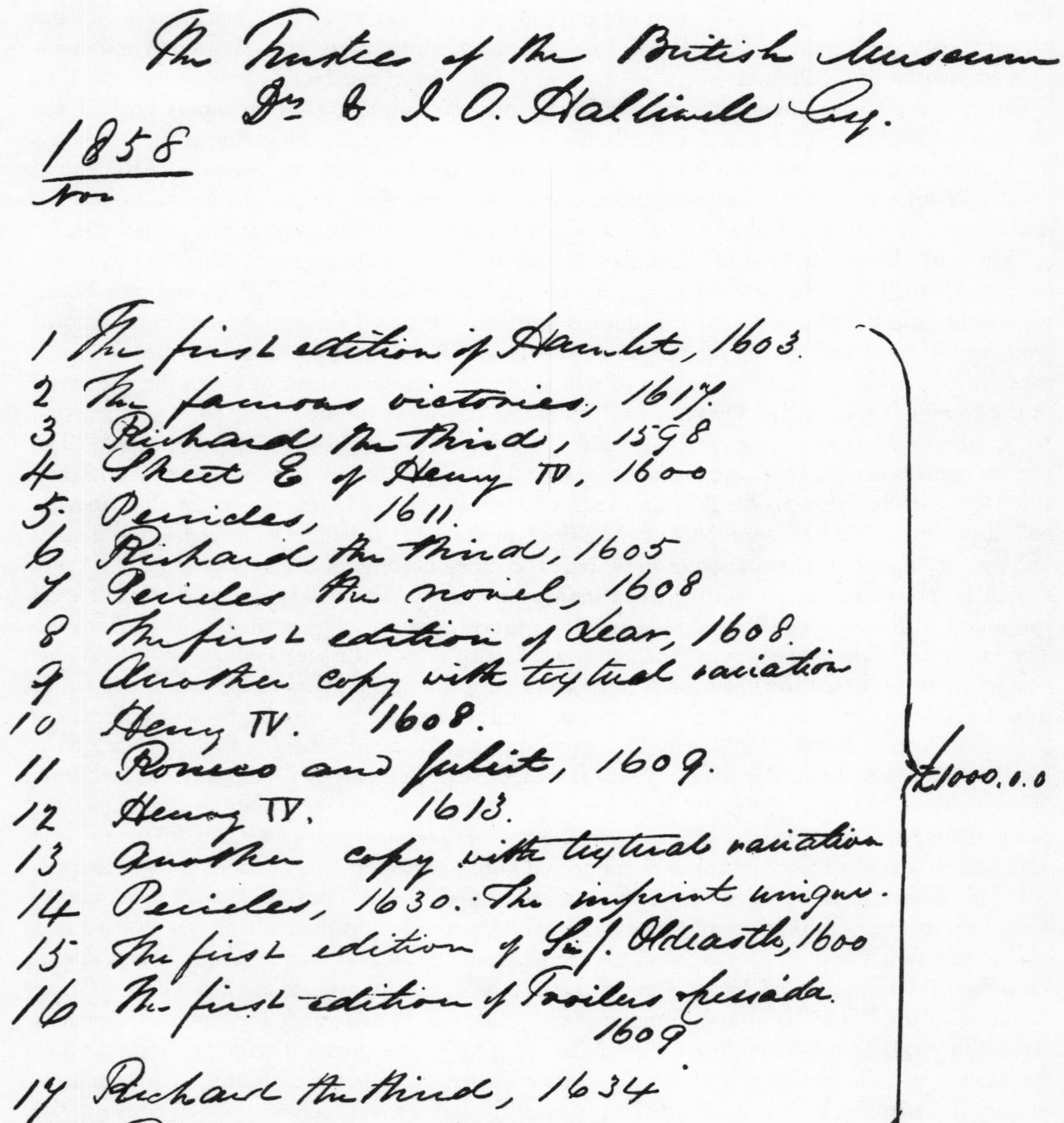

The Trustees of the British Museum
Dr. to I. O. Halliwell Esq.

1858
Nov

1 The first edition of Hamlet, 1603.
2 The famous victories, 1617.
3 Richard the Third, 1598
4 Sheet E of Henry IV. 1600
5. Pericles, 1611.
6 Richard the third, 1605
7 Pericles the novel, 1608
8 The first edition of Lear, 1608.
9 Another copy with textual variation
10 Henry IV. 1608.
11 Romeo and Juliet, 1609.
12 Henry IV. 1613.
13 Another copy with textual variation
14 Pericles, 1630. The imprint unique.
15 The first edition of Sir J. Oldcastle, 1600
16 The first edition of Troilus & Cressida.
        1609
17 Richard the third, 1634
18 Richard III. 1622

9 NO 58

£1000.0.0

£1000..0..0

Fig. 1. Halliwell–Phillipps' invoice to the British Museum, 1858.

46

THE MUSEUM'S HOLDINGS OF QUARTOS AND FOLIOS

The Museum collection of the early quartos was, with almost undue modesty, described by Pollard, in his introduction to the *Shakespeare Exhibition Guide* (1923),[6] as "adequate to the needs of students and not unworthy of a national library". It is in fact a fairly comprehensive collection, its greatest weakness being the lack of the original editions of the six plays in which Shakespeare collaborated or which were revised by him: *The First part of the Contention betwixt the two famous Houses of Yorke and Lancaster* (1594), *The true Tragedie of Richard Duke of Yorke* (1595), *The Troublesome Raigne of John King of England* (1591), *A Pleasant Conceited Historie, called The taming of a Shrew* (1594), *The Famous Victories of Henry the fifth* (1598) and *The Most Lamentable Romaine Tragedie of Titus Andronicus* (1594). Apart from this serious deficiency, the only quartos up to 1709 not represented in the Museum, basing the survey on the *Census* by Pollard and Bartlett, are the following:

> *Hamlet*, 1604, 1695—with the 4-line imprint.
> 1 *Henry IV*, earliest edition, of which only a fragment is known, and 1604.
> *Henry V*, 1602.
> *Julius Caesar*, fourth, fifth and sixth editions.
> *Othello*, 1681.
> *Richard II*, 1598, the third edition, of which two copies only are known, and 1608 (later title).
> 2 *Henry VI*, 1600.
> *Richard III*, 1612—a copy of the 1605 edition in the Museum has been wrongly perfected with the title from this edition.
> *The Taming of a Shrew*, 1607.
> *Titus Andronicus*, 1600; only two copies known.

While the Museum unfortunately has no copy of the '1619' volume containing the nine plays printed by Jaggard, it seems likely, as has been pointed out already, that the copies of these plays which came with the Garrick collection were once bound together like those in the Gwynne copy in the Folger Library. Copies of these plays are also included in George III's library, but here there is no doubt that they were acquired separately from different sources.

The Museum has five copies of the First Folio. The best is that acquired in 1922 with the aid of a generous gift of about five-sixths of the substantial cost from an anonymous benefactor. It is one of three copies with the portrait in the first state, the others being in the Bodleian and the Folger. There is also at least one copy of the title-leaf alone with the portrait in this state. It is a 'large' copy, measuring $12\frac{7}{8} \times 8\frac{3}{8}$ inches (as compared with $13\frac{3}{8} \times 8\frac{1}{2}$ inches of the largest copy known). The Grenville copy, long regarded as the finest copy extant, is to modern taste something of a tragedy. Bought by him "in its first binding and in its original state" (as he describes it himself), he proceeded to have it rebound, by Lewis, in a uniform binding with his other three folios! Cracherode's First Folio is not perfect, having the verses opposite the title supplied from a copy of the second. The fourth and fifth Museum copies are mainly of association interest: George III's copy is a poor one and sorts ill with his collection of the quartos, and the last copy derives its interest from having belonged in turn to Theobald, Johnson, Tonson and Steevens.

Steevens summarized its history in a manuscript note in the book itself: "G. Steevens. Ex dono Jacobi Tonson Bibliop: 1765. It belonged to Mr Theobald. From him it devolved to Dr Johnson, who did not much improve its condition." This copy came to the Museum in 1818 with the collection of Charles Burney.

Of the later Folios, there are four copies of the Second, two with the Allot no. IV imprint (using the classification put forward by R. M. Smith), one with Allot no. V and one with the Smethwick imprint. The earlier Allot imprints and the imprints of Aspley, Hawkins and Meighen are not represented. George III's copy of the Second Folio, an interesting one which had belonged to Ben Jonson and to Charles I—it contains an autograph inscription, "Dum spiro spero.—C. R." —acquired for the King at the Steevens sale, did not come to the Museum, but was one of a number of books from the King's library retained and transferred to Windsor. A story with a moral attaches to this copy: Charles Burney is said to have been keen to buy it, but refrained from bidding when he knew that the King was in for it. As a reward the King gave him another copy of this edition—a first issue, with the portrait overlapping the imprint. This copy came to the Museum with Burney's books, but was sold as a duplicate at the sale of duplicates in 1819! It is now in the New York Public Library.

The three Third Folios include the Grenville copy in the second state, without the portrait on the title-page, but dated 1663, and King Charles II's copy, which has the additional plays and is dated 1664. The four copies of the Fourth Folio unfortunately all bear the commonest imprint: Printed for H. Herringman, E. Brewster, and R. Bentley. The two other variant title-pages are not represented.

Of the apocryphal plays the Museum shows a complete collection of seventeenth-century editions with the following exceptions: of *Arden of Feversham* it lacks the first two editions (1592, 1599); of *Fair Em*, the first edition (c. 1592); of *Mucedorus* it lacks the second (1606), fourth (1611), seventh (1618), ninth (1621), tenth (1626), eleventh (1629?), fourteenth (1639), sixteenth (1663); of the *Merry Devil of Edmonton* it lacks the first two editions (1608, 1612).

The early editions of *Venus and Adonis* are extremely rare, but the Museum has the editions of 1594 (Grenville's copy), 1596, '1602' (1608/9?), 1627 and 1636. *The Rape of Lucrece* is represented by the first edition (1594), the sixth (1616), the seventh (1624) and the ninth (1655) with the Faithorne portrait. The Museum's three copies of the *Sonnets* show the two variant imprints, while its copy (Grenville) of the *Poems* is a very fine one, with the Marshall portrait and both titles.

LATER EDITIONS

If the Museum holding of eighteenth- and nineteenth-century editions of the separate works is compared with a list, such as that in Jaggard's *Shakespeare Bibliography*, of the published editions, it will be found, after making all due allowances, that there are very many gaps in the collection. It is to be expected that the main editions will be present, and that a large proportion of those editions not in the collection will be of little or no value, but it is none the less worth while pausing to consider this matter more closely, for it brings to light a point of great interest and importance. One of the problems which face the large general libraries in these days of specialization is that of making the best of the many 'special collections' which are concealed within their all-embracing assemblages of books. The British Museum Shakespeare collection is a case in point. Because of its integration in a large general library, both its strength and its weaknesses tend to be obscured, and that not only from the user, but also to some extent from the staff. On the other hand, the strength of the Folger Library and its value to students has lain as much in its singleness of purpose as in the great treasures it possesses. By its original terms of reference, set forth by its founder and strengthened by its first director, J. Quincy Adams, the Folger Library has become in this field a standard by which other libraries can measure the scope of their collections. Such a measuring rod is of the greatest value to the large libraries I have referred to. We are grateful to Folger and the staff of the Folger Library for showing how a Shakespeare library can be developed and what the student can expect to find in a collection got together for one purpose. This is the first step towards maintaining and developing a special collection within the general library.

Lest I should be thought to paint too gloomy a picture of the Museum collections in this period, let me quote a paragraph or two from the passage in the *Guide* to the British Museum Shakespeare Exhibition of 1923 which summarizes the Museum's holdings of later printed Shakespeariana:

Dating from the beginning of the eighteenth century, under such editors as Rowe, Pope, Theobald, Warburton, Johnson, Steevens, Malone and so onwards to the editors and critics of the present day [that was in 1923], there are in the British Museum some 340 editions of the collected works of Shakespeare in English and about 100 editions in other tongues....

In editions and translations of separate works of Shakespeare's the British Museum is very rich, possessing over 3000 such texts and translations. Of the plays that furnish the larger number of items towards this total, *Hamlet* is easily first with 90 editions of the original text.... *Macbeth* comes next in bulk, with 78 editions of text....

The collection of biographical and general critical works relating to Shakespeare, and of miscellaneous 'Shakespeariana', comprises upwards of 2000 publications. Of these, biography and criticism occupy over 1000....

All the same, the Museum's collection of eighteenth- and early nineteenth-century editions is unworthy of the fine collection as a whole. It has undoubtedly suffered from being part of a large collection.[7]

Among the interesting copies from this century are a number with manuscript notes by the great eighteenth-century editors. There is, for example, Malone's copy of Capell's edition of 1768, in which he "restored the ancient readings" and "marked such emendations as deserve to be admitted into the text with the initial letter of the commentator by whom each emendation was proposed". By this, he continued, "the reader may observe the falshood and imprudence of Capell's assertion that his emendations are more numerous and more valuable than those of all the other commentators put together"! There is a copy of *Antony and Cleopatra* from Pope's edition of 1728 which contains copious notes assigned by Dawson Turner to Theobald. There is the copy of Johnson and Steevens's edition of 1778 which was used as 'copy' for the printer by Isaac Reed—as is clear not only from the nature of the interpolations and markings, but also from a note in his hand, "send proofs to Mr Reed No 11 Staples Inn". Markings by Ludwig Tieck in his copy of Reed's edition of Johnson and Steevens show him to have been a close and careful student of the texts he translated. Substantial annotations, particularly to *Hamlet*,

Macbeth and *King Lear*, in the hand of S. T. Coleridge occur in copies of Theobald's duodecimo edition of 1773 and in the 1807 octavo edition. Caldecott's interleaved copy of Johnson and Steevens, 1813, is copiously annotated, as are his copies of the 1819 and 1820 editions of his "specimen of a new edition of Shakespeare" containing *Hamlet* and *As You Like It*. There are also Richard Warner's extensive Shakespearian collections, including his emended copy of Tonson's edition, the very large collections of Joseph Hunter, letters from Theobald and Hanmer to William Warburton, notes by Malone and many similar items in the Department of Manuscripts.

ELIZABETHAN AND JACOBEAN MANUSCRIPTS

All the Museum's manuscript Shakespeariana, however, pale into insignificance by the side of *The Booke of Sir Thomas Moore*, three pages of which, containing part of a scene in which More is represented as quelling by his eloquence the riots on 'Ill Mayday' 1517, have been claimed to be in the hand of Shakespeare himself. The manuscript is made up of twenty folios, thirteen from the play as originally written and seven insertions made in the course of an extensive revision. The results of the intensive examination to which the manuscript has been subjected seem to indicate that the original is in the hand of Anthony Munday and that four of the hands concerned in the revision are those respectively of (*a*) Henry Chettle, (*b*) possibly Thomas Heywood, (*c*) the writer of the plots of *The Seven Deadly Sins* (*c*. 1590) and *Fortune's Tennis* (*c*. 1597–8), and (*d*) Thomas Dekker. The fifth hand has been claimed to be that of Shakespeare, on many grounds, though none of them is, unfortunately, conclusive. Pollard, in the *Guide* to the Museum Exhibition previously referred to, sums up his attitude to the problem in the following words:

> To press an official claim that the manuscript should be recognized as of this supreme importance would be out of keeping with the traditions of the British Museum, but a Keeper of Printed Books, who has no official responsibility for the manuscript, but happens to have worked at the problem in conjunction with other students, may perhaps express his personal feeling that the arguments now available will ultimately be found conclusive, unless an unknown author is to be believed to have written a hand which can be shown to possess the same characteristics as Shakespeare's, to have used an old-fashioned spelling every word of which can be paralleled from the 'good' Shakespeare Quartos, and to have anticipated alike the words, the thought, and the temper with which Shakespeare handled similar situations in plays as late as *Coriolanus* and *Troilus and Cressida*.

W. W. Greg's view is similar. He has declared that the claim in Shakespeare's favour rests on "the convergence of a number of independent lines of argument, palaeographic, orthographic, linguistic, stylistic, psychological"; the palaeographical evidence is, he considers, sufficient to "incline the balance of probability in favour of identification". With this judicious summing up we must perforce be content, but we may wish with all our hearts that, in Pollard's words, we had here "the original composition of William Shakespeare, written with his own hand as the thoughts came to him".

The Museum possesses one of the six undoubted specimens of Shakespeare's handwriting still in existence. This is a mortgage by "William Shakespeare of Stratford vpon Avon in the countie of Warwick gentleman", and others, to Henry Walker, "citizein and Minstrell of

London", of a dwelling-house within the precincts of "the late black ffryers". This deed contains four labels with seals, on the first of which is the signature "Wm Skakspe^a". It was found in 1768 among the title-deeds of a Rev. Mr Fetherstonhaugh and was presented by him to David Garrick. It was acquired by the British Museum in 1858.

It is convenient, at this point, to draw attention to the wealth of manuscript material in the Museum which has bearing upon the study of Shakespeare and the theatre in his time, particularly the numerous Elizabethan and Jacobean dramatic manuscripts. These have been extensively dealt with by W. W. Greg in his *Dramatic Documents from the Elizabethan Playhouses* and *The Editorial Problem in Shakespeare*, and I do no more than mention them in the briefest manner, summarizing his conclusions. Of twenty-nine plays in manuscript written between 1590 and 1642 mentioned by Greg in the second of these two works (pp. 23-4, and 22-48 passim), no fewer than nineteen are in the British Museum. I mention these and other plays briefly in the following groups: autographs, 'prompt-books', presentation copies, and plots. The earliest autograph is *Charlemagne or the Distracted Emperor* (c. 1605) which, like the similarly anonymous *The Two Noble Ladies and the Converted Conjuror* (1622/3 ?), Greg considers on internal evidence to be in the author's hand. *Charlemagne*, despite the fact that we have no record of its performance, bears annotations in the hand of Sir George Buc, the Master of the Revels. The manuscript of *The Two Noble Ladies*, as has already been mentioned, is probably in the anonymous author's hand; it has a detailed title and a list of dramatis personae on a blank page and may, Greg has suggested,[8] have been edited for printing. Thomas Heywood's *The Captives* which has extensive annotations and cuttings by the 'book-keeper', may be a prompt-book, but is perhaps more likely to be an author's rough copy prepared for the playhouse scribe. Another of Heywood's plays, *The Escapes of Jupiter*, is autograph, but it bears no signs of playhouse use. Massinger's *Believe as you List*, carefully prepared for the stage by the book-keeper of the King's Company, offers valuable evidence for the study of stage-directions. This play bears the licence of Sir Henry Herbert, as does Mountford's play about the East India Company, *The Launching of the Mary*. Besides these there are several other 'prompt-books' which are not autograph: *Thomas of Woodstock* (c. 1592-5); *Edmond Ironside, or War hath made all Friends* (1590-1600 ?)—this manuscript contains a list of the names of actors taking part in a revival in the 1620's; *Sir John van Olden Barnavelt* (1619), written by the professional scribe, Ralph Crane—also contains a list of actors' names, which have been identified by Greg; like *The Second Maiden's Tragedy*, also in the Museum, it was 'allowed' by Sir George Buc, and has annotations in his hand. *Thomas of Woodstock* and *The Two Noble Ladies* show signs of censorship as does *The Lady Mother*, ascribed to Glapthorne, which bears the allowance of William Blagrave, Herbert's deputy. *The Booke of Sir Thomas Moore* has notes, but not a licence, by Edmund Tilney. Besides his annotations in the plays already mentioned the Museum also possesses the rough draft, mostly in his hand, of Buc's *History of Richard III*. The autograph presentation copy for Prince Henry of Jonson's *Masque of Queens* is preserved in the Royal manuscripts, as is the presentation copy of the *Masque of Blackness*; in the latter, how-ever, only the subscription is autograph. Presentation inscriptions in Jonson's hand to Queen Anne also appear in a copy of the *Masque of Queens*, 1609 (C. 28. g. 5) and in *Two Royal Masques*, 1609 (C. 34. d. 4). Also in the Royal manuscripts is a copy of Sir John Suckling's *Aglaura* (1637-8), prepared for presentation at Court in 1638. Cartwright's *Royal Slave* (1636?) is a calligraphic copy also possibly made for presentation on a similar occasion.

"Stage-Plots of old Plays, viz.—the Deade Man's Fortune, Frederick Basilea, the Battle of Alcazar, etc. Originals. Large folio" is the bald catalogue description of Additional Manuscript 10449, which is of particular interest and value for the study of the drama of the period. It contains no fewer than five of the seven known (six extant in manuscript) stage 'plots'. W. W. Greg, who has devoted considerable study to these plots,[9] shows that they fall into two groups: (1) *Seven Deadly Sins* (this is the only one now extant not in the Museum collection) and *Dead Man's Fortune*, both written about 1590 for Lord Strange's or the Lord Admiral's Company, and (2) *The Battle of Alcazar, Frederick and Basilea, Troilus and Cressida, 2 Fortune's Tennis*, and 1 *Tamar Cam* (no manuscript of this is now known); the latter were prepared for the later Admiral's men about 1597–1602. These outlines of the plays record, on large sheets of cardboard, entrances and sometimes exits for every scene; they indicate properties and attempt to mention the actors of every part. They often preserve information about the plays which occurs nowhere else.

The remarkable collection of plays in Egerton 1994, which includes *Thomas of Woodstock, Edmond Ironside, Charlemagne, The Two Noble Ladies, The Captives, The Escapes of Jupiter, The Launching of the Mary*, and *The Lady Mother* already mentioned, also contains R. Daborne, *The Poor Man's Comfort* (1617?), *Nero* (1624?), *Dick of Devonshire* (1626?), Beaumont and Fletcher, *The Elder Brother, The Fatal Marriage or a Second Lucretia* (c. 1630–40) and *Love's Changelings' Change* (c. 1630–40). Other dramatic manuscripts which call for mention are: Jane Lady Lumley's *Iphigenia in Aulis* (1555), *The Marriage of Wit and Wisdom* (1579), perhaps by Francis Merbury, two manuscripts of *Tancred and Ghismonda* (1600?), Ralph Crane's calligraphic manuscript of Middleton's *A Game at Chess* (1624–5), Fletcher's *Bonduca* (c. 1625) and the autographs of Arthur Wilson's *The Swisser* (1631?), and *The Country Captain* (1635?) by W. Cavendish, Duke of Newcastle. Academic and University plays are also well represented with *Sapientia Solomonis* given by the boys of Westminster School in 1565–6, George Gascoigne's *Jocasta* (1573), *Solymannidae* (1582), Walter Hawkesworth's *Leander* (1598), one of several manuscripts, Thomas Legge's *Richardus Tertius*, also one of a number of manuscripts, Gager's *Dido* and *Oedipus*, both imperfect, *Fatum Vortigerni, Romeus et Julietta, The Birthe of Hercules* (attributed by G. C. Moore Smith to Richard Bernard), and Phineas Fletcher's *Sicelidae*.

Masques and entertainments include *Gesta Grayorum* (1594), possibly in the hand of Francis Davison, the songs possibly by Thomas Campion, *The Twelve Months* (1608–12), George Peele's autograph *Anglorum Feriae, Englandes Hollydayes* (1595), his verse description of a tilt on the anniversary of Elizabeth's accession, 1595, Marston's description of the pageant presented to James I and Christian of Denmark (1606) and the six plays and masques given at Apthorpe (1640–50), possibly in the hand of the author Mildmay Fane, 2nd Earl of Westmorland.

Autographs of many of Shakespeare's contemporaries, in addition to those already mentioned, are to be found in the Museum's collections, some of them in fragments of Henslowe's diary which have been separated from the main part of the work at Dulwich. There are presentation, though probably not autograph, manuscripts of John Day's *Peregrinatio Scholastica* and *The Parliament of Bees*, the latter having a text differing from the printed version of 1641; Thomas Kyd is represented by autograph letters connected with Marlowe's indictment, including articles of accusation against him. And so one might go on multiplying examples where the manuscript collections of the Museum can aid in the study of Shakespeare himself and his life and times and the history of the drama.

Of perhaps slighter interest but more specifically relating to Shakespeare are the many early allusions to his works. Royal MS. 8 A. xxi, which is a thirteenth-century theological compilation, has two lines, in an early seventeenth- or late sixteenth-century hand, quoted from *Venus and Adonis*, probably one of the earliest quotations known:

> Fayer flowers that are not gathered in there prime
> Rot and consume themselues in littill Tyme.

The eighth Sonnet, "In laudem Musice et opprobrium Contemptorii (*sic*) eiusdem", is found in an early seventeenth-century common-place book (Add. MS. 15226). The character of Falstaff is discussed by Richard James, librarian to Sir Robert and Sir Thomas Cotton, in a dedicatory letter to Sir Henry Bourchier prefixed to "The Legend and defence of ye Noble Knight and Martyr Sr John Oldcastel" (Add. MS. 33785). John Manningham's diary from January 1601/2 to April 1603 (Harley MS. 5353) contains an account of a performance of *Twelfth Night* in the Middle Temple Hall on 2 February 1601/2:

> At our feast wee had a play called Twelue night or what you will much like the commedy of errors or Menechmi in Plautus but most like and neere to that in Italian called Inganni.
>
> A good practise in it to make the steward beleeue his Lady widdowe was in Loue wth him by counterfayting a letter as from his Lady in generall termes telling him what shee liked best in him and prescribing his gesture in smiling his apparraile &c. and then when he came to practise making him beleeue they tooke him to be mad.

A contemporary record of a performance of *Othello* (Globe Theatre, 30 April 1610) also occurs, in the journal of the Secretary, Hans Jacob Wurmsser von Vendenheym, of Duke Louis Frederick of Württemberg (Add. MS. 20001). Similar items are Richard Carew's essay of 1595/6 suggesting a parallel between the classical and English writers, including Shakespeare; the autograph manuscript of George Cavendish's *Life of Cardinal Wolsey* (1558), which is held to have inspired Shakespeare's conception of Wolsey in *Henry VIII*; a letter from Thomas Lorkin, afterwards Secretary to the Embassy at Paris, describing the fire which burnt out the Globe Theatre in 1613 while Burbage and his company were playing *Henry VIII*; several manuscript copies of William Basse's epitaph on Shakespeare including one (Add. MS. 15227) written not long after 1630.

To conclude this section on the manuscript material, a word should be said about the material dealing with the Ireland and Payne Collier forgeries. Additional Manuscripts 30346–50 contain papers and correspondence of Samuel Ireland relating to his son's Shakespeare 'discoveries', correspondence with the managers of Drury Lane Theatre relating to the production of *Vortigern*, including letters from R. B. Sheridan and J. P. Kemble and one from Mrs Siddons, and finally "The Divill and Rychard", a mystery play on Richard III "as it was donn onn Sonday last att the Pallace att Westminster by the Clarkes and Boyes of Powles" before Henry VII, 1485—in the handwriting of S. W. H. Ireland. A later collection (Add. MS. 37831) came from William Till who had it from Ireland himself: it contains a copy of a letter from Shakespeare to "Anna hatherrewaye". Collier's fabrications are instanced in Egerton MS. 2623 which contains a fragment of a late sixteenth-century play with words added at the end by Collier intended to convey a covert allusion to Shakespeare.

SOURCE AND ALLUSION BOOKS

It is not easy to treat of the printed Shakespeariana which the Museum can place at the student's disposal, without repeating information which will be thoroughly familiar to readers of *Shakespeare Survey*. To get round this difficulty I have attempted to indicate the range of the Museum collections in this field by comparing its holdings with the books mentioned by Miss Henrietta Bartlett in the two sections 'Source Books' and 'Contemporary Notices' in her *Mr William Shakespeare*. In the former section Miss Bartlett describes "all the important books to which Anders refers" (in *Shakespeare's Books*, 1904)—some ninety items; the latest book referred to is dated 1610 and all of them are rare, some very rare indeed. Of these ninety the British Museum has all but eighteen—I refer of course to the original editions, taking no account of reprints—and several of the eighteen are excessively rare, being known only by single copies or by two or three copies. The most important source-books in the collection include the first edition of Bandello (1554), Painter's *Palace of Pleasure* (1566), Daniel's "Delia" sonnets in *Syr P.S. his Astrophel and Stella* (1591), North's *Plutarch* (1579), Warner's translation of the *Menaechmi* (1595), Luigi da Porto's early version of the story of Romeo and Juliet (1535), Brooke's *The Tragicall Historye of Romeus and Juliet* (1562), Montemayor's *Diana* (1598), Sylvain's *Orator* (1596), the *Pecorone* of Giovanni Fiorentino (1558), Harrington's translation of *Orlando Furioso* (1591), Whetstone's *Promos and Cassandra* (1578), *The Counsellor* of Laurentius Grimaldus Goslicius (1598), with its suggestion of the name of Polonius, Harsnett's *Declaration of egregious Popish Impostures* (1603), *The True Chronicle History of King Leir* (1605), *The Metamorphoses* in Golding's translation of 1567, Montaigne's *Essays*, both French (1580) and English (1603), Silvester Jourdan's *A Discouery of the Barmudas* (1610), and Sir William Alexander's *Tragedie of Darius* (1603), both of which may be echoed in *The Tempest*, Greene's *Pandosto* (1588), Storer's *Life and Death of Thomas Wolsey* (1599), *The Æthiopian Historie* of Heliodorus (1569?), Lyly's *Euphues* (1578?), Marlowe's *Hero and Leander* (1598), and, to conclude this tedious recital of exciting books, the ballad of "The Crowe sits upon the wall, Please one and please all" referred to in *Twelfth Night*.

Miss Bartlett's 'Contemporary Notices' are some 110 in number; of these ninety-four are in the Museum, with another three cases in which the Museum has editions of the same year as those mentioned by Miss Bartlett. Nashe's *Pierce Pennilesse* (1592), Greene's *Groats-worth of witte* (1592), Chettle's *Kind-Harts Dreame*, undated but also of 1592 are the earliest references, and all these are in the Museum in first editions; *Willobie his Avisa* (1594), contains the earliest direct reference to Shakespeare; William Covell's *Polimanteia* (1595), *Colin Clouts Come home againe* (1595), *Palladis Tamia* (1598), the very rare *Cephalus & Procris* of Thomas Edwards (1595), *Englands Helicon* (1600), and *Sir Gregory Nonsence His Newes from no place* (1622), are all worthy of mention. The anthologies, *Englands Parnassus*, with ninety-five extracts from Shakespeare, Bodenham's *Bel-vedére*, and *Englands Helicon*, in which ninety-nine extracts are assigned to Shakespeare (eight of them erroneously) are present in first editions; Shakespeare as an actor is supposedly mentioned in John Davies's *Microcosmos* (1603), and as a poet in Camden's *Remaines* (1605) and elsewhere. It would be possible to continue the list indefinitely: this I refrain from doing, trusting that I have sufficiently indicated that the Museum offers unrivalled stores for the student of the early allusions to Shakespeare and of Shakespeare's library and reading.

BACKGROUND LITERATURE

I have previously suggested that when it comes to the proper organization and development of a special collection the big general library is in some respects at a disadvantage as compared with the special library, whose collections are largely devoted towards one particular end. There is one respect, however, in which the general library has a great advantage over the specialized library. This is in its large array of what can be called 'background' literature. There is no need, in this connexion, to dwell at any length on the resources of the British Museum in English and Continental literature of the fifteenth, sixteenth and seventeenth centuries, in all fields. Some idea of the range and depth of its holdings in English books can be obtained from its now out-of-date *Catalogue of Books...up to 1640,* and by noting the number of times the letter 'L' appears at the head of the location symbols in the *Short-title Catalogue*; for foreign books of the fifteenth and sixteenth centuries there is the *Catalogue of Books printed in the Fifteenth Century*— the Museum has about 10,000 incunabula—and the *Short-title Catalogues* of French, Spanish, Portuguese and Spanish-American books up to 1600 which were compiled in the 1920's under the direction of Sir Henry Thomas, whose services to scholarship by extending the Museum collections in these fields should be remembered with gratitude. It is a pity that the Museum has never published a similar catalogue of its Italian books, for it has notable collections, including those of King George III, Sir Thomas Grenville and Sir Richard Colt-Hoare. Not only are Shakespeare's foreign 'source-books' all present—the *Saxo Grammaticus* (Paris, 1514), the *Decameron* (Florence, 1527), the *Nouella...d'uno Innamoramento* of da Porto (Venice, 1535), the *Novelle* of Bandello (Lucca, 1554), the *Pecorone di Ser Giovanni Fiorentino* (Milan, 1558), the French translation of Bandello (Paris, 1559), the *Hecatommithi* of Giovanni-Battista Giraldi Cinthio (Monte Regale, 1565), the Montaigne (Bordeaux, 1580)—not only are these to be found in it, as a matter of course, but it is no exaggeration to say that for the literature of this period it is probably unsurpassed by any library.

Further light can be thrown on the richness of the Museum's collections for the student of Elizabethan literature and drama by mentioning some of the collections which have been incorporated in it. The Cotton, Harley, Lansdowne (which includes the Burghley papers), Egerton, Arundel, Stowe, Royal and King's collections of manuscripts; the Bagford, Roxburghe and Helmingham-Huth collection of printed ballads, the Thomason 'Civil War' collection, the Garrick collection, the Cracherode library of fine copies of the classics and later Latin literature, the King's library with its classics and Italian and Spanish literature, the Grenville library of classics, English literature, travels and voyages, and Italian and Spanish poetry and romances, the Huth bequest, and in more recent times the Ashley library. The possession of these superb collections carries with it an implied responsibility to maintain the Library as a whole at the highest pitch of efficiency—a responsibility which successive librarians have been quick to recognize.

EARLY MUSIC

A word in conclusion ought to be said of the possessions of the music department of the Museum. This owes a great deal to William Barclay Squire, who was in charge of the printed music in the Museum from 1883 to 1930. Squire was specially interested in the madrigals and motets of the English school of the sixteenth and seventeenth centuries and greatly enriched in this respect the music collections which had come from the Old Royal Library, Sir John Hawkins, Dr Charles Burney and others. He was the author of the *Catalogue of Printed Music published between the years 1487 and 1800 now in the British Museum* (1912). King George III's collection of music did not come to the Museum with the rest of his library in 1823; in 1911, however, King George V deposited it on permanent loan in the Museum. Apart from the fine collection of autographs, contemporary copies and printed editions of Handel, which is the chief glory of this Library, George III's Queen, Charlotte, added many musical manuscripts of the sixteenth and seventeenth centuries. The Library has the John Baldwin volume of motets, madrigals, and the like by various sixteenth-century composers, written *c.* 1600, the Cosyn Virginal Book (*c.* 1600), the Forster Virginal Book, 1624, autograph works by Elway Bevan, Coperario and other seventeenth-century English composers. The Royal Music Library also has its own catalogue, begun by Squire and completed after his death.

Music in the Manuscript Department contains the series of volumes of motets and songs written for Henry VIII and his Court, which came to the Museum with the Old Royal Library. Its collection of sixteenth- and seventeenth-century English music, which includes Thomas Mulliner's book, consisting of airs, chants and similar pieces for the virginal by Tallis and his contemporaries, is perhaps relatively stronger than that of any other period. Among the manuscripts of Shakespearian interest may be mentioned an early seventeenth-century book of songs with lute accompaniment in tablature which contains a poem attributed to Thomas, Lord Vaux, from which the lines sung by the First Clown in *Hamlet*, "In youth, when I did love, did love", were adapted; a book of vocal part music which has the cantus part of a setting of "Then death rock me asleep" from 2 *Henry IV*, Act II; and finally another early seventeenth-century book of songs with lute accompaniment containing "The poor soul sat sighing".

The printed music books to which Shakespeare refers, or which have contemporary or later settings of songs from the plays, include Thomas Est, *The Whole Booke of Psalmes* (1592), Robert Jones, *The First Booke of Songes & Ayres*, 1600 (containing a setting of "Farewell, dear heart", alluded to in *Twelfth Night*), Thomas Robinson, *The Schoole of Musicke*, 1603 (an edition for the lute, containing the setting for "My Robin is to the greenwood gone" from which Ophelia's song may have come); the catch "Hold thy peace, thou knave" in *Twelfth Night*, occurs in Ravenscroft's *Deuteromelia* (1609); William Corkine's *Ayres* (1610) and *Second Booke of Ayres* (1612) contain songs referred to in *The Winter's Tale* and *The Merry Wives*; Morley's *First Booke of Consort Lessons* (the second edition, 1611) containing "O mistress mine", Playford's *Dancing Master* and *English Dancing Master*, Hilton's *Catch that Catch can*—and so on to later arrangements for special productions such as John Wilson's of "Where the bee sucks" and "Full fathom five" in Playford's *Select Ayres and Dialogues* and Wilson's *Cheerful Ayres* respectively and that of Ariel's songs (London, 1675?) probably written for the Dryden-Davenant production of 1667.

It is impossible to detail, within the limits of an article, the books of outstanding interest for the student of Shakespeare. Nor is it possible to do full justice to the varied richness of the Museum's collections. While it would most emphatically not be true to suggest that the Museum's Shakespeare collection has been brought together without skilful direction from the librarians, it does remain the fact that its richness is in a manner of speaking accidental, that it forms just one part of its great wealth in a multiplicity of subjects. The assessment of its wealth in Shakespearian material, and the appreciation of the ways in which it can be increased, is now more possible than it has ever been, thanks largely to the work of the Folger Library. When A. W. Pollard wrote his introduction to the *Guide*, the Folger Library was no more than an idea in the mind of Henry Clay Folger, and his collection, though largely assembled, was an unknown quantity. It was the Huntington Library, then recently enriched with the Bridgewater plays, which was compared with the British Museum and was found to have "a slight but distinct advantage in numbers". Now the Folger Library, by a whole-hearted determination to provide *all* the books which the scholar needs to produce the definitive account of Shakespeare's life and work, has shown how a collection can be built up into a properly planned instrument of research. The richness of the Museum collections, in this as in other subjects, can be measured only by the best that the specialized libraries can offer and it is worthy of all the care and organization that can be bestowed upon it.

NOTES

1. The present writer hopes to collect material for a more detailed account of it in the near future.

2. The letter is quoted in full in Henrietta C. Bartlett and A. W. Pollard, *A Census of Shakespeare's Plays in Quarto*. This copy of 1 *Henry IV* is referred to by Steevens in a letter to Garrick as enabling him to "retrieve two readings" (Steevens to Garrick, 1771).

3. Not quite all, apparently, for a number of volumes of 'Plays' appears in the sale catalogue of his library (with modern books added by Mrs Garrick) on 23 April 1823.

4. George III's library also includes a 'set' of these nine plays, but they are not uniform in size or appearance and were evidently bought separately.

5. Grenville had one quarto, according to the catalogue of his collection, *The First and second Part of the troublesome Raigne of Iohn King of England* (1611).

6. *British Museum Shakespeare Exhibition, 1923. Guide to the MSS. & Printed Books exhibited in celebration of the Tercentenary of the First Folio Shakespeare* (1923).

7. Of *Hamlet*, for example, out of forty-two eighteenth-century editions mentioned by Jaggard, the Museum has only five; of forty-one editions of *Macbeth*, only fourteen.

8. *Op. cit.* p. 45.

9. *Dramatic Documents from the Elizabethan Playhouses* (1931), pp. 1–172 and *Two Elizabethan Stage Abridgements* (1923), p. 21.

THE STRUCTURAL PATTERN OF SHAKESPEARE'S TRAGEDIES

BY

MARCO MINCOFF

The subject of this paper is not, on the whole, one to which scholars have devoted much attention, and the results of this lack of interest have in some ways been unfortunate. Shakespeare's tragedies seem to conform outwardly to the conventional Aristotelian triangle well enough to foster on the one hand the impression that the triangular scheme is the only possible one and that playwrights such as Fletcher who have worked on other principles are lacking in form, while on the other certain un-Aristotelian tendencies, such as the frequent disappearance of the hero during the decline, or the rather abrupt episodic nature of the structure, have been overlooked and even, for instance in discussing the doubtful plays, been regarded as un-Shakespearian while in fact they are typical.

Of the four great tragedies it is *Hamlet* that seems to exhibit the Shakespearian pattern most perfectly. The opening scene is a wonderful piece of atmosphere: a solitary sentry pacing up and down, muffled in an inky cloak to suggest the dark and the cold; to him another figure, similarly muffled, a hasty snatch of conversation in muffled tones, betraying a sense of uneasiness—then more figures, more talk, and out of it, abruptly dropped, the cause of the uneasiness—"What, has this thing appear'd again to-night?" Gradually the thing begins to take shape—it is a dreaded sight, then an apparition, we are about to hear more of it, the atmosphere for a description is carefully prepared, and then, freezing the words on the speaker's lips, the thing itself—the ghost of the newly dead king—appears in the background. The tension rises to a peak—agitated whispers, the thing is challenged but speaks no word, vanishes again, and the muffled figures, shaken to the soul, are left to ponder the portent. Suggestions are made, suggestions that miss the true mark entirely, yet serve to introduce one of the secondary themes of the coming tragedy and underline the deep significance of the apparition, political events, war preparations, a general unrest. Then the Ghost once more, a fresh surge of horror, a more solemn challenge, and just as we hope to have our questions explained the cock crows, the apparition vanishes, and the feelings of horror are now allayed with the calm and lovely poetry of the closing speeches. The whole scene is almost a complete work of art in itself, with its introduction, climax and resolution. Its closest analogy is the overture of a modern opera. It has stirred us deeply and soothed us again, yet leaves us expecting more; it has, towards the close, mentioned the titular hero of the play, and it has introduced the Ghost, who is to start the action, but actually it has told us nothing, it has not even offered us a situation out of which dramatic action can arise, it is purely atmospheric.

And what happens now? We expect the arrival of the watchers to tell young Hamlet what they have seen. Instead a brazen flourish of trumpets shatters the calm of the early morning and the whole court, in the magnificent apparel of state ceremony, sweeps on to the stage, a magnificent effect of sheer contrast. Only the one solitary figure, accentuated by his isolation, strikes a jarring note in this gorgeous throng, awakening for the hardened playgoer, even if the story of

58

the play were not already familiar to him, associations with the familiar theme of the melancholic revenger, awakening too perhaps a vague sense of unfitness—why is the place on the throne not occupied by the young prince, the dead king's son, rather than this man who might in years be his father? But there is no time to think of these matters, we are swept at once into the political complications that have been exercising the watchers on the battlements with the King's clear explanation of events; we are introduced indirectly to Fortinbras and directly to Laertes, who are to play an important part as contrast figures, to Polonius too, and the memory of last night's watch sinks more and more into the background; it has been made to seem more than ever the prelude to the coming war. And now at last the attention turns to the hero, the listless figure in black, and already the contrast with Laertes is stressed—Laertes has had leave to continue his studies abroad, Hamlet must stay at home; and even in the seat of their studies—Paris and Wittenberg—a typical contrast is stressed. And now, with the prince's sardonic comments, his evident hostility towards his uncle's advances, the emotional tension begins to rise. It reaches its peak with the hero's first monologue, while at the same time we are given a marvellous glimpse into the inner man; we feel his disgust and bitterness, his frayed nerves, his desire for death. And when the watchers, whom by now we have almost forgotten, arrive, his sardonic humour and almost hysterical excitement come into play. But there is still no dramatic situation, no germ of action. If the first scene was a piece of static atmosphere, this is static portraiture. The hero is fully introduced to us before the action begins to modify his character. But now the news that the watchers bring cuts across the prince's overwrought tension, and again the scene ebbs away emotionally to its end. The need for a decision imposes restraint, Hamlet becomes collected, a little abstracted perhaps, but the decision is made as it should be, and the scene seems to be leading over to a return to the battlements.

Instead of that, however, what follows is another strong contrast—a simple domestic interior, the introduction of the last of the more important figures of the tragedy and some fresh light on Hamlet, even something that might develop into a theme for action, but action which is only to play a subordinate part. The scene serves also to mark the passage of time till night shall fall again, but that interval scarcely needed stressing in itself. The importance of the scene is more intrinsic as the beginning of a minor action and as a point of contrast, a relaxation of the tension, leading in its turn to tension of another kind. The result is that when we return to Hamlet the atmosphere of the battlements has to be built up anew with a fresh introduction.

We are now approaching an important point, the inception of the action, and here at this crucial moment Shakespeare makes a clear statement of the theme of his tragedy—

> So, oft it chances in particular men,
> That for some vicious mole of nature in them—

a fine piece of dramatic irony that the hero, just as the action is about to start, the conflict about to be defined, points already to the flaw in his own character out of which the real tragedy will grow. Thereupon follows in two scenes, which are in reality but one, the disclosure of the Ghost; the hero is at last precipitated into a really dramatic situation with all the latent possibilities of a development of conflicts, and we are present at the very creation of that situation. But the act does not close at that moment of extreme tension—the cellarage scene brings a gradual relaxation of the tension, a cooling off of Hamlet's wild and whirling words and of his hysterical excitement

5-2

down to collected thought and decision, and finally to the melancholic lethargy of his generalization "the time is out of joint".

This analysis already brings out some of the most salient features of Shakespeare's structural methods. Each scene tends to follow in itself a pyramidal structure, beginning on a low note with a deliberate introduction even, rising to high tension and dropping once more towards the end, forming thus a separate unit, and these units are carefully played off against one another to produce a maximum of contrast. Contrast plays its part, too, in the grouping of the characters within the scenes. Much care is given to a gradual preparation and building up of effects, some of which will not actually be made use of till the later acts. Hints that can only be taken up by one familiar with the play as a whole are introduced, hints that do not in themselves rouse curiosity or anticipation but which will rather serve as an unconscious preparation for what is to come, making things drop into place as parts of an inevitable pattern. The action is slow in getting under way, yet, although the scenes might almost be termed static, at least by comparison with Shakespeare's more baroque successors, the emotional tension is extremely high. There is throughout the act scarcely any action really connected with the central conflict, indeed that conflict does not even exist until the very close, yet there is an effect of action, of forward motion, which is on the whole spurious if closely examined. Practically every scene ends on a note which seems to be leading over to the next, but what follows is in sharp contrast, and generally starts us off along a new path—the transitions are in fact made purposely abrupt. There is a constant holding back of the point to which we wish to come, which results in a great increase of the tension, but also in a very steady rhythmical pulsation.

From the inception onwards the tension rises fairly steadily in the main but with the same rhythmic movement in a series of separate units up to the climax. The main tendency of the next two acts is to present Hamlet in a series of separate encounters, carefully graduated, with Polonius, with his old friends Rosencrantz and Guildenstern, with Ophelia, with the King (in the play-scene) and finally with his mother. It can hardly be said that any of these encounters advances the action, though that is largely due to the theme of delay, which naturally excludes any true action. Nor do they rise naturally out of one another in a chain of cause and effect, producing a clear flow. What they do is rather to illuminate the hero and the situation in which he finds himself in a series of static glimpses which only by their steadily increasing tension give an effect of progress. It is, in fact, the structure of *Tamburlaine*, a series of semi-independent, episodic units held together by a certain parallelism (in the play-scene the parts are reversed, it is the King who is being probed, not Hamlet) and by the personality of the hero, but not by any interdependence or running line of action. Artistically any other order would of course be unthinkable, but as far as mere logic is concerned the position of any of the encounters in the series—except the last—might easily be altered. Even the play-scene might logically head the list and provide a stronger motive for the King's attempts to pierce Hamlet's disguise.

One may note, too, the careful preparation of events, and their delay and interruption. The series sets in with the Reynaldo-scene, a scene unique in Shakespeare in that its main purpose is to underline a time gap, a gap, too, caused not by any necessity of the action but introduced for the sake of the portraiture, to make clear the objective nature of Hamlet's procrastination. Ophelia's disclosures start a train of action, but this action does not move forward smoothly. The transition to the palace is what we expect, but instead of a short introduction leading up to

Polonius's entry we have the preparation for a later unit of the series with Rosencrantz and Guildenstern, and even the purposeful delay with the business of the embassy, before Polonius can bring out his news, and the train is laid actually for a third encounter before even the first has taken place. The first two encounters follow then in quick succession, but with the arrival of the players the series is interrupted to prepare for the fourth, and then, and not till then, are we allowed the peep into Hamlet's mind for which by now we have begun to feel impatient. With his soliloquy the emotional tension, which has already shown two marked pulsations of increasing strength, shoots up to a peak and ebbs even more swiftly with the final resolution to action, a clearly marked peroration cutting the action short for the moment. In the third act the pulsations are considerably stronger—hectic almost. The thread, as usual, is not taken up where the preceding scene left it, but harks back to Rosencrantz and Guildenstern, and the tension rises slowly at first. Hamlet's new soliloquy is subdued in tone, and it is not until the Ophelia-scene that a sharper rise occurs, followed by a slackening as the eavesdroppers exchange their impressions. The opening of the play-scene drops even further, then rises in a steady crescendo to Hamlet's moment of wild exultation, and slowly ebbs again, closing with his preparations to face his mother. And again that forward movement at the close of the scene with the introduction of a new theme is not carried through—the scene in the King's closet interrupts it sharply and is woven into the main movement only by Hamlet's rather illogical appearance. But the comparatively low tone in which the whole scene, including its own distinct apex, is pitched serves as a breathing space and contrast before we reach the last lap of the ascent. In fact every turn of the action is anticipated long ahead, but the sequence of cause and effect is consistently interrupted. We have several episodes running concurrently, overlapping and interrupting one another while the plot threads its way between them. The plot is in fact a network of separate elements.

With the bedroom-scene the highest peak of the action is past, and it is noteworthy that here at the apex of the action the Ghost is reintroduced, recalling its inception. Hamlet has played his cards almost as badly as he could, and failed, and the counterplot of the King now takes the centre of the stage while Hamlet is eliminated during the greater part of the fourth act—even his appearance in IV, iv was apparently cut out of the final version. Instead, the two 'contrast'—or rather 'reflector'—figures of Fortinbras and Laertes, introduced directly or indirectly already in the first act, are developed, each with a father to revenge, and each in his way solving his problem more successfully than Hamlet. This naturally produces a more obviously episodic effect than the actually equally episodic rise of the action, an effect still further increased by the episode of Ophelia's madness.

Even after Hamlet's return, the whole churchyard-scene with its comic interlude is still a markedly separate unit and more evidently static than any of the others. And then, with the final scene, the various threads are drawn together—and there are more of them than one might be inclined to admit off-hand. Hamlet has both achieved his revenge and failed, the sub-plot of Ophelia's love, its disaster and her brother's revenge—almost a separate tragedy in itself—has also worked itself out, and Fortinbras's ambitious energy, which throughout has been more spoken of than represented in action, is also satisfied. And yet these three sequences during the play do not stand out as clearly defined strands, because each step in their development has at the same time been made an element of the main plot too. Ophelia's love has been used as a means of probing Hamlet's disguise, the murder of her father is an essential part of the main plot, only her resulting madness and death break apart as an unconnected episode until they are worked into the main theme by employing Laertes's thirst for revenge to bring about the catastrophe, while her burial serves as an effective setting for Hamlet's reappearance. And in the same way each mention of the Fortinbras theme has its part to play in the main plot. It is first introduced as a red herring to explain the Ghost's appearance, in II, ii it is made use of to stress the time gap—the embassy has had time to go and return—it serves as the subject of one of Hamlet's soliloquies, and finally it rounds the play off on a note of triumph. The result is still further to increase the effect of a closely woven network rather than a clear, bold line of action. Indeed, one could put it better the other way about and say that each element of the plot, each episode, has the tendency to become a centre of its own, to send out filaments which catch hold of the secondary characters too, and force them into prominence. Each person is in fact a separate entity, the centre of a little world of his own, with his own individuality and his own fate, developed far beyond the limits of what the mere plot demands, and there is a certain struggle between the desire to portray, to dwell on the separate personality, on the separate situation, and the need to proceed with the action. Hence the abruptness of the transitions from scene to scene, from episode to episode, hence even a certain diffuseness which does not make itself unpleasantly felt only because each scene or episode is given a centre of interest of its own, a rise and fall of tension and succeeds in capturing the imagination.

Noteworthy, however, is it that the play is given a definite apex, and that the tensions are graduated so as to lead up to and down again from that peak, and this, though we may be inclined to regard the Aristotelian analysis of the parts of a drama as universal in its application, is by no means true either of Shakespeare's predecessors, like Marlowe and Kyd, who on the whole left the pattern of the play to take care of itself, or at least paid small attention to a centring climax or definite turn of the action and still less to making such a turn coincide with the maximum of emotional tension, or his successors from Fletcher down to Dryden, who preferred, not a single climax but a whole series with a corresponding number of turns, but who insisted on the other hand on a flowing, uninterrupted line to join them.

Essentially the other three tragedies follow the same pattern as *Hamlet* though each shows certain modifications of it. In all, owing to the interest in character rather than plot, the tendency towards more or less static portrayal of character and states of mind is closely connected with the treatment of the scene as a definite unit and the absence of a clearly marked flow. The flow is on the whole strongest in *Othello*, since here the story demanded a rapid development which would leave the hero no time to stop and consider probabilities, and this sense of speed is increased by the comparatively high proportion of scenes that begin in the middle of a conversation which we are to imagine has been going on before the entry of the speakers. Here the effect of hurry is insisted on from the first, rapid, crowded events, quick decisions, no time for delay or thought.

On the other hand, in no other of the tragedies is the introduction so long and complex, for the basic character of the hero, his nobility, calmness and self-control before Iago's poison has destroyed it, had to be impressed firmly on the audience's mind. And so the introduction is not so much a separate overture as a separate playlet, connected with the main tragedy chiefly by Brabantio's premonition. Yet the introduction is peculiar in that it seems to drop us without warning into an already developed situation, and even the first scene begins abruptly in the middle of a conversation and with the lever of the action, Iago's malignant hatred of his general, ready to hand. That is due partly to the fact that the hero is actually a passive character, a puppet in the villain's hands, and in fact, as far as Othello is concerned, the inception comes remarkably late in the play with Iago's "Ha, I like not that!" and the accompanying dramatic irony of "When I love thee not, Chaos is come again", so that Iago's ready created motive—of which in actual fact not much is made, the stress being laid rather on the absence of true motive—is rather an example of character-drawing and anticipation than of a true dramatic situation.

From the inception in the third act the main action rises with extreme rapidity, sustained tension and comparatively few pulsations to the climax, Othello's trance, and falls almost as swiftly. And with the turn of the action the usual procedure is reversed, from passive the hero becomes active, and so *Othello* is the only one of the tragedies in which the hero does not disappear during the greater part of the descent. But up to the inception the building up of the play in separate blocks or episodes is even more marked than in *Hamlet*, and the introduction in Venice, the storm, the plot against Cassio, each with its own rise and fall, is a series of separate events. There is also the same complexity of texture, the effect of a network rather than a line, and as in *Hamlet*, and in *Macbeth* too, one may note how in the opening scenes a double tension is achieved through the subsidiary theme of war.

In *Macbeth* the pattern of the opening scenes of *Hamlet* is repeated almost exactly—the purely atmospheric opening with the introduction of the supernatural instigators—much shorter, however, and without any effect of tension—the flourish of trumpets and succeeding bustle of the camp-scene, the keeping back of the hero, even more markedly than in *Hamlet*, the *ab ovo* inception, the dramatic irony of Duncan's remark at Macbeth's entry and Macbeth's own fear of "bloody instructions". Also there is the reappearance of the supernatural agents at the turn of the action, more clearly motivated now and more organic, since it is their change of attitude that is the chief cause of the turn, and the disappearance of the hero in the fourth act as the counterplot sets in. The marked pulsation too, achieved here very often by such 'empty' scenes as the arrival of Duncan, the porter's interlude, the comments of Ross and the old man or Lennox and the other lord, and the tendency to present the hero's development—especially towards the end—in a series of separate flashes.

Yet *Macbeth* has its own peculiarities too, which set it apart from the other plays even more decidedly than *Othello* stands apart—above all the concentration on the hero and his wife, whose parts are parallel, to the exclusion of all other characters, whose personalities and private concerns are reduced to an absolute minimum. It is often supposed that *Macbeth* has been much abridged, yet in view of the absolute nonentity of most of the subsidiary characters this seems doubtful. Lennox is given a certain satirical twist at his appearance as a chorus figure, but not otherwise, Ross not even then, and more important figures like Macduff and Malcolm are entirely un-individual. The only figure with a more definite personality is the genial, earth-bound Banquo, to whom one might add, with reservations, the gentle Duncan, but those are the victims who had to be made to live if their death was to be felt. This absence of any care for the minor figures suggests that the play was in fact planned from the first on a much smaller scale than the other. However that may be, the result is that in *Macbeth* we have not that richness of texture, the complex network of the other plays; it is indeed the only one of Shakespeare's plays in which the action follows a clear, simple line without deviations and complications. Yet it is no more than in the other plays an unbroken line; indeed, the abruptness of transitions, common to all the tragedies, has called forth more comment here and been taken, not very justifiably, as a proof of abridgement. And though *Macbeth* has fewer breaks perhaps than the others, those breaks are sharper. From the inception the action rises in strong, rapid pulsations to a sort of climax in the second act, and falls again with a single pulse beat—the discovery of the murder—down to the news of Macbeth's election, skilfully avoided in direct presentation since it would inevitably form a climax as with the parallel case in *Richard III*. Instead, a certain tension is preserved by Ross's harping on the portents and the horror of the deed. With Act III, however, an entirely new sequence sets in, rising again in bold pulsations to the banquet-scene, the true climax, in which Macbeth appears for the first time at the full height of his glory—it was on that account that a coronation or election scene was avoided—and at the same moment loses his nerve and becomes an object of suspicion to his thanes. By a skilful combination of these two points with the high emotional tension of the Ghost's appearance an apex is formed that almost miraculously out-tops the peak of Duncan's murder.

Rather more use is made of reflection to point a comment, through the contrast figure of Banquo, than in *Othello* where it is practically only Iago's cool attitude towards his wife's supposed lapse that offers an example of this method. More important than the reflector figure in this connexion is, however, the use of recurrent themes, which is much more developed here than in the other tragedies—another pointer to show that the shortness of the play is not primarily due to abridgement—the themes of "fair is foul," "nothing is but what is not," equivocation, the topsyturvydom of this world and unreliability of outward appearance, "out of nature"— themes which melt into one another and provide a continuous series of comments.

King Lear again shows certain peculiarities of its own—the absence of a lengthy introduction; the action starts almost straight off with the inception, which is in itself the most typical example of Lear's wilfulness and easy rage, and thus makes a preliminary portrait superfluous, though it may be noted that there is still no ready created situation lying outside the framework of the play —and the reflector figure of Gloucester is developed into the hero of a fully developed plot. All this is clearly due to the comparatively undramatic, narrative nature of the main plot with its fairy-tale character, and it leads to a fairly regular alternation of abruptly contrasting scenes and an even greater complexity of network than in the other plays, but also to a kind of double climax in two succeeding scenes—the farmhouse and the blinding of Gloucester. One may note how the farmhouse-scene with its imaginary trial of Lear's daughters harks back to the opening scene, just as in *Othello* Lodovico's arrival just after the trance-scene brings with it the atmosphere of Venice and the ducal palace; how the climax is in fact inverted, a climax of despair with a subsequent turn towards renewed hope; and how Lear, remaining a technically passive figure after as before the climax, is eliminated for most of the fourth act, while the rather disappointing intrigues of Edmund and the sisters are used to fill out the waning interest of the descent. Also the irony of the comment "Nothing will come of nothing", taken up both in the inception of the Gloucester plot and in the Fool's later speeches, is worth noting.

In short, in these tragedies, although Shakespeare has no rigid structural pattern as in classical tragedy, and alters the structure freely according to the demands of circumstances, he has a fairly definite pattern in mind, following it most strictly in *Hamlet*. Every structural feature of that tragedy can be matched in the majority of the remaining ones, while each deviation from the pattern of *Hamlet* stands alone and can easily be explained through the special circumstances of the play in question. Much of this pattern can be found in Shakespeare's contemporaries, in Chapman and Jonson, for example—the clearly separated scenic and episodic units, the building up of the play in separate blocks, the network, the lengthy careful introduction and *ab ovo* inception. That in which Shakespeare seems to differ chiefly from the men of his generation is in his use of emotional tension to achieve a rhythmic pulsation—an effect which he had not arrived at in *Romeo and Juliet*—to lend excitement to the introduction, and to mark the catastrophe, which generally comes squarely in the centre of the play.

This centring and emotional stressing of the turn of the action might easily be ascribed to classical influence, but there are no definite signs that Shakespeare learnt anything directly from classical models, while it is noteworthy that the more confirmed classicists like Chapman and Jonson did not attain the classical triangle, and the later seventeenth century, much more classical in outlook than the sixteenth, rejected it altogether. It would seem therefore more correct to ascribe this effect rather to that completeness of structure, demanding a regular introduction and a conclusion to balance which we find exemplified in so much sixteenth-century art, in the closed, symmetrical composition of the Renaissance painters and—a much nearer parallel—in so many of the more complex lyrics of the sixteenth century such as Wyatt's *To his Lute*, Surrey's *Complaint of the absence of her Lover*, Spenser's *Prothalamion*, *Epithalamion* and his *Ditty in Praise of Eliza*, which work up to the height of lyrical emotion in the exact middle and then fall slowly to the end, often in such a way that the first and last, second and penultimate verses or groups of verses are parallel. In the simpler form of the lyric this balance and stress on the centre was more easily attainable, in the more complex forms of the drama and especially the epic it was rare.

THE 'MEANING' OF *MEASURE FOR MEASURE*

BY

CLIFFORD LEECH

The nineteen-twenties, distrustful of 'enthusiasm', strove to see Shakespeare as above all the practical dramatist, led to the choice and the manipulation of his stories, to his manner of theatrical speech and character-presentation, by the stage-conditions of his time and the passing fashion of dramatic taste. This approach strengthened our understanding of Elizabethan stage-technique, and it was a useful corrective to the heavily romanticized Shakespeare of earlier years. But when the student of stage-conditions set up as the complete interpreter, the limitations of the approach were obvious enough. The poetic and the dramatic power were only foster-children of the industrious apprenticeship to the stage: the heart of the matter was not to be weighed in a Shakespeare laboratory.

The realization that the greatness of the poet lies, partly at least, in the scope of his mind has led in recent years to a close study of the ideas communicated through the plays. We now tend to see the histories as dramatic essays on a political theme, the final romances as embodiments of religious truth. Even the tragedies are dredged for underlying 'meanings'. But in one characteristic these searchers for theses do not differ from the stage-conditions men of a generation ago. They, too, emphasize the Elizabethanism of Shakespeare, and relate the significance of his plays to the general current of Elizabethan thought on political and religious themes. In the two tetralogies, we are told, Shakespeare speaks after the fashion of Halle and the Homilies; in the romances he is at one with the Christian attitude, adding—as G. Wilson Knight has it [1]—his *Paradiso* to complete the structure of his collected works. And Miss Elizabeth M. Pope, in her article on "The Renaissance Background of *Measure for Measure*",[2] has set out to demonstrate that Shakespeare's handling of this dark comedy gives a thoughtful examination of the Christian views of justice and pardon. If we accept these interpretations unreservedly, we may see Shakespeare as the superb expositor of his age's thought, but perhaps we shall be giving both to the Shakespeare plays and to the Elizabethan age a consistency of texture that they can hardly claim. Historically it was a time of important social transition, and the birth-pangs of the new order often induced doubt of old premise and new practice: the Homilies are of necessity orthodox, but we would do violence to *Tamburlaine* to interpret it exclusively in their light; Chapman's tragedies and Jonson's comedies are the products of independent minds, ever ready to scrutinize an accepted code; in *Troilus and Cressida* the traditional values of Hector and Ulysses are seen as unavailing in a world given over to disorder. If, then, we are to think of Shakespeare as the dramatic champion of the Tudor supremacy and the Anglican Church, we must recognize that this makes him, not the complete Elizabethan, but the sturdy partisan.

Yet it would appear particularly strange for Shakespeare's plays to be the embodiments of theses. In all matters of detail we find contradictions between one part of a play and another: the time-schemes are hardly ever consistently worked out; the manner of the dialogue may be rhetorical, intimate, sententious, euphuistic, compact, staccato, orotund, facetious, according to the particular demands of the individual scene; the statement of one passage may be at odds with others in the play, as with the differing accounts of Ophelia's death, the riddle of Macbeth's children, and Prospero's claim that he has raised men from the dead on his enchanted isle. Of course we can argue that contradictory time-schemes will fuse in the theatre, that the style in the best plays brings diversity into unity, and that incidental contradictions of statement will go unnoticed by an audience under a poet's spell. It remains significant that there are these discrepancies, for they may lead us to expect to find contradictory 'meanings' juxtaposed in the plays, to see the ending of *Macbeth* as simultaneously the destruction of a brave spirit and the reassertion of a political and moral order. In fact, when Shakespeare wrote *Macbeth*, he was thinking with part of his mind in the fashion of the Homilies, and at the same time he conveyed something of Seneca's concern with the individual's destiny, something of Euripides' cosmic challenge. For this reason, perhaps, *Macbeth* and the other tragedies leave us uneasy, in suspense. If we can, we shall escape from our uneasiness by disregarding certain parts of the dramatic statement, we shall claim *Macbeth* as first cousin either to *Gorboduc* or to *Jude the Obscure*, according as the fashion of the moment and our personal inclinations may lead us. But to escape in either direction is to do violence to the play.

In Miss Pope's account of *Measure for Measure* we have, I think, a corresponding simplification. Her relation of certain utterances in the play to Elizabethan statements of Christian doctrine does indubitably throw light on those utterances, and on the strands in the play's thought and feeling that they represent. But the total impression she leaves with us hardly coheres with the effect produced by the play in the theatre or when read as a whole. We are disturbed by it, not because its Christian doctrine is strict and uncompromising—as we may be disturbed by François Mauriac or Graham Greene—but because the very spokesmen for orthodoxy in the play repel us by their actions and the manner of their speech: they are not too hard for us, but rather too shifty, too complacent, too ignorant of their own selves, and for these failings they are nowhere explicitly reproved. That there is a Christian colouring in the play Miss Pope has securely demonstrated, particularly in the prayer of Isabella for Angelo's life and in the ultimate transcendence of justice by mercy. But this Christian colouring is, I hope to show, not more than intermittent in the play: it wells up, as it were, from Shakespeare's unconscious inheritance, and it does not determine the play's characteristic effect.

We should note first of all that *Measure for Measure* is not free from those incidental contradictions of statement that are to be found in almost all of Shakespeare's plays. Dover Wilson has observed gross inconsistency in the time-references and has drawn attention to the way in which Mistress Overdone in I, ii first tells Lucio and the others of Claudio's imprisonment and immediately afterwards, in her talk with Pompey, displays ignorance of it.[3] A much more serious puzzle is provided by the Duke's statements about Angelo in different parts of the play. In I, i the Duke is presumably serious in his profession of trust in Angelo. If he were not, the appointment of Angelo would be inexcusable. Moreover, he professes that Angelo's high character is fully manifest:

> There is a kind of character in thy life,
> That to th' observer doth thy history
> Fully unfold;

and he adds that such merit should not go unused. Yet, in his conversation with Friar Thomas, the Duke is by no means so sure: part of his object in deserting his post and turning spy is to find out whether Angelo is all that he appears:

> Lord Angelo is precise;
> Stands at a guard with envy; scarce confesses
> That his blood flows, or that his appetite
> Is more to bread than stone: hence shall we see,
> If power change purpose, what our seemers be.   (I, iii, 50–4)

We will not stay to consider whether, in view of these suspicions, the appointment of Angelo should have been made. In III, i, however, the Duke professes himself amazed at Angelo's fall from grace:

> but that frailty hath examples for his falling, I should wonder at Angelo;

and then, some forty lines later, tells Isabella of Angelo's former relations with Mariana. We should in particular note the Duke's assertion that Angelo, wishing to escape from his dowerless bride, pretended "in her discoveries of dishonour": his past conduct is, in fact, here presented as so infamous that Isabella is moved to cry:

> What corruption in this life, that it will let this man live!

Yet the Duke knew all this long before, we must assume. Not only, therefore, does Angelo's appointment reflect on the Duke, but we must find Shakespeare curiously engaged in deceiving his spectators: we have been led to believe that Angelo was honest in his puritanism, was convinced of his own strength against temptation, was horrified when Isabella was used to bait vice's hook. It is difficult to see how even a revision-theory could explain these inconsistencies. Rather it seems likely that, as so often, it was the immediate situation that primarily engaged Shakespeare's attention.

If that is the case, however, should we expect to find consistency of thought and feeling through the play? Are we to try to reconcile the deeply Christian cry of Isabella:

> Why, all the souls that were were forfeit once;
> And He that might the vantage best have took,
> Found out the remedy;   (II, ii, 73–5)

with the Duke's speech on death in III, i? In this connexion we should remember that, though Miss Pope will not accept Roy Battenhouse's view of the Duke as representing "the Incarnate Lord", she does see him as the good ruler, doing God's work and moving through the play as "an embodied Providence".[4] Yet, despite his Friar's gown, the Duke offers no hint of Christian consolation: Claudio must welcome death because there is no real joy to be found in life: he denies even personality itself:

> Thou art not thyself;
> For thou exist'st on many a thousand grains
> That issue out of dust.

Man, he says, is not master of his own mind:

> Thou art not certain;
> For thy complexion shifts to strange effects,
> After the moon.

And there could hardly be a more dreadful or more sober denunciation of human lovelessness than we are offered here:

> Friend hast thou none;
> For thine own bowels, which do call thee sire,
> The mere effusion of thy proper loins,
> Do curse the gout, serpigo, and the rheum,
> For ending thee no sooner.

We can, of course, see the dramatic reason for this speech. It provides the thesis to which Claudio's shrinking from death is the antithesis. But it cleaves too near the bone to be regarded as a mere dramatic convenience. We have to recognize that the ideas in the speech reverberated in Shakespeare's own mind, that they could co-exist with echoes of redemption and of a human as well as divine forgiveness.

The Duke, ultimately the dispenser of pardon, has something of Prospero's magisterial place and nature, is indeed at certain moments a morality-figure, a god out of the playwright's pigeon-hole. G. Wilson Knight assures us that "Like Prospero, the Duke tends to assume proportions evidently divine",[5] while W. W. Lawrence argues that the Duke is but "a stage Duke", a mere instrument in the play's economy.[6] Both these judgements, however, overlook the strong antipathy which the Duke has aroused in many readers during the past hundred years. The contrast between Wilson Knight's view and that, for example, of H. C. Hart[7] suggests an ambivalence in the character, a contradiction between its dramatic function and the human qualities implied by its words and actions. As F. P. Wilson has briefly shown, the character's morality-outline cannot be preserved in a play where other characters are as fully realized as Isabella, Angelo, Claudio and Lucio.[8]

Raleigh pointed out how the Duke plays at cat-and-mouse with Angelo in the last act,[9] and indeed his supreme indifference to human feeling is as persistent a note as any in the play. In II, iii he catechizes Juliet, and in bidding her farewell casually breaks the news of Claudio's imminent execution:

> Your partner, as I hear, must die to-morrow,
> And I am going with instruction to him.
> Grace go with you! *Benedicite!*

We should note perhaps that as yet there is no hint that the Duke will interfere with the sentence: he has no criticism of Angelo's severity to make here, and in IV, ii he insists that the sentence would be unjust only if Angelo fell short of the standards he is imposing on others. If, however, we are to assume that the Duke undergoes a 'conversion' which brings him to the exercise of mercy, we should be given some clear token of this in the play: as things stand, it appears as if the Duke pardons because he has not the strength to be severe and because he enjoys the contriving of a last-minute rescue. He is indeed like Prospero in this, who pretends sorrow for Alonso's loss of his son, and then extracts a stage-manager's thrill from the sudden discovery that Ferdinand is safe. When Lucio refers to "the old fantastical duke of dark corners", he gives us a phrase that our memories will not let go: it comes, too, most appropriately in IV, iii, just after the Duke has told us that he will proceed against Angelo "By cold gradation and well-balanc'd form." and has informed Isabella that Claudio is dead. Of course, he gives us a reason for this behaviour:

Isabella shall have "heavenly comforts of despair, When it is least expected", but this implies an odd principle of conduct, which we should challenge even in "an embodied Providence". Indeed, it appears that there is nothing the Duke can do directly. After he has spied on the interview between Isabella and her brother in III, i, he tells Claudio that Angelo has merely been testing Isabella's virtue: one can see no reason for this beyond the Duke's love of misleading his subjects. Having, moreover, hit upon the Mariana-plan, he still urges Claudio to expect immediate death. We should note, too, that he claims to know Angelo's mind by virtue of being Angelo's confessor. One does not have to be deeply religious to be affronted by this piece of impertinence, but later we find that the Duke takes a special delight in the confessor's power which his disguise gives him: in Angelo's case he doubtless lied, but in IV, ii he is prepared to shrive Barnardine immediately before execution and in the last speech in the play he recommends Mariana to Angelo as one who has confessed to him. We have reason to believe that the home of Shakespeare's childhood was one in which the old religion was adhered to:[10] be that as it may, however, it is difficult to believe that he could look with favour on a man who deceived a condemned criminal with a pretence of priestly power and who tricked Mariana into giving him her confidence.[11]

But mystification is his ruling passion. He sends "letters of strange tenour" to Angelo, hinting at his own death or retreat into a monastery (IV, ii); he gives Angelo a sense of false security at the beginning of v, i, announcing:

> We have made inquiry of you; and we hear
> Such goodness of your justice, that our soul
> Cannot but yield you forth to public thanks,
> Forerunning more requital.

Then he orders Isabella to prison, calls Mariana "thou pernicious woman", and then, in his Friar's disguise, tells them both that their cause is lost. Later he laments with Isabella that he was not able to hinder Claudio's death:

> O most kind maid!
> It was the swift celerity of his death,
> Which I did think with slower foot came on,
> That brain'd my purpose.

Apart from considerations of common decency and kindness, we must assume at this point that Isabella is a woman he loves. Later he pretends to discharge the Provost for beheading Claudio, though here presumably only the standers-by were deceived.

It may be argued that we are taking the last act too seriously, that here, as Raleigh put it, we have "mere plot, devised as a retreat, to save the name of Comedy".[12] Indeed, there is evidence that Shakespeare's mind was not working at full pressure in this part of the play: Isabella tells Mariana in IV, vi that the Friar may "speak against me on the adverse side": this he does not do and we may assume that when writing IV, vi Shakespeare had not fully worked out the conduct of the final scene. Nevertheless, the stage-managing Duke of v, i is of a piece with the man we have seen eavesdropping and contriving throughout the play. But now he forsakes his 'dark corners', focuses the light on himself as Richard did at Coventry, gives pardon to all, even to

Escalus for being shocked at the Friar's seeming impudence, and promises himself an added delight in further discourse of his adventures.

We should not forget in this last scene that the Duke is still outraged by the manner of Viennese life. Speaking as the Friar, he puts forward the same view as at the beginning of the play:

> My business in this state
> Made me a looker-on here in Vienna,
> Where I have seen corruption boil and bubble
> Till it o'er-run the stew: laws for all faults,
> But faults so countenanc'd, that the strong statutes
> Stand like the forfeits in a barber's shop,
> As much in mock as mark.   (v, i, 318–24)

Apart from his desire to spy on Angelo, his whole object in abandoning his ducal function was that the law should be exercised with greater rigour; yet at the end all are forgiven—except Lucio, whose punishment is grotesque rather than stern—and it would seem inequitable to discriminate between Barnardine and Mistress Overdone. But perhaps at the end, like the Duke himself, we forget Vienna and the governmental function: it may be that a *coup de théâtre* should not supply a legal precedent.

There is, moreover, something odd in the relations between the Duke and Lucio. Miss Pope, in exalting the Duke's ultimate dispensation of mercy, says that Lucio has to make amends "to the girl he has wronged".[13] This is a sententious way of putting it, for Shakespeare seems to take it much less seriously: in III, ii Mistress Overdone gives us the lady's name, and 'wronging' seems too romantic a term for Lucio's association with her. Our reaction to the Duke's punishment of the one man he could not forgive is compounded of amusement at Lucio's discomfiture and astonishment at the intensity of the Duke's spite. When Lucio protests against the sentence, the Duke's reply is "Slandering a prince deserves it": this is a different matter from righting a wrong done to Mistress Kate Keepdown. Before that, I think, most readers and spectators have frankly enjoyed Lucio's baiting of the Friar. Not only do his words "old fantastical duke of dark corners" bite shrewdly, but it is amusing to see how the Friar tries in vain to shake Lucio off when he is garrulous concerning the Duke's misdemeanours. Critics, searching for ethical formulations, are apt to forget that in the theatre the low life of Vienna and Lucio's persevering wit can arouse our sympathetic laughter.[14] And because we have earlier tended to side with Lucio against the Duke, we are amused when the Duke is petulant at Lucio's interruptions in the final scene. As for the judgement, we may remind ourselves as we hear it that, about this time, Shakespeare wrote in *Lear* of a judge and a condemned thief who might exchange places.

But much in this play seems to provide a comment on the administration of justice. The law's instruments include Abhorson, Elbow and, as a recruit from the stews, Pompey: their combined efforts take something away from the law's majesty. During Shakespeare's middle years he made much use of trial-scenes and other ceremonial unravellings. There is the Venetian court in *The Merchant of Venice*, the dismissal of Falstaff by the newly crowned Prince in 2 *Henry IV*, the King's putting of things to rights in *All's Well*, and the Duke's similar exercise of his function in this play. In each instance the sentence given can be justified; some clemency is allowed to mitigate the letter of the law; the way is cleared for the return of common conditions. And yet in every case our feeling is hardly of complete satisfaction. Shylock, Falstaff, Lucio arouse some resentment on their behalf, and we have little pleasure in the assertion of the law. It is frequently argued that we are too sensitive in our attitude to these victims of justice, and Miss Pope[15] suggests that Shakespeare's first audience would have been at least as well contented if Angelo, Lucio and Barnardine had been, like Shylock, punished severely. But perhaps the attitude of the audience is not so necessary to an understanding of Shakespeare's purpose as his own attitude must be, and it is in *Measure for Measure* that we are given one of the clearest statements of his wide-reaching sympathy: Isabella herself reminds us that

> the poor beetle, that we tread upon,
> In corporal sufferance finds a pang as great
> As when a giant dies.   (III, i, 79–81)

We may remember too that Barnardine, a convicted malefactor, seems to be introduced into the play for the sake of providing a substitute for Claudio's head: that he is not executed and that Ragozine dies so conveniently would suggest that Shakespeare could feel the horror of execution in the case of the common ruffian as well as in that of the gentlemanly, merely imprudent Claudio. It would be dangerous to base a judgement of Shakespeare's purpose on the assumption that his feelings were less fine than ours.[16]

No more than the other plays incorporating 'trial-scenes' is *Measure for Measure* to be interpreted as a dramatic satire. It is indeed the overt purpose of the play to demonstrate, as Miss Pope has suggested, a governor's duty to practise mercy, to requite evil with forgiveness or with the gentler forms of punishment. Even the Duke's cat-and-mouse tricks with Claudio and Angelo may be justified as the mitigated punishment for their wrongdoing. Miss Pope has judiciously drawn attention to the Duke's soliloquy at the end of Act III, where in gnomic octosyllabics he speaks with chorus-like authority:[17] here, indeed, the morality-element in the play is uppermost, and Wilson Knight has noted the resemblance of these lines to the theophanic utterances of the last plays.[18] But, as so often with Shakespeare, the play's 'meaning' is not to be stated in the terms of a simple thesis: there are secondary as well as primary meanings to be taken into account, and the secondary meanings may largely determine the play's impact. We can see 2 *Henry IV* as a play with a morality-outline, with the Prince tempted by disorder and finally won over to the side of Royalty. At the same time, that play seems a dramatic essay on the theme of mutability, with sick fancies, the body's diseases, senile memories, and lamentations for a lost youth constituting its lines of structure. And we can see it, too, as part of the great historical design, of the chain of actions that led from Gloucester's murder to Bosworth Field. There is a satiric element as well, which appears uppermost when Prince John teaches us not to trust the word of a noble, and which is perhaps latent in Falstaff's rejection-scene.

It is this complexity of meaning that makes it possible for us to see and read these plays so often, that enables the theatrical producer to aim at a new 'interpretation'. We are tempted always to extract a meaning, and the undertaking may be profitable if it leads us to inquire into the bases of Elizabethan thought and does not limit our perception to those things in the play that are easy to fit in place. In *Measure for Measure* in particular we should be careful of imposing a pattern on Shakespeare's thought, for the silence of Isabella in the last hundred lines suggests either a corrupt text or a strange heedlessness of the author. But we should always be ready for

PLATE I

A. PORTRAIT OF WILLIAM SHAKESPEARE painted for and presented to
JOHN DRYDEN, 1693

B. THE 'NEW' SIGNATURE OF SHAKESPEARE, in a copy of
WILLIAM LAMBARD'S *Archaionomia*, 1568

PLATE II

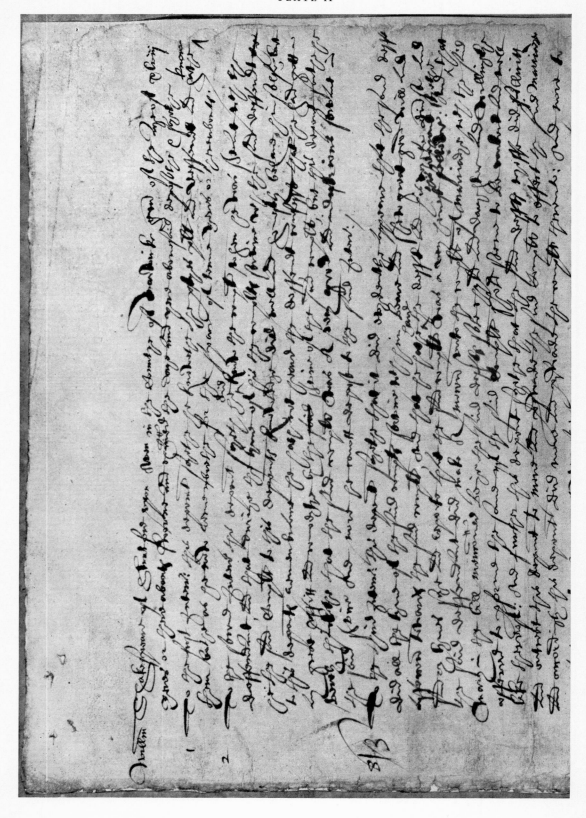

SHAKESPEARE'S DEPOSITION in the Belott-Mountjoy Suit

PLATE III

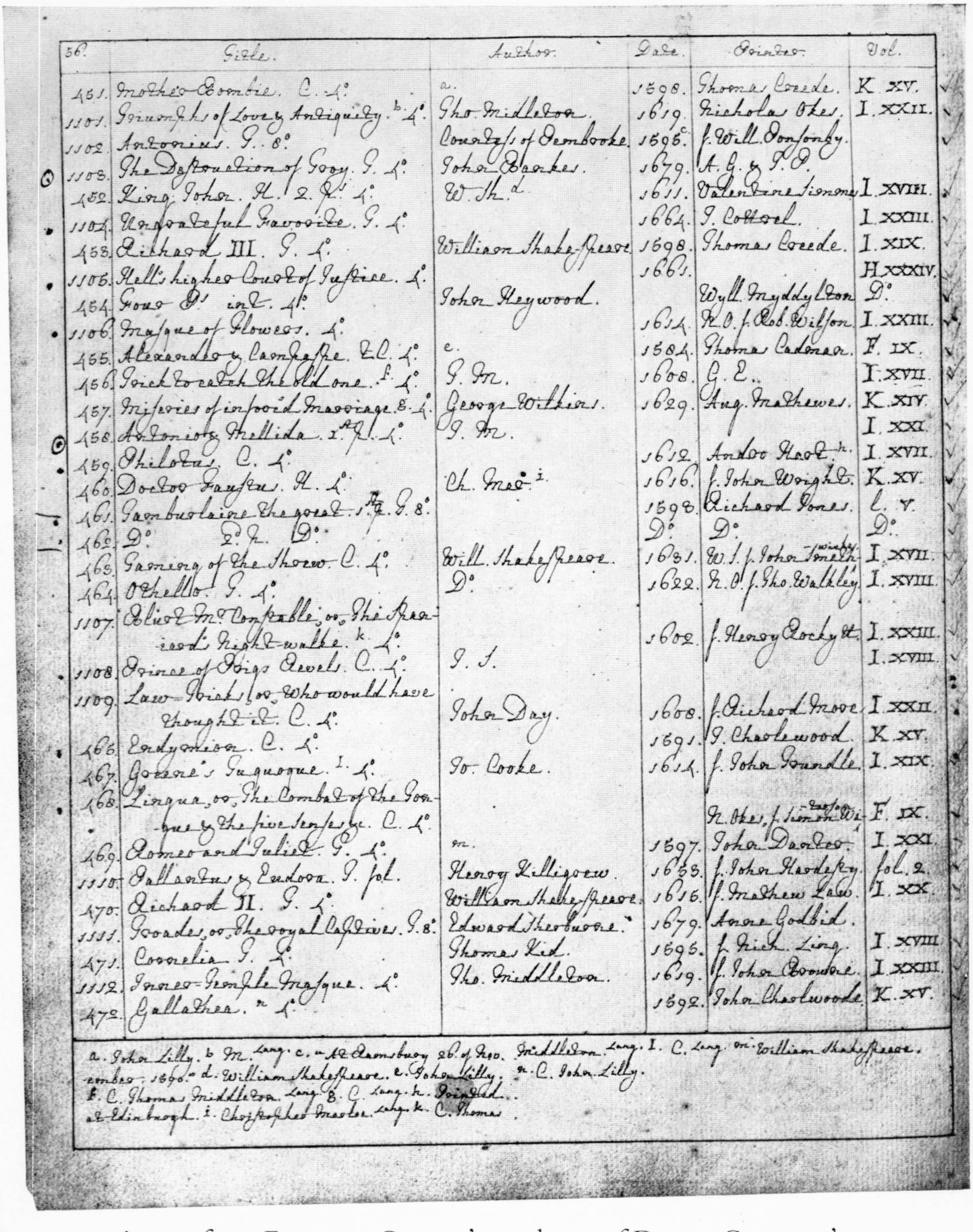

PLATE IV

A page from EDWARD CAPELL's catalogue of DAVID GARRICK's
library of 'old plays'

the by-paths which Shakespeare's thoughts and feelings may take at any moment of a play. If we would penetrate into his state of mind during the composition of *Measure for Measure*, we should not, I think, overlook the name he gave to Claudio's young mistress [19] and the light thrown on Isabella's childhood when she cries that she would rather think her mother a strumpet than her father Claudio's begetter. Shakespeare cannot have forgotten an earlier Juliet when he used her name again, and the words of Isabella illuminate her cult of chastity. In our search for the play's 'meaning', we should not neglect these hints of a suppressed but deep sympathy with Juliet and of an almost clinically analytic approach to Isabella. In *Measure for Measure* we have a morality-framework, much incidental satire, a deep probing into the springs of action, a passionate sympathy with the unfortunate and the hard-pressed. Only if we concentrate our attention on one of these aspects will the play leave us content.

NOTES

1. *The Crown of Life* (1947), p. 30.
2. *Shakespeare Survey*, II (1949), 66–82.
3. New Cambridge edition (1922), pp. 99–100.
4. *Op. cit.* p. 71.
5. *The Wheel of Fire* (1930), p. 87.
6. *Shakespeare's Problem Comedies* (1931), pp. 104–5.
7. Arden edition (1905), pp. xxii–xxiii.
8. *Elizabethan and Jacobean* (1945), p. 118.
9. *Shakespeare* (English Men of Letters), ed. 1939, p. 158.
10. Cf. J. H. de Groot, *The Shakespeares and 'The Old Faith'* (1946).
11. W. W. Lawrence, *op. cit.* p. 105, is at pains to convince us that the Duke did not confess Angelo, but he does not consider the implications of his exercise of priestly function with Mariana and (in intention) with Barnardine.
12. *Op. cit.* p. 169.
13. *Op. cit.* p. 80.
14. Raleigh, *op. cit.* p. 166, is here as so often an exception.
15. *Op. cit.* p. 79.
16. Even with the trick of the substituted bed-fellow, we should not too readily argue that its frequency in earlier literature would make it acceptable to Shakespeare. It is noticeable that the Duke broaches the subject with some hesitation and seems to anticipate opposition from Isabella. He has, indeed, to suggest that the end justifies a doubtful means: "If you think well to carry this, as you may, the doubleness of the benefit defends the deceit from reproof. What think you of it?" Isabella's quick assent is in sharp contrast to the Duke's laborious persuasions.
17. *Op. cit.* p. 73.
18. *The Wheel of Fire*, p. 87.
19. In Whetstone her name is Polina.

HAMLET AND THE PLAYER WHO COULD NOT KEEP COUNSEL

BY

J. M. NOSWORTHY

It is well known, not only to scholars, that besides the good texts of *Hamlet* preserved in the Quarto printed in 1604 and in the Folio of 1623 there is a strange version of Shakespeare's tragedy which has come down to us in a quarto dated 1603. This quarto boldly proclaims that it represents the play "as it hath beene diuerse times acted by his Highnesse servants in the Cittie of London: as also in the two Vniuersities of Cambridge and Oxford, and else-where". Few, if any, of the other Shakespeare quartos can boast a title-page quite as impressive as this one, and few are more pretentious or misleading in their claims. It is possible that *Hamlet* was played at both the Universities and in the city of London, though the Globe Theatre, the normal habitat of the King's Players, was in Southwark. What appears manifestly impossible is that the version preserved in this particular quarto was performed in any of these places. There is virtue, how-ever, in the 'else-where', which we may take to be the operative word. Modern research has rendered it highly probable that the 1603 Quarto perpetuates the attempt to portray something resembling Shakespeare's *Hamlet* before provincial audiences.

The theory that it represents an earlier form of the existing play—a notion which, no doubt, led William Poel to put on his "*First Quarto Hamlet*" at St George's Hall in 1881—nowadays finds few adherents. It has become evident that this brief and halting text cannot represent a reputable version of the play, and equally clear that Shakespeare can have had no direct con-nexion with it.

Another explanation may also be put aside—that it was a piracy by someone who took down by shorthand as much as he could of the play which appears in its full form in the Quarto of 1604. Recent investigation has shown, beyond any reasonable doubt, that there was no system of shorthand in existence in 1603 supple enough to reproduce this or any other 'bad' quarto. Fortunately twentieth-century scholarship has been able to demonstrate that many of the 'bad' quartos are memorial reconstructions set down for provincial use by one or more actors. This explanation of 'bad' quarto origins was triumphantly pressed home in 1910 by W. W. Greg, who showed that the short and incoherent quarto of *The Merry Wives of Windsor*, printed in 1602, was reported by the actor who had played the part of Mine Host of the Garter. *Hamlet*, pirated not very much later than this, is, almost certainly, an outcome of the same methods, possibly by the same delinquent. It seems desirable to say here what has seldom been said—that we should not assume that there were several such rogues when one will suffice.[1]

The person responsible, then, may be assumed to have been a man who had taken a part, no doubt a minor one, alongside the great Burbage in the original London production and who had been commissioned to prepare a text suitable for use by a touring company. This 'pirate' actor is unknown to us by name, but it is possible not only to distinguish the role he sustained in the play but also to watch him engaged in his task.

74

Since the pirate would obviously reproduce his own lines accurately, it is fitting that we should begin by segregating those sections of the quarto which are suspicious by virtue of their excellence. The following emerge:

I.   Voltimand's part.
II. Marcellus's part.
III. The Prologue to *The Murder of Gonzago*, together with the speech of Lucianus.
IV. Sporadic passages in Acts IV and V, usually in crowd-scenes.
V.   Most of the lyric snatches spoken (or sung) by Hamlet, Ophelia and the Clowns.

This represents fairly wide distribution and suggests at first sight that several agents must have been involved. However, a certain amount of elimination is possible at the outset. The Voltimand actor was not involved; Dover Wilson has demonstrated that the pirate had access to a manuscript copy of Voltimand's part.[2] The lyrics, too, are immaterial. They are easy to remember as verses, easier still as songs, which they doubtless were in stage performance, and as some of them belong to folk tradition they were probably familiar as household words. The remaining sections call for consideration.

In 1915, H. D. Gray made a conspicuously successful attempt to establish the guilt of the Marcellus actor.[3] Marcellus's speeches are reproduced in the 1603 Quarto with almost complete accuracy, while a remarkably high standard prevails in the speeches of other characters who appear in scenes in which he is present. The first act is the only one in which he is concerned, and analysis shows that I, i, in which he is present practically throughout, is very full and accurate. So, too, are the second half of I, ii, which involves Horatio, Marcellus and Bernardo, and I, iv. In I, v the reporting of the dialogue between Hamlet and the Ghost is quite good, but even so there is a remarkable improvement after the entry of Horatio and Marcellus. On the other hand, Marcellus's absence spells disaster even at this early stage in the play. The first half of I, ii is a mere skeleton paraphrase, and I, iii, which involves only Polonius, Ophelia and Laertes, and runs to a hundred and thirty-five lines in the 1604 Quarto, is reduced to a mere seventy lines which include a good deal of inept paraphrase. Since, therefore, it can be shown by inductive methods that the presence of Marcellus and excellence of reporting are co-extensive, it seems merely perverse to question the correctness of Gray's diagnosis.

Gray further suggested that the pirate had a part in *The Murder of Gonzago*, and was led to the dubious surmise that "it is entirely possible that the play within the play as first given was almost exactly as we find it" in the first Quarto. In a later article Gray identified the pirate as the Lucianus of the inner-play.[4] His summing-up is relevant to the present investigation: "the facts", he says, seem to indicate that the pirate was "Marcellus in Act I and the Second Player (Lucianus in the play-within-the-play) in Acts II and III. After that he served, apparently, only as a supernumerary, and would inevitably have been used in most if not all of the crowd scenes."

Gray finds that the three-line Prologue and the six-line speech of Lucianus are both given correctly in the earlier quarto, but sporadic accuracy in such short sections can, of course, prove nothing unless there is a relatively high standard in what may be termed the surrounding speeches. These, as it happens, are not well reproduced. On the contrary, they are, for the greater part, so unlike the corresponding speeches in the full text that Gray thinks that they may represent an earlier version. This point, however, may be reserved for later consideration, for we have now to return to II, ii, to the point at which our suspect enters.

In spite of the Folio stage-direction, "*Enter foure or fiue Players*", we may doubt whether so many were employed in actual performance. Their subsequent entry is given in the 1604 Quarto as "*Enter Hamlet, and three of the Players*", and the Folio suggests further reduction to "*two or three of the Players*". *The Murder of Gonzago* involves, at most, four players and probably made do with three. We need not be too curious about all this. The important thing is to decide whether the pirate was included in these groups of Players. It seems highly likely that he was.

We find that the pirated quarto reports the "little eyases" section very imperfectly, but with the entry of Polonius (called here by the name of Corambis) there is a sudden change to almost total accuracy, and the dialogue between Hamlet and Polonius compares very favourably with the full version.

> *Cor.* My lord, I haue news to tell you.
> *Ham.* My Lord, I haue newes to tell you:
> When *Rossios* was an Actor in *Rome*.
> *Cor.* The Actors are come hither, my lord.
> *Ham.* Buz, buz.
> *Cor.* The best Actors in Christendome,
> Either for Comedy, Tragedy, Historie, Pastorall,
> Pastorall, Historicall, Historicall, Comicall,
> Comicall historicall, Pastorall, Tragedy historicall:
> *Seneca* cannot be too heauy, nor *Plato* too light:
> For the law hath writ those are the onely men.

There are omissions, of course, and one or two very obvious specimens of piratical ignorance, but as a piece of parrot-fashion reporting this ranks high. We may take it, I think, that the pirate remembered these lines because he was standing behind one of the stage-doors, awaiting his entry and listening intently for his cue. His actual cue-line would be Polonius's,

> What followes then my Lord?

At this point he would prepare to enter, and his actual entry accounts for his imperfect recollection of Hamlet's reply:

Why as by lot God wot, and then you knowe it came to passe, as most like it was; the first rowe of the pious chanson will showe you more, for looke where my abridgment comes.

which he corrupts into:

> Why by lot, or God wot, or as it came to passe,
> And so it was, the first verse of the godly Ballet
> Wil tel you all: for look you where my abridgement comes.

Thereafter, throughout the Pyrrhus section we may detect a gradual decline. Its first twenty-five lines are excellently reported. Then the pirate's memory fails and he omits twenty lines, while his account of "the mobled queen" tails off into a mere garbled paraphrase. Evidently he has lost interest, and now simply waits until he hears the cue for his exit. This cue he reports tolerably well:

> O farre better man, vse euery man after his deserts,
> Then who should scape whipping?
> Vse them after your owne honor and dignitie,
> The lesse they deserue, the greater credit's yours.

And so he leaves the stage with Polonius, and we notice a falling-off in the report of Hamlet's brief dialogue with the First Player. From the distance he hears Hamlet declaiming his long soliloquy. He grasps the general sense of it, and recalls a word or two here and there, but that is all.

III, i calls for little comment. The pirate is well out of the way. He dislocates the scene and shows no recollection of Shakespeare's wording. Claudius's opening speech, for example, is mangled thus:

> Lordes, can you by no meanes finde
> The cause of our sonne Hamlets lunacie?
> You being so neere in loue, euen from his youth,
> Me thinkes should gaine more than a stranger should.

In III, iii Hamlet enters with three of the players according to the 1604 Quarto, but the pirated text has the direction "*Enter Hamlet and the Players*". This seems to imply that the pirate was one of the players. He is once again guilty of dislocation, but there is, on the whole, very little that he omits, while he preserves, in garbled form, a few lines that do not appear in the 1604 Quarto or the Folio. We may assume that he was present on the stage but somewhat inattentive to dialogue, virtually monologue, in which he was not actively concerned. After the stage-direction "*exeunt players*", he presents quite accurately Hamlet's lines,

> *Horatio*, thou art euen as iust a man,
> As e're my conuersation cop'd withall.

Presumably the pirate made his exit with these words ringing in his ears. The ensuing dialogue between Hamlet and Horatio is very feebly reproduced, probably because the pirate was too busy preparing for his part in *The Murder of Gonzago*.

The reporting remains bad for several lines after the entry of Claudius, Gertrude, Polonius, Ophelia and the rest, but there is a marked improvement after Hamlet says to Polonius,

> My lord, you playd in the Vniuersitie.

This line I take to be the pirate's initial cue, warning him to stand in readiness for the Dumb-show. He listens attentively for a while and is able to reproduce the section down to "heere's a mettle more attractiue" with almost complete accuracy. After that he forgets several lines which turn up in the wrong place later. At first sight, it looks as if he has forgotten his own cue, but this is not so, his entry being, of course, determined by the entry of the King and Queen in the Dumb-show. In his report of the Dumb-show he supplies his own name, Lucianus, for the poisoner. The 1604 Quarto terms him "an other man" while in the Folio he is simply "a Fellow".

If Lucianus spoke the Prologue, he must have returned to the stage immediately after his Dumb-show exit. This is not impossible. Certainly the Prologue is perfectly reported and the surrounding dialogue between Hamlet and Ophelia fares quite well. The ensuing dialogue between Albertus (Gonzago) and Baptista is quite different from that given in the 1604 Quarto and the Folio, and this, as we have noted, has led Gray to postulate two Shakespearian versions. I do not think that Shakespeare would have wasted his time preparing two versions of deliberately pedestrian verse. There was no need for the pirate to be very attentive so long as he did not miss his cue, and, in any case, he would have some difficulty in remembering the involved and long-winded speeches. He recalled, however, that these were in rhyme and it is rhyme that he supplies: I think that it is his own rhyme and not Shakespeare's. Lucianus nods for a while, but pricks up his ears at speech-endings, and we find him on the alert as his entry cue approaches. The lines warning him to stand ready are given perfectly:

Duke   T'is deeply sworne, sweete leaue me here a while,
               My spirites growe dull, and faine I would beguile the tedious time with sleepe.
Dutchesse Sleepe rocke thy braine,
               And neuer come mischance betweene vs twaine.

He hangs on every word now, and reports the conversation between Hamlet, Claudius and Gertrude correctly, entering promptly on his cue—which is,

                    this is one
          Lucianus nephew to the King,

but taking his own entry so much for granted that he does not even bother to mark it in his report.

At this point a curious thing happens. The pirate recalls that Ophelia several times addresses to Hamlet sentences beginning with the words "You are". Through sheer bad luck he hits on one of these sentences which had occurred earlier in the scene,

              Y'are very pleasant my lord,

and follows it up with tolerably correct versions of the "Jig-maker" and "Devil wear black" speeches which also belong to the earlier section. Then comes Ophelia's further protestation, presented not quite accurately as,

              Your iests are keene my Lord,

and the pirate is once more in control of the situation. He now reports,

Ofel.   Still better and worse.
Ham.   So you must take your husband, begin. Murdred
        Begin, a poxe, leaue thy damnable faces and begin,
        Come, the croking rauen doth bellow for reuenge.

And it seems possible that his memory is here a little more reliable than Shakespeare's handwriting or the compositor's eyesight. We have seriously to ask ourselves whether his "So you must take your husband" is not an essentially better reading than the 1604 Quarto's: "So you mistake your husbands" and the Folio's: "So you mistake Husbands."

This apparent authority extends to Lucianus's own lines which are given thus in the pirated text:

> Thoughts blacke, hands apt, drugs fit, and time agreeing.
> Confederate season, else no creature seeing:
> Thou mixture rancke, of midnight weedes collected,
> With *Hecates* bane thrise blasted, thrise infected,
> Thy naturall magicke, and dire propertie,
> One wholesome life vsurps immediately.

This excellence supports the view that Lucianus was the pirate very powerfully indeed, and if we accept this view we must, once again, view both the 1604 Quarto and the Folio with suspicion. The version in the former is not very satisfactory. The compositor sets up 'Considerat season' in the second line, and, because he associates what he prints as '*Hecats* ban' with invective, he makes the midnight weeds 'thrice inuected'. For the last line he produces,

> On wholsome life vsurps immediatly.

The Folio corrects 'Considerat' and 'inuected', but retains 'Hecats ban' and renders the last line,

> On wholsome life, vsurpe immediately.

We may ask, therefore, whether 'Hecates bane', a poisonous plant, does not preserve Shakespeare's intention, and whether the antithesis between the poisonous weeds, the many and unwholesome, and the Player King's life, the one and wholesome, is not also intentional. Such speculations are dangerous, however, for the whole page of the pirated text on which this speech figures has a crop of errors for which we must blame not the pirate but the printer. Thus, we find 'phy' for 'play', 'Mouse-trap' with the article omitted, 'trapically' for 'tropically', 'guyana' for 'Vienna', 'Epitithe' for 'Epitaph' and 'Murdred' for 'murtherer'. The safest course for an editor would be to rely on the Folio at this point.

Immediately after this speech the 1603 Quarto marks an exit for Lucianus. There is no such direction in the 1604 Quarto or the Folio, possibly because the inner-play in actual performance was shut off by curtains. However, Lucianus should, strictly speaking, leave the stage immediately after he has committed the crime. The Dumb-show in all versions indicates as much.

However this may be, it is quite clear that Lucianus, if he was the pirate, made his exit at this point, for in the ensuing commotion he gathers very little of the dialogue and what he does gather he corrupts. He transfers Ophelia's "The King rises" to her father, and as a result misplaces Hamlet's "What, frighted with false fire". Moreover, he stupidly supposes that Claudius rises because he is tired, and so gives him the line,

> Lights, I will to bed.

Presumably he associates Claudius's departure with a vague recollection of Hamlet's line,

> For some must watch while some must sleepe,

which is perverted in its turn to,

> For some must laugh, while some must weepe.

It is noteworthy that, once Lucianus has made his own exit, he has very hazy ideas about the dispersal of the other characters. His direction "*Exeunt King and Lordes*" does not account for Gertrude and Ophelia who must also leave the stage at this point. The remainder of the scene calls for little comment. The pirate is off-stage. He picks up scraps of dialogue here and there, but his report degenerates into a flabby and inept paraphrase with serious omissions and wholesale corruption.

Thus one man, in his time, has played two parts and has said all that Shakespeare gives him to say. *Hamlet*, however, has still rather more than two acts to run, so that it is quite reasonable to surmise that the pirate will emerge once more as a super. There is nothing in the remainder of the pirated quarto version of Act III to suggest his presence, and it is not, in fact, until we reach IV, iii, that we catch a glimpse of him. In the Folio this scene is simplified in the interests of cast economy, so that only Hamlet, Claudius, Rosencrantz and Guildenstern appear, but both quartos agree in admitting a number of attendant lords, of whom our pirate may well have been one. There is some tolerably close reporting of this scene's rather intricate dialogue in the pirated text. The pirate does not seem to have been present all through the scene, and I think that he served as one of Hamlet's guards, for the reporting becomes good immediately upon Hamlet's entry and lapses again when he goes out. I see no reason for supposing, as Dover Wilson once did, that the pirate passed over the stage in Fortinbras's army at the start of IV, iv.[5] The 1603 Quarto certainly gives the gist of Fortinbras's brief speech, but in the form of a rather loose paraphrase, and the rest of the scene is wanting.

Corruption is at its worst in IV, v. The pirate recalls only a few scattered lines of dialogue, and Ophelia's songs are presented in a disorderly fashion though they are verbally accurate. Of IV, vi the pirate seems to have remembered nothing. He substitutes a bogus dialogue between Horatio and Gertrude which looks like a desperate and uninspired attempt on his part to give some kind of coherence to the surrounding tract of unintelligible fragments. IV, vii is reduced from a hundred and ninety-six lines to no more than fifty-five and is wretchedly presented. The pirate has scarcely remembered a phrase of the original. His rendering of Gertrude's account of the death of Ophelia makes amusing reading:

> O my Lord, the yong *Ofelia*
> Hauing made a garland of sundry sortes of floures,
> Sitting vpon a willow by a brooke,
> The enuious sprig broke, into the brooke she fell,
> And for a while her clothes spread wide abroade,
> Bore the yong Lady vp: and there she sate smiling,
> Euen Mermaide-like, twixt heauen and earth,
> Chaunting olde sundry tunes vncapable
> As it were of her distresse, but long it could not be,
> Till that her clothes, being heauy with their drinke,
> Dragg'd the sweete wretch to death.

In thus presenting Ophelia "pledging with contented smack, The Mermaid in the zodiac" the pirate seems oddly to have anticipated Keats, and, imbecile though it is, it is also an interesting recollection for it tells us that he had acted in *Twelfth Night*. Hence Ophelia is made to sit (in water) "like patience on a monument, smiling at grief".

v, i is difficult. Dover Wilson's former suggestion that the pirate played the Second Grave-digger and also the churlish Priest is certainly wide of the mark. The first half of the scene

PLATE V

A Seventeenth-Century Triumphal Car. One of a series in a procession honouring the Archduchess Isabella in Brussels, 1615. From a painting by Denis van Alsloot

PLATE VI

A. A TYPICAL STREET-THEATRE STAGE. Detail from the title-page
of SCARRON's *Comical Romance of A Company of Stage Players*, 1676

B. BASQUE FOLK-DANCE STAGE AT TARDETS

PLATE VII

A. Castle of Kronborg, Elsinore, Denmark

B. *As You Like It*. Stage design by Salvador Dali for the
Luchino Visconti production, Rome, 1948

PLATE VIII

A. *Henry VIII*. Permanent set by TANYA MOISEIWITSCH for TYRONE GUTHRIE's production, Shakespeare Memorial Theatre, 1949

B. *Henry VIII*. THE TRIAL-SCENE. Shakespeare Memorial Theatre, 1949

involves only the two Gravediggers, Hamlet and Horatio, and it is not possible to find a place for the pirate. The second half could very well admit him as one of the courtiers present at Ophelia's funeral. Yet, oddly enough, the reporting of the Gravedigger section is fuller and more exact than that of the funeral. The pirate, standing in readiness for his entrance as a mourner, would, of course, hear a good deal of the earlier part of the scene, and I can suggest two reasons why he should remember it. In the first place, there is a fair amount of broad, if grim, humour, and our pirate seems, in general, to have remembered the comic speeches far more accurately than the rest. In the second, the meditations on life and death in this scene are a memorable stuff which has burned itself into the minds of many people who are not pirates, actors, scholars or even Shakespearians at all. These considerations seem relevant but are, I concede, hazardous, and I do not press them.

The pirate may, I think must, have been one of the mourners at Ophelia's maimed rites, yet his report is hopelessly vague and confused. So much so, that I would deny his presence, were it not for a lucid interval. He remembers that Laertes leaps into the grave and that Hamlet leaps in after him. The stage-directions in the 1603 Quarto are, in fact, the sole authority for the full action. He also recalls tolerably well part of the accompanying dialogue, thus:

> Ham. Beholde tis I, *Hamlet* the Dane.
> Lear. The diuell take thy soule.
> Ham. O thou praiest not well,
>   I prethee take thy hand from off my throate,
>   For there is something in me dangerous,
>   Which let thy wisedome feare, holde off thy hand:

It would seem, therefore, that our pirate, though present, has been inattentive, but that his interest, and consequently his memory, have been aroused by violent and exciting action, and we imagine that Burbage was peculiarly effective here. I am not satisfied that this is the full explanation, for it seems possible that this section of dialogue is, in a sense, a cue. The pirate, in other words, is one of the supers who must now hold themselves in readiness to obey Claudius's behest:

> Pluck them a sunder.

After this there are one or two trifling reminiscences, but the scene tails off miserably.

The first sixty lines or so of v, ii are a blank. After that the pirate recalls isolated fragments very vaguely. The first half of this long scene furnishes, in fact, no more than a handful of lines, all dreadfully garbled. The second half suffers a good deal of omission and dislocation, but there is, at least, a reasonably substantial section reported with some show of accuracy. We may take it that the stage-direction, "*Enter King, Queene, Leartes, Lordes*", which serves in the 1603 Quarto in place of the far fuller directions given in the 1604 Quarto and the Folio, covers our pirate in the humblest of these roles. Once again, he has no speaking part, and once again his reporting displays nebulous paraphrase with flashes of excellence. Thus, we find sporadic passages such as the following, which, despite lineal dislocation, preserves the matter and expression of the original fairly closely:

> Ham. Iudgement.
> Gent. A hit, a most palpable hit.

Lear.	Well, come againe.	*They play againe.*
Ham.	Another. Iudgement.	
Lear.	I, I grant, a tuch a tuch.	
King	Here *Hamlet,* the king doth drinke a health to thee	
Queene	Here *Hamlet,* take my napkin, wipe thy face.	

At one point this is superior to the 1604 Quarto text which offers the almost meaningless, "I doe confest" for "I, I grant, a tuch a tuch". The Folio supplies what is, presumably, the correct reading at this point:

Laer.	A touch, a touch, I do confesse.

Once again the pirate recalls a piece of dialogue that is associated with violent and arresting action, and it is, again, possible that this was his cue to hold himself in readiness for the performance of some minor office. For the rest, the most accurate sections are those dealing with the duel, with Hamlet rounding on Claudius, and with the entry of Fortinbras and the ambassadors. The obvious general improvement after this last entry led Dover Wilson to assign to the pirate a place, as in IV, iv, in Fortinbras's train, but this leaves the earlier sections of accurate reporting unexplained. I think that the pirate's memory reacted to the exciting moments that end the play.

This analysis, then, lends ample support to Gray's conclusions. The pirate sustained, successively, the roles of Marcellus, Lucianus and an Attendant Lord, thus performing just such functions, both for quantity and quality, as we should expect to find allotted to a minor actor in an Elizabethan presentation. His reporting exists on three levels: the good, the bad and the indifferent. This may seem an obvious and not particularly intelligent classification, but I think it a necessary one in 'bad' quarto analysis, since it enables us to judge, within certain limits, the extent to which the reporter was involved in the various scenes. The middling sections of reporting in the pirated quarto of *Hamlet* are, in several respects, the most interesting, since they tell us something about the reporter's personal habits. His tolerably close rendering of the Polonian 'sententiae' in I, iii and of the eschatological musings in V, i suggests that he was a person of philosophical parts or, at least, an amateur of moral saws. It seems likely, too, that his interest was held by vivid and exciting action, so that he remembered a fair amount of the dialogue connected with it. He had, alas, very little feeling for poetry, and does not seem to have been particularly interested in the play. He was content to remain in ignorance about the scenes in which he did not appear and was not always eager to understand the meaning of those in which he did. On the whole, one would hardly suppose that he was a credit to the company, and is left with the pious hope that his fellows among His Majesty's servants were rather more intelligent and very much more conscientious.

NOTES

1. In *The 'Bad' Quarto of Hamlet* (Cambridge, 1941) G. I. Duthie has decisively proved that this Quarto represents a garbled version of the text which the Quarto of 1604 preserves in its Shakespearian fullness.
2. "The Copy for *Hamlet* 1603 and the *Hamlet* Transcript 1593", 3 *The Library*, IX (1918), 153, 217.
3. "The First Quarto *Hamlet*", *Modern Language Review*, X (1915), 176.
4. "Thomas Kyd and the First Quarto of *Hamlet*", *PMLA* XLII (1927), 721.
5. *Op. cit.* It is quite evident that Wilson no longer holds this view.

UNWORTHY SCAFFOLDS:
A THEORY FOR THE RECONSTRUCTION OF
ELIZABETHAN PLAYHOUSES

BY

C. WALTER HODGES

In the many attempts that have been made during the last fifty years to establish a convincing reconstruction of the Shakespearian public playhouse the main force of effort and controversy has nearly always ranged around that area at the back of the stage which we call the 'tiring-house façade'. The uses and appearance of this feature have occupied the keenest attention of reconstructors ever since the publication of the de Witt sketch of the Swan Playhouse, in 1888—particularly, of course, because this famous drawing tended so unhelpfully to disagree with certain theories held at that time, just as it has done, in one way or another, with all other theories held ever since. In their various assessments of the tiring-house façade most reconstructions disagree with one another, except in their universal, though somewhat apologetic, disagreement with the observations of Johannes de Witt. Yet while students have been concentrating with more and more eagerness upon this area of disagreement, they have accepted without much question a number of preconceived opinions about the nature of the actual stage, the platform structure, itself. In estimating the character of the Elizabethan theatre we are constantly being betrayed by the habits of our modern theatrical experience. We try, seemingly in very spite of our better knowledge, to find some sort of a proscenium somewhere upon the Elizabethan stage; to open up an inner-stage, no matter how questionable the evidence for its existence, and to thrust back into it a greater and greater portion of the action of the Elizabethan plays. In this way the tiring-house façade has seemed, like a magnet, to draw back both actors and students alike into itself, leaving the great stage before it empty and unattended. But let us change our point of view for a while; let us turn our backs upon the tiring-house, leaving its problems and disagreements unresolved, and inspect some details of the stage, Shakespeare's 'unworthy scaffold' itself. There is reason to suppose that we have misinterpreted some of its features, which, if we can come to see them more clearly, may assist us when we return again to examine the tiring-house.

We cannot begin better than by examining the de Witt drawing. We must try to bring to this not only the knowledge gained from all the research into theatrical history that has taken place since this drawing was first discovered, but also, if we can, a 'fresh eye', as painters say, with which to try and see it as though for the first time. Looked at in this way it may seem to us that one of its most remarkable features is also one which has been so long accepted as a commonplace that it now passes as a thing not worth further inquiry. This is none other than that the drawing shows a large rectangular stage set out into a round arena, a square peg in a round hole. If we could come fresh to this arrangement, surely it would strike us at once as a rather clumsy and uncomfortable feature. Those two wedge-like spaces upon either side of the stage, how awkward they are, how offensive to the general sense of architectural fitness! One asks oneself, why did not the builders of the Swan carry the stage right across from one side of the yard to the other? What is the purpose of those wedges? To accommodate the 'groundling' spectators in the yard? One supposes so, disregarding for the moment the familiar dandies sitting on the stage, who, by all logical analysis, would be sitting just here along the sides, in the way of just those very groundlings. Surely it cannot have been a very advantageous place for groundlings to stand? Or let us look at this same feature at the Fortune. This, it will be recalled, was a square playhouse; here at least the square peg was fitted in a square hole, and since we have the builder's contract for it, we can expect some very precise information as to how it was done. And yet here again the effect is most surprising. Here, by any logical interpretation of the contract, there is a space of ground running along each side of the stage between the stage and its neighbouring galleries, which, while it measured only 6 feet wide from stage to gallery, was no less than 27½ feet long. In other words, these two spaces, one on each side of the stage, have the dimensions of corridors or gangways rather than of convenient parts of the auditorium: and when we consider, as we shall a little farther on, that the Elizabethan stage was probably set up much higher than modern stages are, so that spectators, to get a comfortable view, would be apt to stand a little way off, and not close up against it, we are led again to think that whatever their uses may have been, the spaces at the sides of the Fortune stage could hardly have been *designed* for the comfort and convenience of spectators.

The general feeling that these stage-side spaces are awkwardly managed is reflected in the readiness of scholars to abandon them as untrue. On the face of it, it would seem to make a much better general design, as well for the round playhouses of the Bankside as for the square Fortune, if these stages were to taper, narrowing towards the front, thus opening out the side spaces, and allowing better movement and more room for spectators in the yard. Two well-known Caroline engravings, the title-pages to *Roxana* and *Messalina*, appear to give some countenance to this notion, which has been adopted in a number of important reconstructions, the two most notable being Albright's in 1909, and J. Cranford Adams' in 1943. But still it will not do: it is not convincing enough. The combined evidence of the de Witt sketch and the Fortune contract alone, without counting any lesser arguments and deductions, is very strong, and the value of *Roxana* and *Messalina* is too unsure. When the balance of the evidence is made, and all the likelihoods assessed, one is left with the probability that the typical Elizabethan stage was a rectangular one, just as de Witt has shown it. In other words, we are left with an architectural design which we do not like very much, which we feel to be unsatisfactory, requiring some further explanation. It is a problem; and to attempt to alter it, to rectify the design to suit ourselves, is to shirk the problem at just that point where, if we pursue it, if we press it hard where it appears so clumsy and inexplicable, it may prove that we have hit upon the very root and spring of the matter, which will there open up and reveal the explanation. For instance, the word 'design' has been used above: it was said that we feel something unsatisfactory about the *design* of the stage...; and here we should pause, for surely in the modern sense there was no such thing as a *design* for an Elizabethan stage, nor yet for the playhouse it stood in. We have been betrayed by our modern approach. We should know well enough that these places were not designed on drawing-boards as they would be to-day, but erected according to rule-of-thumb and traditional methods by master masons and their craftsmen. We are not concerned here with designs, but with traditions. Is it not possible that both the stage and the house it stood in were *traditional* in form, and that the only innovation made by James Burbage, when he erected The Theatre in 1575, was to make a rough-and-ready combination of the two?

We have long been taught that the Elizabethan playhouse derived its form from that of the galleried inn-yards in which, in earlier days, the old stages were set up; and that the stage itself, then an improvised affair, adopted certain features, doors, windows, and so on, which it found most useful and usual at those inns. This theory has been given more credit than it deserves. Certainly it was common at one time for plays to be performed in inn-yards, but more than this we do not know, and we are not justified in assuming that the inn-yard gave any other feature to the theatres than the convenience of the use of galleries; a feature which could in any case have been seen already in use at the bull- and bear-baiting arenas on Bankside, some years before the first theatre was built. In any case the first theatres, it is generally agreed, were round or polygonal buildings, which does not argue very strongly for their resemblance to the yards of any known kind of inn. Surely the more apt problem is: what sort of a stage was it that was set up, in the early days, in those inn-yards? Are we perhaps justified in supposing that it was some traditional form of stage which was later transferred, perhaps with a few modifications, but substantially the same, to the round-shaped Theatre, then to the Curtain, and to all the other playhouses, of whatever shape, round, polygonal or square, modifying, enlarging, aggrandizing itself perhaps in one way or another, but always remaining within touch of a tradition whose conventions were fixed long before Burbage was a baby? There are things which lend some colour to this possibility. For instance the Fortune builder's contract provides that this theatre shall be fitted with a stage "contryved and fashioned like unto the Stadge of the saide Plaie howse called the Globe". It seems to bother no one that the Globe was a round or polygonal building, while the Fortune was square. Evidently the character of the stage derived nothing from the roundness of the one nor the squareness of the other, but had its own nature to keep to, and kept to it in spite of all. Besides this it may be noted that contemporary visitors to the London playhouses appear to have been very impressed by them; but not for the technical reasons by which, if they had vouchsafed them, their descriptions could have been so useful to us to-day. What impressed them was simply the then unusual business of providing a public auditorium; of the stages, and how plays were performed on them, and, for instance, whether there was such a thing as an inner-stage or not, they have nothing whatever to say. One is tempted to think that in this regard they found nothing essentially different from traditional practices they had seen elsewhere, even in other countries.

The inferences, slender though they may seem, are worth pursuing, because we can at once point to the existence, in full flourish, of a traditional stage of the very type we are seeking. It is none other than the old street theatre, the booth stage of the market-place, the *théâtre de foire*. This is perhaps most familiar to us in engravings of seventeenth- and eighteenth-century strolling players, especially of the Commedia dell' Arte. But its lineage, as Richard Southern has pointed out in his study of the subject, is much older than that, and its descendants more recent. Its earliest portraits are found in Greek vase-paintings of phlyax comedies, while some photographs taken a few years ago at Tardets, in the Pyrenees (Plate VI B), show Basque peasants dancing their traditional folk dances on this same traditional stage. Its form does not vary much between one century and another. Basically it consists of no more than a platform supported on posts or trestles, behind which is some sort of small house or tent from which the actors come out. Here we may recognize, if we will, an early form of the Elizabethan tiring-house. The picture of this basic stage given in Fig. 2 is general rather than particular: it purports to show a typical structure of which all the specific instances of which we have record are variations in one degree or another. Sometimes, as shown in the English engraved title-page to Scarron's *Comical Romance*, of the Restoration period (Plate VI A), we see it in its simplest manner, though with some small additions it can quickly take on the more ornamental appearance of the Lyons *Terence* stages of

Fig. 2. Basic platform stage.

the fifteenth century: or, elaborated almost out of recognition, but still fundamentally the same thing, it can present us with those baroque towers and arcades of the Flemish Rederyker stages of the sixteenth century, which may be studied in George R. Kernodle's book, *From Art to Theatre*. Here again we are on the threshold of the Elizabethan playhouse, as Kernodle has shown.

There are two special characteristics of this traditional street theatre, which recur so frequently in pictures of it as to deserve our special attention. One is, that it seems not to have had any fundamental qualms about revealing the naked trestles that supported its stage. True, these were often hidden behind draperies; but when, as often happened, they were allowed to show, this would seem not to have been necessarily from lack of means (for in the Lyons woodcuts illustrating Terence's *Andria*, which show a pleasantly ornamented stage facade, not lacking for the necessary decorative skill or expense, we find at the same time that the naked timbers beneath the stage are plainly represented) but simply, we must suppose, because an audience was willing, at need, to accept the convention of turning a blind eye upon things which did not come within the action of the play. The stage was a mere scaffold for actors, differing little if at all from that other scaffold upon which, perhaps in the selfsame market-place, the public executioner performed his own mystery; and in both cases the scaffolding itself might be either draped or left bare as occasion dictated; and in any case it did not matter much, so long as the performers were raised up high enough for all the crowd to see them.

Fig. 3. Mountebank stage at a fair. Sketch made from a seventeenth-century engraving by Callot. Note height of trestles.

This brings us to the second characteristic feature we are to notice as typical of the street theatres; which is, the unusual height of the stage, as compared with our modern custom. It varies, of course, and not every contemporary picture will support the claim; but the evidence is good and plentiful enough to show that the stage-floor of a typical street theatre was set level with the tops of the heads of the spectators standing around it, if not a little higher (Fig. 3). The reason for this is obvious. The shows were meant to be seen by large crowds standing on flat ground, and if the people at the back were to be able to see, then the spectacle had to be raised up high enough for them to do so: the only alternative would have been to have the spectators themselves raised on stands, or on a raked floor, which was here out of the question. This, as we know, was the case with the medieval street-shows, where the stages, either static or on waggons, were frequently set high enough to allow for a dressing-room underneath. One of the best pictures we have of the pageant cars of the old medieval tradition is "The Triumph of Isabella", an early seventeenth-century Flemish painting now in the Victoria and Albert Museum (Plate V). This shows a procession of ten splendid cars, part of the celebrations in honour of the Archduchess Isabella of the Netherlands in 1615. The picture is skilfully and realistically painted, and from it we can judge that the floor-level of the various cars was set at about 5 feet 6 inches above the ground. Another picture, van der Meulen's painting of a static theatre set up in a market-place, a very circumstantial and fully detailed record dating from the 1660's, gives a similar result—though here 5 feet 6 inches would appear to be the minimum height, and one might even put it a little higher. In general, a reasonable guess would put the normal stage height for a street theatre playing to standing spectators as somewhere between 5 feet 6 inches, and 6 feet above the ground.

These then are some of the characteristics of a traditional stage which we here suggest was the immediate parent of the Elizabethan one. We can imagine it, quite small at first, erected in the yards of the London inns; then with room to expand in Burbage's newly built arena, enlarging itself; and that little tabernacle at the back, the rudimentary tiring-house, enlarging itself also, adding an upper story, or even two, incorporating itself into the structure of the main building and presently with the further addition of a canopied Heavens, becoming the façade we know— or think we know (Fig. 4). We must recall, however, that this is not the course of development that has hitherto been supposed; according to that theory the features of the tiring-house were originally adapted from the existing gallery framework of the playhouse, and its general design was fundamentally conditioned by this framework. But it must be remembered that this is no more than a conjecture; there is no special evidence for it; and although the theory here offered as an alternative is also conjecture, there are a few indications of something which, if they are not evidence to support it, at least nod in that direction. For instance, it will be remembered that in the Fortune contract the builder is first given his instructions for building the playhouse 'frame', i.e. the general structure of the auditorium, and is then given further directions for a "Stadge and Tyreinge howse to be made, erected & sett upp *within*[1] the saide fframe", very much as though not only the stage but the tiring-house also was thought of as a separate structure. Furthermore, it is quite clear in the de Witt drawing that the tiring-house façade is flat and that it stands forward and apart from the round structure of the auditorium, in which it may be incorporated, but of which it is *not* an essential member.

However it is not with the tiring-house but with the stage that we are now concerned. We will assume, at least for the time being, that this theory as to the origin of the Elizabethan stage structure is correct; approaching it from this angle, let us see what new light is thrown upon the business of reconstruction. First, let us go back to the street theatre where we left it just now, considering the height of the stage.

If it is agreed that, in the period we are studying, an outdoor stage for a standing audience would tend to be a high one, about on a level with the top of a man's head, may we not assume that this characteristic was continued in at least some of the Shakespearian playhouses? There is a strong argument for this. We know that an indispensable feature of these theatres was the space under the stage called the Hell, and to allow for this most, if not all, reconstructions hitherto (which provide for a stage between 4 and 5 feet high, and no higher) have had recourse to an excavated cellar beneath the stage, to give the necessary headroom. This immediately raises a number of problems. For instance, with the stage assumed to be below head-level it has at once been necessary to consider whether the floor of the surrounding yard would not need to be set on the rake, so as to give the spectators at the back a better view; and many reconstructors, notably G. T. Forrest, Walter Godfrey and J. Cranford Adams, have taken this course. But the evidence of the Hope Theatre is certainly against it; here, we are told, the stage was made "to be carryed or taken awaie, and to stande uppon tressels", so that when desired the arena could be left free for "the game of Beares and Bulls to be bayted in the same": this means that in this case

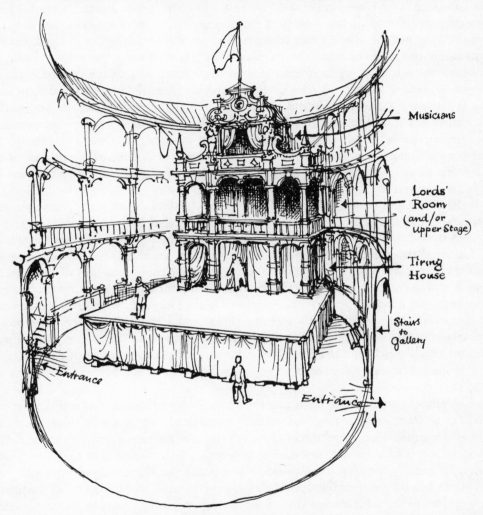

Fig. 4. **A conjectural sketch of Burbage's Theatre (1575).** The tiring-house booth of the street theatre has here been built up to correspond with the galleries, but the Heavens canopy has not yet been added.

neither a sloped arena nor a dug cellar can be considered as at all probable. But in any case, to have gone digging cellars on the Bankside of Shakespeare's day was to go digging for trouble. Whenever the Thames was at high tide this locality was then little better than a marsh, and the rising water was collected in ponds and ditches which, as the tide went down, discharged it again into the river. The Globe Playhouse itself was, as Ben Jonson tells us, built upon piles, "Flancked with a ditch, and forc'd out of a Marish". We can imagine, if we must, that the builders, being determined to provide Burbage with a cellar, may have dug down 1 foot or, with some ingenuity and a good deal of pumping, 2 feet. Deeper is unlikely: and in view of the fact that for their pains they would have needed the extra trouble of building up the surrounding floor—and in view of what we have seen at the Hope, and of what we have seen of the street theatres, is it not more likely that they dug no cellar at all, left their yard flat, and built their stage up, like other stages, high?

In a speculation like this where exact evidence is all too rare, we are often obliged, for want of better, to accept the most reasonable probability: which is in this case that a typical Elizabethan public theatre stage was apt to be much higher than we have formerly imagined, and that the activities of the Hell took place on a level with the groundling spectators around it, in the same way that it had always been done in medieval times. The actor had the heads of his groundlings not at his knees but at his feet, and Ben Jonson's pun about the "*under*standing gentlemen o' the ground" gains point when we see his speaker standing so high above them.

Turning now to the actual structure of these stages, we find that we have evidence of four of them, and that these are all different. In three of these cases the evidence is direct; in the fourth, the Globe, it is inferred.

First is the Swan, and our evidence is, of course, the de Witt sketch. It appears clear enough to be acceptable that the draughtsman intended to present what we will call an open stage, that is a stage left open beneath, so as to reveal its supports. We have already seen that this was not an unusual feature in the street theatres, and so its presence here at the Swan is no freak, but a direct link with tradition. We wish, however, that we could make more sense out of those two great baulks with which the front of the stage appears to be supported. Presumably there were two others farther back, beneath the two pillars supporting the Heavens, where they would certainly have been needed. A reconstruction along these lines would make sense, except that some sort of modification would be needed to provide support for the two forward corners of the stage. But these are details which tend to take us beyond the thread of our present study. Having found at the Swan some evidence for an open stage, we will pass on to the Fortune, where we can be certain of the opposite.

From the builder's contract we learn that the Fortune stage measured no less than 43 by 27½ feet, and since no other reference is given we must understand it to have been rectangular in plan. Its height above ground is not specified. However, we are told that it is to be "paled in belowe with good stronge and sufficyent newe oken bourdes...", and soon after this there follows a further detail about this, which seems hitherto to have been misunderstood, judging from previous reconstructions based upon the contract. The passage in question provides that "all the princypall and maine postes of the saide fframe [i.e. of the house] and Stadge forwarde shalbe square and wroughte palasterwise with carved proporcions called Satiers to be placed & sett on the topp of every of the same postes...". From this it must be assumed that the stage was all supported underneath with posts, of which those on the outer or 'forwarde' side were to be cut square, ornamented at the tops with the famous carved Satiers, and set 'palasterwise' against the paling of oaken boards previously referred to. The effect thus produced is shown in Fig. 4 (and it may be noticed in passing that it is very like the front of the stage in the well-known woodcut from Parabosco's *Il Pellegrino*). The significance of this is that the stage is *seen* to be carried on posts in the traditional manner. The paling appears only as a sort of curtain wall between the posts.

As was said above, however, other reconstructions have interpreted this passage differently. In these the "princypall and maine postes of the . . . Stadge forwarde" have been judged to belong not to the stage proper but to the tiring-house façade, and there, 'palasterwise', some posts have been duly arranged. The point is important to us here, and in a further instance which will arise later, because it involves our interpretation of the word 'stage' as the Elizabethans understood it. In the modern sense it is an elastic word involving not only the boards and timbers of the stage itself, but, if need be, the whole area in which it is set, the atmosphere with which it is invested, and indeed the very profession of those who act upon it. Not so to the Elizabethans. To them a stage was a scaffold, a raised floor, and no more; and we ought not to interpret their

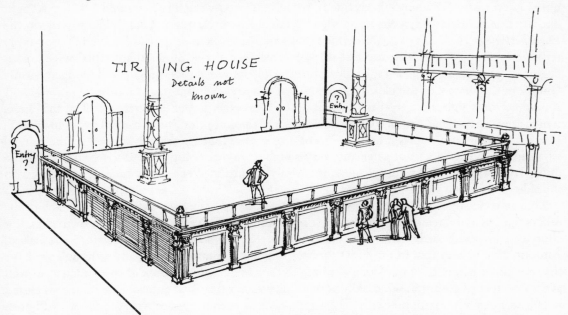

Fig. 5. Reconstruction of the Fortune stage, showing probable arrangement of pilasters.

use of the word in any wider sense. The tiring-house was an adjacent but separate thing, and did not come within the meaning of the word stage.

With all this in mind we will look at those parts of the Fortune contract which refer to the stage of the Globe. It will be remembered that the Fortune was built to rival the Globe, and the builder was directed to copy many of its arrangements. Certain differences are particularized, however. For instance, after the clause where it says that the Fortune stage was to be paled in below with oaken boards, it then goes on to say that it was to be "in all *other* proporcions . . . contryved and fashioned like unto the Stadge of the saide Plaie howse called the Globe". The word 'other' seems to imply the possibility that at the Globe the stage was *not* boarded in below, an implication which is later reinforced in a passage (already partly quoted above) which goes like this: "To be made & doen to be in all other contrivitions, conveyances, fashions, thinge and thinges effected, finished and doen according to the manner and fashion of the said howse called the Globe *saveinge only* that all the princypall and maine postes of the saide fframe and Stadge forwarde shalbe square and wroughte palasterwise...". In other words, the principal and main posts of the stage at the Globe were *not* square as they were at the Fortune; therefore presumably they were round. And they were not set pilasterwise, as indeed, not being square, how could they have been? How, then, was the stage boarded in below? There are two possibilities: either the boards were set fully behind the outer posts in such a way as to leave them standing free or else they were set fully in front of them, to make a continuous panelling in which the posts did not feature. Either is possible; but neither seems to be quite in tune with the tradition we are following or, indeed, with the likely practice of an Elizabethan joiner in this case. At any rate we ought to consider a third possibility, which is that the stage was not boarded in at all, but was left open. "They might distinctly perceive a goodly stage to be reared (shining to sight like the bright burnished gold) upon many a fair pillar of clearest crystal." The passage in the *English Wagner Book* of 1594, from which that sentence is taken, is quoted by Chambers as aptly reflecting—though in glorified terms—the general effect of the Elizabethan public stage, and it begins by emphasizing those ranks of supporting pillars which, we suggest (allowing for some fantasy in the matter of the clearest crystal!), were a well-known stage feature.

And not only pillars but trestles. The last of the four stages in our evidence is that of the Hope, which as we have already noticed, was made to stand upon trestles "to be carried or taken away". Here, if the stage was boarded in, there is nothing in the Hope contract to suggest it: the general structure of trestles does not offer any very suitable way of doing it: and the character of the thing, from a traditional point of view, is entirely against it. Probability here again inclines on the side of the open stage.

Thus of our four stages only one is known for certain to have been paled in. With each of the others there is some reason to believe that the structure was an open one of posts or trestles, not concealed behind boards. But this is not to say that the structure was therefore left naked. Although we believe that in the street theatres this was sometimes done, and although we have the immediate evidence of the Swan drawing to the same effect, the bulk of the evidence, as well as the comfort of common sense, tells us that this was not the usual course. The stage was closed in below, not with boards but with hangings. This had been a practice with the street and booth stages from the very beginning, and its vestiges are hanging upon every Punch and Judy show to this day. For Elizabethan times, there is quite a deal of familiar textual evidence which will back up a theory that the Fortune stage, in being panelled, was not typical, but an innovation. The evidence for hangings has been misunderstood because, as stated above, scholars have allowed themselves to believe that the word 'stage' could be read as applying to the façade of the tiring-house. Thus when Shakespeare gives us:

Black stage for tragedies and murthers fell

we have been told not that the stage, the scaffold, was all hung round with black, like the scaffold for a public execution, but that some black draperies were used behind or over the stage. Indeed, this may also have been done, but first Shakespeare tells us that it was the *stage*, not the tiring-house, which was black. Again, in the Induction to *A Warning for Fair Women* we have the lines:

The stage is hung with black, and I perceive
The auditors prepar'd for tragedie.

Or there is the quotation from Sidney's *Arcadia*, describing the clouds coming over the sun, which "blacked over all the face of heaven; preparing (as it were) a mournful stage for a Tragedie to be played on". But if none of this is unambiguous enough, the following from Heywood's *Apology for Actors* leaves no doubt as to where the hangings were placed. He is speaking in the person of Melpomene and is purporting to describe the theatre of ancient time. His terms, however, as G. R. Kernodle says, are altogether those of a glorified Elizabethan stage, and in one sentence he refers to the matter of stage-hangings: "Then did I tread on arras, cloth of tissue *hung round the fore-front of my stage.*" Taken in conjunction with what we know of medieval practice, of the street theatres, of the stage-structures at the Swan and the Hope, and even possibly at the Globe, and remembering that Heywood's own theatrical connexion was with the Red Bull, so that he may have had that theatre most in mind when he wrote the passage given above, are we not justified in supposing that if there was ever such a thing as a 'typical' Elizabethan stage, we ought to imagine it as being hung all round with a great skirt of cloth, one of several sets of hangings of different colours suitable to different types of play, hangings which had been much used and rough-handled like the shabby splendours of some travelling circus to-day, and which sometimes hung loose so that the draughts would stir its fringes a little in the dust, or maybe sometimes was lashed tight from post to post, to keep the groundlings from peering in too much at the preparations being made for them in Hell?

Or sometimes these hangings would be pulled aside, and the occupants of Hell could run out with fireworks into the middle of the crowd. There is an episode in *The Plot of the Play called England's Joy* which demonstrates this. The Plot, which, it may be remembered, is the only surviving example of an Elizabethan playbill, gives the outline of a spectacular play dealing, in the manner of an allegory, with the glorious victories of Elizabeth. It is entirely reminiscent of those animated triumphal arches and *tableaux vivants* erected for the state entry of James I into London, of the royal entertainments at Kenilworth and Elvetham, and of the mode of the Flemish Rederyker shows; and in keeping with all this it ends with an apotheosis and the display of a Throne of Honour. The Heavenly spectacle is then at once contrasted with a Hellish one. The whole sequence reads:

> ...And so with music both with voice and instruments she is taken up into Heaven, when presently appears a Throne of blessed souls, and beneath *under the stage* set forth with strange fireworks, divers black and damned souls, wonderfully described in their several torments.

Now it can be objected that *England's Joy* is not in the first class of evidence, since so far as we know the play never existed. The existing plot of it refers only to the hoax of March 1602, when one Richard Venner, having beguiled a large audience to the Swan to see this fabulous production, produced nothing, and welshed with the gate-money. The plot is a dud prospectus; but as such it must needs have been written to be convincing to its readers, which it would not have been if it had promised an entertainment which, in the ordinary citizen's view, could not have been accomplished at the Swan. Besides, nothing in the whole document is foreign to what we already know of Elizabethan theatrical practice except this last item of a tableau presented under the stage. But may we not accept this also? It is already corroborated for us by de Witt that the Swan had an open stage. Thus the tableau described would have been presented between those two great supports shown in the drawing, and would, surely, have been revealed when the time came by drawing aside the stage-hangings.

But what of the visibility of this, when there was a mob of groundlings to shut out the sight of it from the galleries? What, then, was the visibility of similar devices in medieval practice? What problems were raised when the street performers of the Mysteries acted simultaneously between their pageant stages and the street ("Herod rages in the pageant and in the street also"; and "the 3 kings speaketh in the street")? Presumably, as in the former time, the spectators would be kept away from that part of the ground needed in the action. A part of the yard could be roped off. Perhaps for a play like *England's Joy* which had an unusually high entrance fee, there were no ground spectators at all, and whole portions of the play (there was to have been "a great triumph made with fighting of twelve gentlemen at Barriers", as well as "the battle at Sea in '88 with England's victory") might conceivably have taken place in the yard. In any case it need not be supposed that, necessarily, for all plays, the whole of the yard was always occupied by spectators. There is more than a little reason to believe that Elizabethan stage practice did occasionally include, if only for its stunt value, a certain amount of action in the yard. The possibility alone is enough to demand research. Is it possible, for example, that the barge in the last act of *Pericles*, in which Marina and her attendants were brought out to Pericles' black-sailed ship, was a practicable boat brought in through one of the gates of the yard and moored alongside the stage, which was the ship? Also, there are a number of references, in early plays, to actors on horseback. ("Enter a spruce Courtier a horsebacke", 1 *Richard II*.) Sir Edmund Chambers has suggested that this effect was simulated by the use of hobby-horses on the stage, but surely it is worth investigating the alternative, that there were occasions when real horses were ridden into the yard? It could so easily have been done.

But all this takes us beyond the scope of this article. We have tried to show that the Shakespearian public stage had its origin in the common scaffold stage of the street theatres; that, like so many of these, it was built high, sometimes head-high to the spectators standing around it, always high enough to allow working space underneath without recourse to digging a cellar; and that it was usually an open structure of posts or trestles, draped round with hangings. We suggest that these conditions were general throughout Shakespeare's time, though with ever increasing degrees of modification (for example, it is probable that stages tended to become larger and more solidly built as the successful career of the public theatres went on), culminating in the large fully panelled-in stage of the Fortune, which, we suggest, was in some respects ahead of its time. But in any case the old style was always just around the corner, and when the Hope was built, thirteen years after the Fortune and for the same proprietors, its stage was a trestled one in the oldest manner of all.

The ancient tradition which nourished the Elizabethan playhouses died when the last of them was pulled down; since when it may almost be said that no play of Shakespeare's has been seen acted, except in adaptation.

NOTE

1. Italics, in this and all other quotations, are mine. C.W.H.

SHAKESPEARE IN THE GERMAN OPEN-AIR THEATRE

BY

KURT RAECK

'Open-air theatres'—a collective term for various types of theatre opposed to the enclosed play-house—have their own peculiar laws of dramaturgy which essentially differ from those of the theatre in the ordinary sense. Here, instead of an auditorium there is a spectators' enclosure; instead of a stage, an open platform.

The facts that there is no curtain and that different dimensions apply to platform and arena, the lack of stage machinery and its capacity for scene changes, and the different acoustic and visual conditions demand that both the method of production and the form of the play chosen for production should be most carefully determined in accordance with the requirements of the stage. So far, however, the open-air theatre in Germany has proved incapable of stimulating the writing of special plays; and there is no 'open-air drama' worth mentioning. Dramas of 'local colour' and indifferent 'festival' plays have fallen quite deservedly into oblivion after only a short life on the stage.

A change of emphasis from the spoken word to the acted visual gesture is the most significant, if not sufficiently considered, feature peculiar to the open-air theatre. The *word*-drama here becomes a show, an action play—and, considering this fact, we must deem it indeed extraordinary that the German open-air repertory has come to rely mainly on Shakespeare's dramas, especially *A Midsummer Night's Dream*, *As You Like It*, *Twelfth Night*, *Much Ado about Nothing*, *The Comedy of Errors*, and *The Taming of the Shrew*—extraordinary because Shakespeare, more than any other dramatist, develops his actions and his plots from and through the spoken word alone.

For this utilization of Shakespeare's plays a specious reason can be advanced. There is a gap in the development between the Elizabethan and the Restoration theatre. The reborn English theatre of the Restoration period shows a strong Continental influence, especially French, and as a result a clear cleavage exists between the earlier stage and the later. A demand for *décor* had been stimulated in the public, and the long and splendid history of Shakespeare performances shows ultimately the full subordination of the Elizabethan stage to the 'illusionary' stage of the baroque theatre, up to the time when the 'Shakespeare stage' has been rediscovered in our own times.

It was indeed this rediscovery of the 'Shakespeare stage', through various experiments in theatre building and in the utilization of the stage, which, at the turn of the century, opened the way for the introduction of Shakespeare's plays to the open-air theatre. Producers observed that in the Elizabethan theatre, plays were given in broad daylight. Since there was no artificial lighting to indicate a change from day to night, and since the stage platform offered none of the opportunities for the display of scenery such as were offered in the contemporary Continental theatre, Shakespeare had his *décor* spoken; when necessary, the locality and the time of the day (or night) were made clear in the dialogue or in the action. Thus, for example, the appearance of an actor carrying a lantern or lamp created the illusion of night even when the performance was held in daytime.

For these reasons, several producers argued that Shakespeare's dramas were best suited for a stage without scenery and for daylight performance: and they thought that the open-air theatre satisfied the conditions. It is the validity of this argumentation that we must carefully examine.

For this purpose we have to distinguish three kinds of open-air theatres in Germany:

1. The first group is that of the so-called 'Nature Theatres' or 'Forest Glade Theatres', built into a beautiful natural setting, amidst forests or mountains—for example, the Harz Mountain Theatre and the Wunsiedl Theatre. Where nature was not 'natural' enough, showing traces of artificial layout, the art of the gardener, based upon English traditions of landscape gardening, helped to create a natural 'back-cloth' artificially.

2. The second group of open-air theatres comprises those erected in an open square, in front of architecturally impressive buildings. Here the most famous examples are the stage in front of Salzburg Cathedral and the theatre in the Salzburg Rock Riding School; the now destroyed Römerberg Theatre in Frankfort-on-Main which used to be built up anew every summer, and which is now accommodated in the ruins of the Carmelite Monastery; and the theatre in the courtyard of the picturesque ruin of the Renaissance Castle at Heidelberg. Such open-air theatres in most cases consisted of mere wooden stands and benches put up for the audiences every summer. Usually the stage was nothing more than an open bare space in front of a beautiful façade, and only occasionally would a special raised platform be erected before it.

3. The third group of open-air stages are those incorporated in the meeting places of the Third Reich. In their basic form, they were shaped like great amphitheatres of ancient Roman type; rather than theatres they were parade grounds for political gatherings. A characteristic example was the vast open-air theatre for twenty thousand spectators built near the Berlin Stadium at the Olympic Games in 1936. Since the acoustic conditions made speaking impossible without the coarsening aid of loudspeakers arranged around the huge area of the auditorium, these stages proved entirely unsuitable for plays from the ordinary theatre repertory. Attempts were made to utilize the structures for productions of operas by Handel, Glück and Wagner, but eventually the unsuitability of such a stage for any kind of theatrical performance was fully and finally demonstrated.

It is, therefore, with the first two groups of open-air stages that we are concerned, since in these alone do we find the repertory made up of Shakespeare's plays.

The first point to be noted is that often the producers of plays on these stages choose to present their selected dramas at night, using artificial illumination for the purposes of delimiting the auditorium, and of adding visual charm by lighting the natural setting or the architectural background.

What is of prime significance here is the fact that the open-air theatre in darkness, with artificial lighting, approaches in its effects those of the enclosed theatre building. The placing of two stages side by side, both with *décor* and strongly lit up against the darkness surrounding them, makes a change of scenes possible, and it is true that occasionally the grandeur of nature itself can assist the producer with a direct effect such as the illusionary stage could never produce.

From performances in these theatres, however, we can hardly deduce many problems peculiar to the open-air theatre, since the artificial lighting creates on the double-stage set the illusion of a peep-show. The principal matter of real interest arises where the auditorium is planned for the accommodation of a very large audience. In such cases, we discover that the playwright's words lose their force and that the actors, trained in the centuries-long tradition of the enclosed theatre, find difficulty in adjusting themselves to the new and different visual and acoustic conditions of the open-air stage.

In addition, there is another, and a more serious, difficulty, a difficulty which perhaps may be sufficiently illustrated by selecting one play for examination. *A Midsummer Night's Dream* has proved by far the most popular drama for open-air production, and just at first it might seem that it is ideally fitted for this purpose: very little consideration is required, however, to convince us how little this and other Shakespearian dramas are artistically suited to open-air production. Not even where the background is composed of perfectly natural surroundings is the plot of this comedy (mainly set in a wood) adapted to the completely natural character of an open-air theatre. The 'wood' in *A Midsummer Night's Dream* is a wood of the imagination; it should exist only in the spectator's imagination. Furthermore, it is a natural setting which has been upset by the quarrel of Oberon and Titania, and only the enclosed theatre can create the stage symbols necessary for its proper interpretation. Here, as elsewhere in Shakespeare's plays, it is true that the less is expressed by *décor* on the stage, the more will the spectators' imagination be kindled by the spoken word. The poet can introduce his listeners to the realm of fancy the more easily, the less their eyes are distracted by the reality of the natural setting. In Germany, the illusionary stage of the peep-show theatre created a tradition of Shakespeare performance which often led far away from emphasis on the word; and, instead of countering that tradition, the experiments in open-air production have merely served to accentuate its faults. At a time when we are beginning to see that the only true way of giving full stage value to these dramas lies in returning to the laws peculiar to the Elizabethan theatre and, in particular, abandoning the use of all gorgeous *décor*, the open-air productions, themselves based on a 'romantic' and false tradition in the presentation of Shakespeare, so far from aiding towards a richer and more valid method, are definitely hindering progress.

OTHELLO IN PARIS AND BRUSSELS

BY

ROBERT DE SMET

[*Translated by* SIR BARRY JACKSON]

Of all the tragedies of Shakespeare, *Othello* is undoubtedly the one which the French theatre-goer has been able to accept with least perplexity. The action is complete, developing with compact logic. Louis Gillet, the French critic, says: "In form, *Othello* is the author's finest work. No play is so simple, so well constructed, or more in accord with the classic spirit. The poet has left us nothing more complete and rounded....All the reactions are of common humanity, entirely comprehensible, with no place for the supernatural or the marvellous." There is truth in this statement: although perhaps it might be better re-phrased in a slightly different manner—in *Othello* the mysterious, always repellent to Latin races, does not immediately make itself apparent, and might indeed in desultory reading be thought to be absent altogether, while the characters are so conceived that French actors, trained by classic discipline, will always be more at ease in this play than in any other of the poet's works.

It is not astonishing, therefore, to find that the earliest tentative efforts to play Shakespeare on the French stage should have started with *Othello*. It was *Othello* that served as model for the first French tragedy in which the influence of Shakespeare can be detected. It was *Othello* in which the first English company playing Shakespeare in Paris made its appearance, and it is *Othello* that the poet Alfred de Vigny chose to launch in the French Theatre one of the offensives of the romantic movement which preceded the battle of Victor Hugo's *Hernani*.

To begin at the beginning. The earliest association of the tragedy of *Othello* and the French public took place on 13 August 1732, when M. de Voltaire presented his *Zaïre* with the actors of the Royal Company. It was fourteen years after this event that Pierre Antoine de la Place published his *Théâtre Anglois* in which we find eleven of the plays, some of them translated, some of them related in detail. Thirty years later, in 1776, Pierre Felicien le Tourneur produced, in conjunction with the Comte de Catuelan and Fontaine-Malherbe, his Shakespeare translated from the English and dedicated to the King, published by the Veuve Duchesne.

Zaïre, of course, is not a translation, and not even what we should to-day call an adaptation of *Othello*, though it might be called an imitation. The public of 1732 was completely ignorant of the source of the play. Voltaire, in his preface, gives no hint of the fact that he had seen *Othello* played during his stay in London, but he seems to have been impressed and remembered some, at least, of its salient points. *Zaïre* has much the same subject-matter as *Othello*, but the treatment is such as might be expected of a French author imbued with classic precepts and to whom variation of time and place was anathema. Orosmane, Sultan of Jerusalem, becomes jealous of a Christian captive named Zaïre. There is no Iago. This Turkish Othello is the victim of a mistake, for he discovers, only too late, that the Cassio of the imbroglio is the brother of his Desdemona, who has been unjustly sacrificed. In this production it is interesting to note that, by chance, the actors were excellently suited to interpret characters of Shakespearian greatness.

98

Quinault-Defresne, thirty-nine years old, of great dignity and bearing, with expressive eyes and magnificent voice, was an obvious Othello. Mlle Gaussin, only about twenty at the time, was a miracle of beauty—and of a tenderness to tear the heart. What more could be wanted for Desdemona?

For Voltaire the appearance of translations of *Othello* was a double annoyance. On the one hand, there were critics who, noting resemblances between *Zaïre* and *Othello*, dared to aver that he had echoed the lines of "a drunken savage" and deplored his extracting even a "few pearls" from what was described as a dung heap. And on the other, Voltaire came to decide that he himself must stand forward as the champion of classic art against the growing army of those who were beginning to find in Shakespeare more than a "few pearls"—were, in fact, inclined to see in his art a peculiar excellence.

In spite of Voltaire's violent opposition, strongly supported by the whole of the Académie, the idea of introducing Shakespeare to the French stage intensified steadily. In 1773, M. Douin, a Captain in the Infantry, issued a *Moor of Venice*, and twelve years later a Procureur Général de Genève, M. Butini, also attempted a version of *Othello*. Both of them worked with the idea of public performance, but neither found artists willing to appear in their translations. It was only in 1792, on the eve of the Terror, that a French Othello made his appearance before a French audience. The adapter was one of the oddest of the many strange figures produced by the eighteenth century. This was Jean-François Ducis, a citizen of Versailles with an engaging character and of an honesty commended by all his contemporaries—but by no means a gifted poet; his verse is of a quite devastating banality and monotony. He devoted himself to a cult of Shakespeare; in crowning the bust of the poet with laurels on the Day of St William, he said: "It was thus that in days of old the ancients crowned with flowers the springs from which they had drunk." He did not understand a word of English, and his translations had to pass through the perilous hands of an intermediary, but he was an enthusiast, and about 1769 he was instrumental in securing the performance of *Hamlet* at the Comédie Française. After that, at intervals, came *Romeo and Juliet*, *Macbeth*, *King John* and, at last, *Othello*. Ducis took textual liberties which appear staggering to the reader of to-day. That a few of the grosser expressions should be softened down and some of the coarser words should be omitted we can well understand, for the audiences of the eighteenth century would never have allowed such without voluble objection. One can also understand that concessions were made to French manners and customs of the day, for, as Ducis says, a tragic poet is "obliged to conform to the uses of the nation for which he writes". But it is more difficult to understand why this 'bonhomme' (the name given him by the Emperor Napoleon) thought it necessary to add to the terrors of Shakespearian tragedy by including, for example, an old Montague made prisoner by an old Capulet, locked up in a sinister dungeon, and tortured by hunger to such a degree that he is forced to eat his own children, or Lady Macbeth who, in the sleep-walking scene, murders her young son. In *Othello*, however, Ducis no longer indulges in additions of the sort. This was the year 1792, and the massacres of the year of Terror were close at hand. It was at this moment that Ducis became rather less inventive. It would not do for his Othello to be a Moor of darkest tint; he is simply an Oriental only vaguely bronzed; reasoning like Bottom and his companions in *A Midsummer Night's Dream*, Ducis decides that he must not "fright the ladies out of their wits". He reduces Iago, whom he calls Pezzaro, to the secondary role of a simple confidant. So long as he is on the stage there is no hint of his evil character, but after his disappearance a minor character expounds his perfidious nature at some length—the reason for his being kept off the stage in the later part of the play being that no audience could knowingly tolerate the sight of such a black-hearted villain. Even with these dubious sacrifices to the taste of the day, the first performance was not well received. In the fifth act, the entire audience rose in disorder and shouted protestations. Several ladies fainted. And what was the result? In order to reassure the most nervous of the spectators, Ducis immediately devised an alternative ending—an ending of complete happiness and peace. But the great actor Talma, who created the role of Othello, did not care much for the character. After a performance during which there were unexpected laughs, he refused to play it any more—this in spite of the fact that Madame de Staël tells us "it was sufficient for him to frown, to pass his hand across his forehead, to become the Moor of Venice". It was only near the end of his life in 1825 that Talma agreed to reappear in the tragedy. In the meantime the theatre-going public had become more accustomed to the plot and the characters owing to Italian operas founded on the subject.

On the Continent, operatic composers have played a very large part in making Shakespeare known among theatre-goers, and in popularizing the plays. Later in the century, Ambroise Thomas did much to accustom play-goers to *Hamlet*, just as Gounod profited by the story of *Romeo and Juliet*. In 1821, Rossini embellished *Othello* with melody. Garcia, the father of Malibran, with Madame Pasta, accustomed the public to witnessing the assassination of Desdemona. Another form of theatre played its part when, in 1818, the brothers Franconi gave a pantomime, intermixed with a few lines of dialogue, "in imitation of the English Tragedy *Othello*", by M. Cuvelier in the Cirque Olympique. I know nothing of this work, but I have a suspicion that there was very little of the original left. The music was by a M. Darondeau, the ballets by a M. Chap; the scenery of Leys and Demay appears to have been the principal attraction. Frederick Lemaître, who later was to become the leading actor of romantic parts and the great attraction of his day, was in the cast. He played the part of Mallorno. Who is Mallorno? The adapters of the period, very much as the adapters in the cinema world to-day, had a mania for changing names. Ducis turned Cassio into Loredan, Emilia into Hermance, and Desdemona into Hedelmone. It would be of interest to know whether, in this extremely curious production, the future idol of Paris was something more than a mere walker-on.

Everything points to growing interest in *Othello* about the year 1825. Three years previously, an adventurous English company had appeared in Paris with unfortunate results. "His Britannic Majesty's Most Humble Servants Mr S. Penley, his Wife and Daughter Rosina, formerly of the Royal Theatre, Windsor" came to the Théâtre de la Porte St Martin, to give "the tragedy of *Othello*, by the most celebrated Shakespeare". Their reception was as bad as could be. The greatest disorder prevailed among the audience. Laughs, imitations of animal noises and comic remarks entirely drowned the voices of the actors, who were also recipients of more solid objects than laughs and cries in the form of potatoes, bad eggs and so forth. It would appear that this behaviour was largely due to political feeling. The Bonapartists, extremely sensitive after the death of the Emperor, turned the performance into an anti-English demonstration and, at the height of the tumult, cried: "Down with Shakespeare! He is one of Wellington's lieutenants!" These incidents, however, were completely forgotten when, on 21 March 1825, a benefit performance for Talma was given at the Opéra, when the great actor once more played the part of the Moor at the request of his many admirers. His first entrance caused a great sensation. The audience expected the richly spangled costume and white turban to which the Italian singers had accustomed them, but Talma, always careful to observe accuracy in costume, played the part as a General commanding the Venetian Army. He wore a red sixteenth-century doublet and a black head-dress with white plumes. His success was immense. Unhappily his example was not followed, and the Opéra continued to present Othello as a Turkish figure of carnival. If one may believe Alexandre Dumas—although his statements should be received with caution—Talma was the prisoner of a standard repertoire which suffocated his genius, and which was imposed upon him by the prejudices of his period. He is said to have told Dumas, then a young man visiting him in his dressing-room, "I ask for Shakespeare, and I am given Ducis". Talma had passed some of his youthful days in London and was well acquainted with the language. There is no doubt that had he lived to have seen the visits of the English company in 1827, 1828 and 1829, he would have been among the many artists of Paris who applauded, for it was these artists who really brought the genius of Shakespeare to the people of France.

This latest English company was a very different one from that of the unfortunate Mr Penley and family. By the enthusiasm they aroused and by the influence they exercised on dramatic literature, this second visit of an English company to Paris was one of the most remarkable events in the history of the French theatre. *Othello* did not perhaps arouse quite such enthusiasm as *Hamlet*, which took the audience by storm. So far as *Othello* was concerned, the Parisians had the good luck to see the title-role played by Charles Kemble, Macready and Edmund Kean in succession. The first performance of the play was honoured by the presence of the Duc d'Orléans (the future King Louis-Philippe) and his family. It would seem that the scene of Desdemona's death was even at this period more than a French audience could contemplate with equanimity. Many ladies left the theatre completely shocked. Kemble was reproached with an excess of ferocity in accomplishing the murder. A contemporary journalist wrote: "We shall never be able to accustom ourselves to see a madman stifle the dying words of his wife with a pillow on which he leans with both hands for more than a minute." One must add that this incident was quite new to the public. Ducis did not dare to risk the pillow. In his version Desdemona was killed with a stroke from a sword, the sword being a weapon of knight-errantry accepted by the classic rules.

The English actors appear to have paid some attention to their critics; another member of the press later calls attention to the fact that "the English actors have learned in Paris to kill themselves with rather more politeness and to suffocate their victims with rather less cruelty". In any case success was incontestable, and, what is even more interesting, French artists evinced a spirit of emulation. Three days after the English company's appearance, the Comédie Française put Ducis' *Othello* in the bill, and it was remarked that Mlle Bourgoin "played with much greater warmth" than previously. She and her companions seem to have been inspired by the visitors. Ligier succeeded Talma. He was a short man of rather plebeian aspect, but of uncommon power. He surpassed himself. One dramatic critic observed that "the terrible outbursts of his voice, the wild expression of his features, the convulsive trembling of his limbs, all conspired to heighten the tremendous effect of the fifth act". Edmund Kean was the next visitor from London, preceded by an enormous reputation. In *Othello* he was far more criticized than Kemble, whose performance was acceptable to the classic mind. Kean was reproached for a rather monotonous voice, tricks of diction, and a bizarre grin. His costume also caused surprise—a sort of muslin tunic and a little red vest, beneath which one could see the blackness of a naked body.

The third Othello to arrive was Macready. The gentlemen of the press received him with unanimity as "an example of the most extraordinary genius that the art of the theatre has ever known". Magnin, critic of *Le Globe*, who had been very reserved in his criticisms of Kemble and Kean, declared: "Macready has at length shown us what we have wanted to see for so long —a real Othello." The public was much struck by the drawing of the bed curtains before the smothering of Desdemona, a scene which hitherto French delicacy had found far too brutal. But the great triumph of this company and the greatest revelation of all the English seasons, was a young actress who had made no name in her own country. Directly she was seen in France, Harriet Smithson was regarded as the greatest actress of her day. Her Desdemona inspired a torrent of tears. One can only regret that many cuts in the play robbed her of much of the text— above all, the Willow Song, although this, twenty-five years before, as set to music by Grétry, was the outstanding success of Mlle Desgarcins, Talma's Desdemona when he played in the Ducis translation. On returning to England, Miss Smithson endeavoured to repeat her success, but in vain. Her talent appeared to vanish after leaving French shores. She later returned to Paris, however, and married Hector Berlioz, who had adored her in almost religious silence from that memorable evening when Shakespeare "fell upon him in unsuspected manner and shook him as if by thunderbolt".

Among the public who witnessed this performance was Alfred de Vigny, aristocrat and poet, who became a close friend of Macready, and it was while watching one of the performances that he conceived the idea of making a translation himself. This translation, produced at the Comédie Française on 24 October 1829, is nowadays treated with undue severity. One thing is certain. His respect for the original text is undoubted. He even worked from the Folio of 1623 and claimed as literal a translation as possible, saying: "I have attempted to work word for word, and after careful search found many astonishing analogies between the English language, implanted by William the Conqueror on the old Saxon, and our own."

Any defects in de Vigny's effort are due rather to his period than to his country. The English company had cut the text by omitting the character of Bianca and by excising any suggestion of coarseness or vulgarity in the dialogue. It is obvious that de Vigny could not do better than follow the English example. As it was, even his cut version left more of the original than was acceptable to patrons of the French theatre, who were shocked by the word 'mouchoir'—a word which seemed to them to have no place in the tragic vocabulary. Ducis had taken the greatest care to supplant Shakespeare's handkerchief by a ribbon ornamented with diamonds, a wedding present from Othello to Desdemona, which she had worn as a head-dress at the marriage ceremony. The utterance of the word 'mouchoir' at the first performance of de Vigny's translation was greeted with whistles and hissing. There was much gossip about it in the auditorium. The press seized on the incident, which in the course of years became legendary, and there is hardly any history of the theatre that does not recall the story. But the victory, for after all it was a victory, lay with the author. This was the birth of French Romanticism. Younger writers of the period were determined to shatter the citadel of the older school and destroy the classicism of the Comédie Française. To enrol Shakespeare among their ranks was brilliant tactics. *Othello* was as a finger pointing in the direction of *Hernani*.

On the whole this version was well played, though the romantic dialogue did not meet with the entire approbation of the actors; they were not young and their training had left them steeped in convention. Joanny, despite a turned-up nose and undignified gestures, was looked upon as the successor of Talma; and Mlle Mars, who, in spite of being fifty years old (though passing for much less) was still admittedly supreme as interpreting the coquettes of Molière and Marivaux. In so far as their talent permitted, they gave of their best as Othello and Desdemona, precisely as they did some few months later in the parts of the old Don Ruy Gomrez and Doña Sol in *Hernani*. There is no evidence that either saw any notable difference in the authors—to them Shakespeare and Victor Hugo were as one.

The success of de Vigny's version was undoubted, but for some incomprehensible reason it completely vanished from the repertoire of the Comédie Française after sixteen performances. To the best of my knowledge, no theatrical historian has endeavoured to explain this fact. And yet the mutilated version of Ducis was played during 1829 and 1830 at the same time as the Vigny version. Even after this was dropped, the version of 1792 received at least fifty performances up to the year 1849. It was half a century before *Othello* reappeared at the Comédie Française.[1]

On 27 February 1899, an adaptation by Jean Aicard appeared at the historic French house. The strife between the poet and the director is old history and too well known to repeat. The well-remembered tragic actor, Mounet-Sully, had for a long time expressed a desire to play the title-role, and made a tentative effort in 1878. The opportunity came at a gala performance when the programme, at Mounet-Sully's insistence, included a fragment of the last act of Shakespeare's play. Sarah Bernhardt, who was just beginning to be recognized as one of those 'monstres sacrés' whose slightest gesture aroused audiences to frenzy, was the Desdemona. The experiment was awaited with vibrant impatience. Alas! any possible triumph was ruined by so simple a thing as a mistake in make-up. Mounet-Sully had decided to blacken himself from head to foot. On his entrance, bedizened so that he closely resembled one of those wooden Eastern figures that carry candelabra, and rolling his eyes from a face streaming with perspiration, the entire audience burst into unbounded merriment from which it never recovered. It was only with the greatest difficulty that the tragedian, consumed with anger, was able to continue to the end.

After such a disaster, the director, only too glad of any pretext to dispose of a work he did not admire, thrust the manuscript back into the pigeon-hole where it remained for twenty years —yet the success which attended its production after that lapse of time amply rewarded Mounet-Sully for his earlier failure. Othello became one of the great parts of his career.

As Sarah Bernhardt had left the Comédie to conquer wider fields, the Desdemona of the 1899 production was Mlle Lara, who was then just beginning her career. Her voice was one that touched her hearers' hearts—they heard, they shed tears and they were conquered.

Jean Aicard's translation is infinitely less valuable than that of de Vigny, despite the fact that the former was rather disdainful of the latter, mocking what he called his "timidity of approach". Comparing the two, it is obvious that one was a poet of genius and the other a mere hack, whose lines, lacking rhythm and colour, would to-day be unspeakable. The contrast between the spirit of 1899 and that of to-day is perhaps nowhere better revealed than through a comparison of Aicard's work with that of Jean Sarment. Sarment is not only a poet, he is also a man of the theatre, an actor as well as an author. His version of *Othello*, acted at Monte Carlo in 1937 and at the Odéon in Paris the following year, is concise and clean-cut, with few embellishments, moving swiftly to the inevitable conclusion. For the first time, a translator dared to include the equivalent of phrases hitherto omitted on the grounds of coarseness. The public was astonished and not a little shocked by such frank expression. After its production, critics even averred that the translator must have added crudities and unpleasant phrases of his own. *L'Illustration* made astringent comments and in its publication of the text the offending words were printed in the original English. Perhaps prudery can go no further.

The most remarkable feature of this production of 1937–8, however, is that for the first time in France Iago received recognition as a character of primary importance. Up to and preceding this date he had been but a shadowy figure. Voltaire, as I have already said, would admit of no rival to his protagonist, Orosmane. Ducis kept him almost entirely in the wings. It was unfortunate that in the English company's performances, the Iago was played by an actor "fat, clumsy, of ruddy complexion, without gesture, without expression, who merely recited his lines like an immature scholar". And in the Vigny version at the Comédie, the Iago was an actor who possessed vitality and intelligence of a sort, but was devoid of grace, making incorrect and meaningless gestures, twisting and turning—in short, perpetual movement in human form. Paul Mounet, the elder brother of Mounet-Sully, who was the Iago of the Aicard version, was not altogether successful. His natural gifts should have raised him to the status of a great tragedian, but it was whispered that he was always overshadowed by his brother and never at ease when playing with him.

Jean Sarment's conception of the part was an Iago of seeming honesty, with a mask of bantering levity and familiarity. This portrayal aroused much comment. Madame Colette, in *Le Journal*, said: "This magnificent role of traitor, so complete in villainy, so lost in his own evil, arouses some sort of pity. The downfall of a being sunk so low in humanity inspires a cry for help." Whereupon Robert Kemp in *Le Temps*, gently reproved her: "The situation of this monster", he wrote, "is so frightful that Madame Colette is worried and almost pities him, as one should pity all evil-doers. I cannot feel so compassionate."

For all the press this Iago became the main theme of criticism; theories abounded and every critic belittled the conclusions of others. Othello, Desdemona, the horror of the last act, which so shocked earlier audiences, were all forgotten. It is the first time such a reversal of opinion expressed itself in France.

I did not see Jean Sarment's Iago, but, about five years ago, I experienced something akin to the change of interest for which he was responsible. This was in Brussels where a young actor, André Berger, who is a fervent admirer of Shakespeare, was much impressed by a translation of *Othello* by Georges Neveux. This is, perhaps, the most theatrical version of the tragedy in French, although peculiarly it has never reached beyond the rehearsal stage in Paris itself. The vocabulary is excellent, inspiring, and its attraction for an actor can be well imagined. Berger put the play on at the Théâtre des Galéries, in Brussels, playing the part of Iago himself. Othello was given to a coloured actor from the Congo, named Paul Fabo. This actor attacked the part with unbounded energy. Conviction emanated from his inmost soul. The audience was moved because he was moved himself. But in spite of his actually being the son of an equatorial king, there was no nobility, none of the dignity we expect in Shakespearian tragic figures. The Iago, on the other hand, was completely equipped in voice and gesture, and, skilfully concealing the evil in his nature, he overshadowed the Othello from beginning to end—further proof of technique's victory over instinct. Though the reasons were different, the results were practically the same when the play was given by the Théâtre National de Belgique in the Neveux translation. This time Iago, heavy, full-blooded and completely master of the situation, was opposed to an Othello weaker in form and figure, who played in trance-like fashion.

In my own opinion, a balancing of the two major parts is essential to the success of the play. If the spectator leaves the theatre with either Othello or Iago uppermost in mind it is proof that the piece has not received proper interpretation. This theory accounts for the profound effect of the visit of the Arts Theatre Company to Brussels in 1947, when *Othello* was given with Hawkins as Othello and Clunes as Iago. In this production, honours were equal and the full meaning of the text made abundantly clear. It is obvious that Iago, the prime moving spirit in the play, must dominate the action up to that moment when Othello escapes from his toils and becomes a blind and irresistible force. The audience, however, must be made aware that this force, though dormant, is present from the outset. The Moor can attain heroic stature only when he has had, from the start, a worthy adversary, and such an adversary is only to be feared when his prey is worthy of being conquered. Retribution descends on the guilty one as his victims engulf him in catastrophic disaster. Something mutual in proportion must exist between the protagonists, otherwise no audience can appreciate the shaping of this imposing tragedy.

The latest translation[2] to be given in Paris was by a Swiss, René-Louis Piachaud, whose *Coriolanus* at the Comédie Française some years ago was given such a stormy reception. His *Othello* was played in 1948 at the Théâtre Marigny by the Municipal Company of Lausanne. This production aroused considerable comment among press and public, and I must confess that I, too, found it somewhat disconcerting. Othello was played by a Swiss actor, Léopold Biberti, and Iago by the well-known French actor Aimé Clariond. The latter's impersonation was on the grand scale, the incarnation of evil, with repulsive grin and eyes from which murder leaped. This Iago suggested venomous hate and perfidy before speaking a word.

As to the Othello, this was Biberti's first appearance in France and consequently something of an adventurous ordeal, especially with such a formidable Iago. Clariond is popular with the Parisian theatre-goers, who come under his spell directly he appears. He is that type of actor who dominates the stage to the detriment of those around him. On his coming, the others, like the witches in *Macbeth*, "vanish into thin air".

Biberti made Othello of such dusky hue that at first I mistook him for a native of the Congo. His proficiency in disguise is, I am told, one of his principal attractions in the theatre where he usually plays. His movements varied from swift to slow, the gestures of his hands varied from twitching nervousness to static benison, his vocal delivery from chant to frenzy, with head and body swaying monotonously. The resultant effect was that of a warlock rather than of a military chief; the murder of Desdemona became a kind of ritual killing rather than the act of a jealous husband. The first reaction to such a portrayal was unsympathetic. After consideration, however, I recalled the theories of the latest translator of Shakespeare, Pierre Messiaen. He advances the theory that, in order to appreciate Othello's character aright, we must consider the religion of his family and race. According to this view, Othello's crime becomes a purifying act rather than the deed of a wronged and passionate husband.

There is perhaps a connexion between this attitude and that of Stanislavski, who bids his actors take care to avoid making the Moor a jealous vulgarian; they should, he declares, rather seek to display the nobler motives underlying his criminal action. And Middleton Murry similarly stresses the revelation that the line "Sure there's some wonder in this handkerchief" had for him when he heard the word 'wonder' emphasized. When one considers such an interpretation one must be struck by the frequency in the text of the words 'witchcraft', 'enchanted', 'charms', 'magic'—and one must allow that Mikhail Morozov, in his essay in the previous volume of *Shakespeare Survey*, is right when he asserts that the allusions to the moon become almost a refrain on the Moor's lips. Louis Gillet is thus not justified in saying that the marvellous and the super-natural play no part in the poet's text; there is reason for such interpretations as that of Biberti.

When I began, I called attention to the fact that of the Shakespeare canon *Othello* is the most easily acceptable play to the French public. Nevertheless, the road has been long and, in the course of years, translations, adaptations and players have had to work with prudence and with patience along paths strewn with difficulty and peril. If *Othello* took so long to obtain recognition, we may well imagine the task that lies ahead for those who would introduce other works at present almost unknown.

In these days when the producer is all-important, my omission of his position may appear negligent, but space forbids, and in addition he is not my subject. *Othello* is not one of the plays that lends itself to audacious or unusual treatment. The action is not helped by more than the traditional setting. With this drama there has been no leaning towards oddity for its own sake, a form of experiment which only too frequently stifles life from the Shakespearian stage. *Othello* has been fortunate in this respect.[3]

NOTES

1. I do not mention the adaptation of Louis de Gramond (Odéon, 1882) or that of Louis Menard (Nouveau Théâtre, 1899). A complete list of any such plays would be tedious. My intention is only to underline the main lines of the history of *Othello* on the French stage.

2. Since this article was written (August 1949) the Théâtre du Vieux Colombier has given an adaptation of *Othello* by Mme Longworth-Chambrun, and the Comédie Française intends to produce Neveux's translation early in 1950.

3. The following are some of the works consulted:

Cours de Littérature Dramatique, ou recueil par ordre de matière des feuilletons de Geoffroy (Paris, 1819).

Les Fastes de la Comédie-Française, et portraits des plus célèbres acteurs qui se sont illustrés et du ceux qui s'illustrent encore sur notre théâtre, par Ricord aîné (2 vols. Paris, 1821).

Petite biographie des acteurs et actrices de Paris (Paris, 1831–2).

Réflexions de Talma sur Lekain et sur l'Art Théâtral (Paris, 1856).

Edouard Noël et Edmond Stoullig, *Annales du théâtre et de la musique* (Years: 1878, 1882, 1894, 1895, 1899) (Paris).

J. J. Jusserand, *Shakespeare en France sous l'Ancien Régime* (Paris, 1898).

Henry Lyonnet, *Dictionnaire des Comédiens Français* (2 vols. Paris).

J. L. Borgerhoff, *Le Théâtre Anglais à Paris sous la Restauration* (Paris, 1912).

F. Baldensperger, "Esquisse d'une histoire de Shakespeare en France", in *Études d'histoire littéraire*, 2e série (Paris, 1910).

Margaret Gilman, *Othello in French* (Paris, 1925).

SHAKESPEARE AND DENMARK: 1900–1949

BY

ALF HENRIQUES

To gain a proper estimate of Shakespeare in Denmark during the first half of the twentieth century one should bear in mind certain facts. The Danish people consists of four million inhabitants only—in 1900 there were only two-and-a-half million. The capital has no less than one million inhabitants. On the other hand, the largest town but four has only 50,000. Even in proportion to this the number of theatres is quite small. The Royal Theatre in Copenhagen, which is subsidized by the State, performs plays, operas, and ballets; but apart from that there are few theatres in the capital and the provinces, and they have great difficulties in maintaining a good literary standard. On the other hand, the Royal Theatre, which is now 200 years old, is regarded with remarkable interest and reverence; according to Danish traditions this theatre is a cultural and not a commercial enterprise. Another proof of the remarkable centralization in Denmark is the fact that, till a few years ago, the country had only one university, situated in Copenhagen. Like other small nations, the Danes have been fortunate in that they were forced to acquaint themselves with foreign languages and influences. The geographical position of the country has meant that these influences have never been one-sided. Quite naturally the German influence has been the strongest; rather early, however, an important contact was established with England, whereas the connexion with France after 1800 has been comparatively weak. Danish literary taste has always been determined by these facts, and it is also of great importance to note that the cultural element is largely fostered by an enlightened middle class. Danish civilization rests on a broad basis and is only to a small extent guided by a little group of high-brows. The taste is bourgeois, with a certain partiality for what is realistic, natural, humorous and idyllic; moreover, it is not doctrinaire, and with all its limitations it is quite healthy.

All this is important if we want to understand the fate of Shakespeare in Denmark. There are features favouring the knowledge of Shakespeare, whereas others have a somewhat restrictive influence. If we want to estimate the results after 1900, however, some knowledge of conditions before that date is important.

THE BACKGROUND

The critical estimation of Shakespeare has been extensive ever since about 1760. Inspired by German and English criticism, the Danish pre-romanticists took an interest in the strange Englishman, and after 1800 the romanticists worshipped him—in a less hectic manner, however, than did the German Shakespeare-maniacs of the same literary movement. A strong adoration is still found in the three-volume monograph, published in 1895 by Georg Brandes, the well-known critic (*William Shakespeare*, English translation in 1896), a popularizing work following Taine, with an attempt to construct a picture of the man behind the poetry and to find its main inspiration in personal matters. At the same time it was a work that displayed its author's best qualities: his intuitive understanding of the world of poetry in a way that makes his readers

8-2

respond too. As a scholar Brandes was open to criticism; as an artistic interpreter he is one of the very greatest.

As regards the translations of Shakespeare, from an early date great accuracy was demanded owing to German influence. Since 1807 (the first Danish translations were made in 1777) the plays have been translated into blank verse, and all translators have endeavoured to find apt Danish equivalents for the characteristic Shakespearian style. During the first decade of the nineteenth century an expert and poetic translation was published by Peter Foersom, an idealistic writer, who introduced Shakespeare on the Danish stage with a performance of *Hamlet* in 1813, in which he himself played the name-part. Others continued his work, above all Edward Lemboke, who produced a complete translation of Shakespeare's dramas in 1873—with the exception of *Pericles* and *Titus Andronicus*. The former play has only been translated in part, the latter never. Lemcbke's translations are found in most Danish homes that take an interest in Shakespeare and they are totally dominant on the Danish stage; they flow easily and smoothly, are in harmony with Danish romantic theatrical diction, but have no dramatic vigour and make no attempt to render the boldness and strength of Shakespeare's verbal art.

Performances of Shakespeare's plays (before 1900 practically speaking at the Royal Theatre only) were encouraged by the energetic propaganda of a small group of enthusiasts, but theatrical managers always feared that they might not be equal to the great task—and there was also instinctive public distrust of 'the grand style'. Several attempts were made between 1813 and 1830, but the results invited caution. On the whole, the texts used were not corrupt, but adaptations were dominant about the middle of the century, and they were often monstrous. It is a characteristic of Danish mentality that it is mainly the comedies that belong to the permanent repertoire. Tragedy is traditionally weak on the Danish stage, whereas we have had a number of comedy actors of great virtuosity. Quite naturally, however, one of the tragedies has excited the curiosity of the Danes—the play about a Danish prince; and *Hamlet* has always been performed in a sympathetic and faithful manner. Towards the end of the century the adaptations began to go out of fashion in favour of more exact renderings of the original dramas, although sometimes shreds of the older tradition even now continue to survive.

As a source of inspiration Shakespeare was of great importance to the romantic movement in Denmark, from the forerunners to the epigones. The study of Shakespeare has proved a vital stimulus to all Danish writers of tragedies, historical dramas and poetical comedies since 1800, and to quite a few of them Shakespeare proved an influence that permeated their entire work—in a few cases the model struck them powerless. Denmark possessed more, and more typical, disciples of Shakespeare than neighbouring Germany. There was, of course, a native reaction, animated powerfully by the fact that Danish dramatists are usually most successful when writing bourgeois realistic comedies. When during the last three decades of the century the naturalistic school of art became predominant, the traditional Shakespeare epigones became almost extinct. The realistic problem drama had little to learn from Shakespeare. Its devotees had other aesthetic principles and other models, even if they did not value Shakespeare less highly than the romantic dramatists had done.

So much for conditions before 1900.

RESEARCH AND CRITICISM

It was no easy task for our literary historians to succeed Georg Brandes; it is true that experts could, and were quite willing to, point out his inaccuracies, and his book was another confirmation of the fact that when dealing with his literary 'heroes', he too often introduced his own feelings and opinions. The main thing was, however, that *the* Danish book on Shakespeare had been written. Since the turn of the century the verdict has not become a milder one, and yet the book is still felt to have vitality. It was a more agreeable task to try new methods, and in this province as well as in so many others the new age was characterized by the work of the specialists. Now, and only now, does a first-hand Danish Shakespeare philology spring up. Otto Jespersen, the English scholar and Professor in the University of Copenhagen, contributes to the study of Shakespeare with skill and common sense, above all with an article on the scansion of Shakespeare's verse (*Reports of the Danish Royal Society*, 1900) and with a chapter on "Shakespeare and the Language of Poetry" in his *Growth and Structure of the English Language* (Leipzig, 1926; written in English). In 1906 Niels Bögholm, who succeeded him at the university, wrote a doctor's thesis on "Bacon and Shakespeare", in which, without admitting the existence of a Bacon problem, he points out to what extent each of the two contemporary writers has his individual mode of expression, thus using the various grammatical variants with different frequency (for instance, the comparison of adjectives or the use of indefinite pronouns).

A few other scholars attached to the university contributed in a small, but important, way to Danish appreciation of Shakespeare. Vilhelm Grönbech, the eminent professor of comparative religion, at that time reader in English in the university, wrote an essay on "Shakespeare and the pre-Shakespearian Drama" (printed in *Edda*, the Scandinavian literary periodical, 1916). It is a most suggestive essay, which is, however, based on the points of view of the previous century; thus, for example, the importance of Kyd is not considered at all. Valdemar Vedel, the literary historian, published an elegant essay on "Shakespeare and the Renaissance" in the *Germanisch-romanische Monatsschrift* for 1911 (in German). Among other articles revealing a certain independence without adding fresh material of any kind should be mentioned an article by Niels Möller, the humanist and lyrical poet, called "Shakespeare at his Work" (*Edda*, 1916), based upon an examination of *The Winter's Tale*.

In Denmark Niels Möller was one among many learned amateurs who made contributions to our knowledge of Shakespeare. The best known modern amateur scholar, however, is August Goll, Solicitor-General, whose main work, *Criminal Types in Shakespeare* (1907), was translated into English in 1909. It is the criminologist and judge of human character who speaks here. Like Brandes, his model, he underrates the practical, 'theatrical' element in the plays. But he tells us subtle things about Macbeth, the occasional criminal, Lady Macbeth, the amoral lover, Cassius, the fomenter of revolution, and Brutus, its theorist, about Richard III with his morbid self-assertion and about Iago with his destructive instinct. Another collection of essays, called '*Romeo and Juliet*', *and other Studies of Shakespeare*, appeared in 1912, but is not of the same importance. It contains a study of Romeo's poetical cast of mind and an essay on the contrast between civilization and culture as expressed in *As You Like It*, *Cymbeline*, and *The Tempest*. Shortly before his death Goll also published a highly sensitive study on *Coriolanus* (*Gad's Danish Magazine*, 1934). Karl Mantzius was another admirable amateur whose achievement for the benefit of Shakespeare on the Danish stage should be mentioned. In his spare time this intelligent and ambitious theatrical enthusiast wrote a history of the stage in five parts, translated into English in 1905: *A History of Theatrical Art in Ancient and Modern Times*. It is true that the book is based on no original research, but it has become known outside its own land because of its wide scope and the manner in which the author has succeeded in presenting a vivid picture of the theatre's history.

A strange contribution to the interpretation of the Hamlet legend—conceived as the wishful thinking of the underdogs—was furnished by Johannes V. Jensen, the Danish poet who was recently awarded the Nobel prize, in his booklet *Hamlet* (1924), the basis of which was a lecture delivered before the Shakespeare Association in 1923.

The most learned Danish Shakespeare philologist is no doubt Valdemar Österberg. In commentaries and introductions to his numerous translations of Shakespeare—*Hamlet, Othello*, and *A Midsummer Night's Dream* being among his finest—he reveals great scholarship and a sound judgement, the latter not at all a matter of course among people who busy themselves with Shakespeare, and quite unassumingly he often produces original contributions, above all in a few essays—one called "Studies of the *Hamlet* texts" (1920) with a critical examination of the earliest Quarto and fresh evidence that it cannot be Shakespeare's first form of the play, and another on "Prince Hamlet's Age" (printed in English in the publications of the Royal Danish Society in 1924). In the latter the author attempts to represent the psychology of Hamlet as that of a disillusioned young man, quite successfully diminishing the importance of the Clown's 'chronological' speeches. Another attempt at textual criticism and determination of authorship was made by Österberg in an article on "The Countess scenes of *Edward III*", printed in English in *Shakespeare Jahrbuch* (1927), where, in particular, parallels from Shakespeare's lyric poetry are used with prudence in an attempt to connect the scenes with Shakespeare's works.

Österberg's methods and views are continued by Paul V. Rubow, the literary historian, professor in the University of Copenhagen, for whom Shakespeare has been an object of constant study. In his work *Georg Brandes and the Critical Tradition in the Nineteenth Century* (1931) he deals with the attitude of Brandes towards Shakespeare, pointing out his dependence on the reading of his early years: the Germans, Rötscher, Ulrici and Gervinus, and, as regards literary method, his French models, Taine and Renan. In 1932 Rubow published his book on *Shakespeare in Danish*, containing penetrating comparative analyses of all existing translations, awarding the first prize to Österberg. The results of a large number of articles for newspapers and periodicals and prefaces for translations—above all the results of discussions with Österberg throughout the years—are contained in two books on Shakespeare by Rubow, *Shakespeare and his Contemporaries* and *Shakespeare in the Light of Current Research*, both of them published in 1948. The first work is mainly a series of studies on the philological determination of authorship, Rubow producing fresh evidence that *Henry VI* was Shakespeare's work by pointing out how parallels that have suggested authors such as Marlowe and Greene may just as well suggest other playwrights of the day, since certain traditions for dramatic diction had already fully established themselves. Following the same principles as Österberg, Rubow corroborates the theory that Thomas Kyd is the author of *Arden of Feversham*, and possibly of *King Leir* and *The True Tragedy of Richard*. It contains an essay on Shakespeare's Sonnets, a reprint of an article in English in *Orbis Litterarum*, the Danish literary periodical (1946), where Rubow accepts the 'anti-autobiographical' theory, adding fresh material on the forms and importance of the dedications of the time. The second book contains a brief chronological survey of Shakespeare's life and works with annotations based on recent research, together with his own reflections, the latter being the result of his penetration and love of contradiction, leading to views now fertile, now heretical: his paradoxical conclusions, based on the revised chronology of the plays, lead him towards an entirely new conception of Shakespeare's relationship to his contemporaries, while at the same time he brings forward original views regarding Shakespeare's psychological treatment of character.

In 1948, Ingeman Ottosen, like Österberg a grammar-school master, published a detailed study on *Shakespeare under Elizabeth*, in which he, too, endeavoured to inform the public of the results of the research of the present century. The book is careful and sober, and slightly reserved, and is meant to supplement and correct Brandes. As was the case with the latter, Ottosen's book is intended for the well-informed general public. But Ottosen does not possess Brandes' ability to make his readers enthusiastic about Shakespeare. In this respect, too, Ottosen's remarkable monograph is thoroughly representative of this century.

In 1941, the present writer completed a study entitled "Shakespeare and Denmark until 1840", the sub-titles of 'Estimation', 'Translation', 'Performance', 'Imitation' defining the fields treated. The author lays special emphasis on the process of inspiration, thus endeavouring to give a more penetrating analysis than that to be achieved by merely discovering external imitations. The analyses are based on a synthesis of structure, diction, matter and idea, together with a consideration of Shakespeare's attitude towards reality and towards his public.

The Translations

Lembcke's old translations have continued in high estimation and are still used persistently. At the same time there have been numerous twentieth-century admirers of Shakespeare who had reason to think that it was worth while trying to get closer to the original texts through new translations less influenced by Danish romanticism. Niels Möller's versions of *Hamlet*, *The Merchant of Venice*, and 1 *Henry IV*, are more faithful renderings than had been seen before, but are—on the other hand—without much sublime poetry. Johannes V. Jensen employed a different procedure when he translated *Hamlet* in 1937, trying to work his interpretation, faithfully based on Dover Wilson, into his very free translation. Jensen intended to bring *Hamlet* closer to us, using a diction that was more influenced by the language of our own day than by that of nineteenth-century romanticism. The result was open to criticism, and was, indeed, violently attacked. Still, certain speeches reveal a poetical sublimity greater than what is found in any other Danish translation. However unphilologically and perversely it may have been done, it is the work of a poet.

The principal figure among the translators of Shakespeare of our time is Valdemar Österberg. As early as 1887-8, when still quite young, he published translations of *Hamlet*, *King Lear* and *Romeo and Juliet*. In 1900-1 he revised these, adding five more: 1 *Henry IV*, *Othello*, *A Midsummer Night's Dream*, *Twelfth Night* and *The Tempest*. Later followed *The Merchant* and *Dramatic Works*, I–IX, containing fresh revisions, and including for the first time *The Merry Wives of Windsor* and *Much Ado About Nothing*. The latter appeared posthumously on Österberg's death in 1945. Österberg also made a translation of all Shakespeare's Sonnets and of what were in his opinion the Shakespearian parts of *Sir Thomas More*, *Edward III* and *Pericles*, together with a translation of Kyd's *Spanish Tragedy*. (It may incidentally be mentioned that there exist very few Danish translations of other Elizabethans, though we have translations of *Arden of Feversham*, *Sir John Oldcastle* and *The Merry Devil*, with the sub-title of "Three Pseudo-Shakespearian Plays", made by A. Halling.) Österberg's translations are all important works of art; with extreme care and invention he tried to reconstruct Shakespeare's text, attempting to find corresponding rhythms, sounds, images and connotations. The connoisseur and the philologist will appreciate his work; the general reader and the actor are less enthusiastic. As is the case with Shakespeare himself, Österberg is not always easy to understand. Certain difficulties in connexion with the recitation of his verse are not exclusively due to the actors. It is, however, most regrettable that the theatres in Denmark have always avoided Österberg. Strange as it seems, no performance of one of them has ever been attempted. Österberg may not have been gifted with the sense of euphony; but owing to his diligent work he came close to assimilating Shakespeare and his art.

SHAKESPEARE ON THE STAGE

The inheritance left to the present century by the Royal Theatre in Copenhagen, the national stage, was anything but glorious. Both actors and producers were in closer touch with the realistic drama; they had a taste for psychological studies and sober veracity. One actor only was in harmony with Shakespeare—Olaf Poulsen, the comic actor, the greatest dramatic genius Denmark has ever had, a man who radiated vitality, was a master of fantastic buffoonery and was endowed with a note of profound human pathos. His Bottom and Sir Toby Belch were impressive comic achievements.

The new century opened with the attempts of Karl Mantzius at a Shakespeare renaissance. Imitating the Munich experiment, he had a sort of Shakespearian stage constructed. The performance took place against a stylized background of three arches, and behind the middle one, the largest, changes of scenes were revealed—in other words a mixture of the abstract and the realistic stage; but the naturalistically-minded public would not even sanction this, nor did the press show any understanding. During the first years of this century *Richard III* and *King Lear* were performed on this stage with the highly intellectual and restrained Mantzius himself in the name-parts; later he played Shylock, and was particularly successful as Sir Andrew Aguecheek, and as Antony in *Julius Caesar*. The weakness of these productions lay in the fact that neither he nor his audience had any instinctive sense of pathos. This is how one of the critics puts it: "Shakespeare does not concern us; his greatness goes over our heads, because our lives are uneventful, without risk, without anxiety." If this is true, Shakespeare ought to have had greater chances of success after 1914 and above all after 1939. To a certain degree the truth of this statement has been established.

When Mantzius became manager of the theatre, this resulted in two great performances of Shakespeare: *Hamlet* and *Julius Caesar*—with traditional settings. Not even these successes, however, could veil the fact that the theatre attempted new productions of old plays with a fear bordering upon aversion. Far too many Shakespearian performances seemed an inevitable tribute to a classic, and if anything there was a slight feeling of embarrassment on both sides of the footlights. The audience unquestionably was bored. There were few actors who believed in what they had to say, and there was no producer to transform the theatre into—a theatre, not by means of settings, but through an exuberant imagination. In 1916, the memorial year, the production of a new play was not even attempted. In the years that followed Mantzius gave guest performances only, while Olaf Poulsen retired on account of old age.

Johannes Poulsen, the nephew of Olaf Poulsen, was the man truly responsible for starting the renaissance. Max Reinhardt inspired him to produce Shakespeare with imagination and liveliness, and there was a potent charm in the attempt to make use of all scenic possibilities for the production of the plays. Between 1926 and 1937 Poulsen staged a series of sensational performances which again made Shakespeare popular, or much discussed at any rate: *The Tempest*, with incidental music by Sibelius, *The Taming of the Shrew*, in a consciously naïve style, *A Midsummer Night's Dream*, in which Titania was played by Johannes Poulsen's wife, Ulla Poulsen, one of the best dancers of the Royal Danish Ballet, and at the same time an accomplished actress; lastly, using Jensen's translation, he produced *Hamlet*, which he imagined in black and white, as did Sir Laurence Olivier in later years, the weakness being that the words were sometimes drowned in the splendour and unrest on the stage. The same comment holds good with regard to his own interpretations of certain of Shakespeare's characters.

Rabelaisian Johannes Poulsen caused a revival of Shakespeare in Denmark, and he was assisted by a number of fellow-actors who also sought for something apart from mere realism. Although it is true that after his death in 1939 it has proved difficult to rival his efforts, his influence still remains. During the German occupation of Denmark, for example, when a national repertoire was aimed at, Shakespeare was not forgotten. A performance of *Macbeth* in 1944 was intended to make Danes and Germans realize the inevitable defeat of bloody tyrants.

It may give readers some idea of Danish taste that out of the sixteen Shakespearian dramas performed at the Royal Theatre since 1813, the following have been given most frequently (listed according to the number of performances): *A Midsummer Night's Dream*, *Twelfth Night*, *The Merchant of Venice*, *Hamlet*, and *As You Like It*—in other words: comedies, and *Hamlet*, 'the Danish play'. Disharmonious tragedies like *Othello* and *King Lear* appear much farther down on the list.

The fate of Shakespeare at the other theatres in Denmark runs along the same lines. Experiments have been few and far between, although there have, of course, been the inevitable performances of Shakespeare in modern costumes—even a Petruchio on a motor-cycle. At a huge and very beautiful open-air theatre in the middle of a beech wood near Copenhagen, Shakespeare's plays belong to the permanent repertoire: *A Midsummer Night's Dream*, *As You Like It*, *Twelfth Night*.

Of some interest are the numerous guest performances by foreign celebrities, sometimes alone, sometimes with their own companies. It is quite understandable that they should have taken a particular interest in performing *Hamlet* before his fellow-countrymen. Since 1900 the part of Hamlet has been played by Sarah Bernhardt, Anders de Wahl (Swede), Ingolf Schanche (Norwegian), Moissi, Katschalov and Gösta Ekman (Swede)—and the guests at Kronborg in Elsinore.

The open-air performances at the old Renaissance castle (Plate VII A) have their own history, which begins in 1916, when a gala performance of *Hamlet* was arranged by the Danish Association of Professional Writers, played mainly by the actors of the national stage. The performance was introduced by old Georg Brandes, who gave a most inspiring talk, and preceded by a short play,

Shakespeare, written specially for the occasion by Helge Rode, the lyric poet, with incidental music by Carl Nielsen, Denmark's greatest composer. The performance took place on one of the old bastions, the advantage being that the castle could be used as a distant setting, the weakness that the attention of the audience was distracted by noises from the town and from the Sound. When Elsinore was going to celebrate its fifth centenary as a borough, and another play to commemorate the occasion was wanted, the performance took place in the large courtyard. Here *The Taming of the Shrew* was performed under the direction of Johannes Poulsen on a stage that was an exact copy of the Swan Theatre in Johannes de Witt's drawing. The performances of Shakespeare that have taken place at Elsinore whenever possible since 1937 have been placed in the same courtyard—an enterprise that has created a wide international interest. They are arranged by a society called "The National Open-Air Theatre", whose purpose it is to perform *Hamlet*, and possibly other historical and classical dramas, in the Kronborg courtyard. Under the protection of the King of Denmark a number of foreign companies of actors have performed *Hamlet* in Elsinore. This is the list of guest performances until 1948: 1937, the Old Vic from London with Laurence Olivier and Vivien Leigh; 1938, Staatliches Schauspielhaus, Berlin, with Gustav Gründgens; 1939, an English company with John Gielgud and Fay Compton; 1946, the National Theatre, Oslo, with Hans Jacob Nielsen; 1947, the Swedish Theatre, Helsinki, with Erik Lindstrom. The idea is excellent; *Hamlet* is performed in so many different ways by the various nations that there is little danger that continual performances of the same play should become monotonous, and foreign actors of Hamlet are more than willing to go to historic Elsinore. In 1949 a company came over from the State Theatre of Virginia, U.S.A. with Robert Breen, and it is maintained that foreign Hamlets are queueing up, all wanting to come to Elsinore.

THE INFLUENCE OF SHAKESPEARE

It may be difficult to ascertain what Shakespeare has meant to this century as a source of inspiration. Only the romantic age imitated Shakespeare's art openly; to do something similar to-day would be felt as an imitation of post-romanticism. It is quite possible to enumerate a few half-forgotten historical plays after 1900 that approach Shakespeare's style, but they are only curiosities, anachronisms. What Shakespeare has meant to artists indirectly by showing them the variety of art, its graceful gaiety and its penetrating knowledge of the world defies analysis.

When, after the first World War, youth reacted against the bourgeois and naturalistic theatre with fresh demands that the theatre should again be a real theatre, though mirroring life in its richness and realism, Shakespeare was their main inspiration. They wanted action and oratory, but they also wanted to experiment with new forms. Very rarely did they echo Shakespeare directly. Traces of his influence are felt in the style of *Palace Revolution* (1923), a satirical play by the intellectual dramatist Iven Clausen—a play dealing with King Christian VII and Caroline Mathilda, his English-born Queen. And Shakespeare's influence is obvious in the work of Kaj Munk.

Munk is the greatest dramatist of the period, and in his case it is quite easy to ascertain Shakespeare's influence, because, contrary to his contemporaries, he accepts the inheritance of the Danish romantic movement with its liabilities, considering the traditional dramatic forms quite sufficient. It is characteristic that his first fully developed play, *Pilate* (1917), dating from his school-days, was written in blank verse. He was stirred to write his first really important work (*An Idealist*, 1928, with Herod the Great as its principal character), because one of his theological text-books complained that Shakespeare had not used that material. Munk immediately determined he would make the attempt instead. In this play Munk imitated Shakespeare in the epic technique, in the many fragmentary characters and in the contrasts between pathos and buffoonery. There is, however, no trace of Shakespeare in the diction, the passion of which reminds us of Strindberg, nor in the view of life, which vacillates between an admiration of the strong man and a Christian humility. Some witty and striking scenes between Cleopatra, Antony and Augustus are more in the spirit of Shaw than of Shakespeare. As regards construction and diction, *Cant*, Munk's Anne Boleyn play, is as closely related to Schiller as it is to Shakespeare; but the eloquence of certain of Shakespeare's villains is perceptible in its speeches of hypocrisy and self-delusion. There is little merit in his strange adaptation of *Hamlet* (1935), a mixture of a free translation and an undergraduate's youthful modernization; in this play Munk's aesthetic judgement was anything but sound, and the message unpleasantly undemocratic. Those who admire Munk because he revived 'the grand style' in Danish drama and because of his gallant fight in the years of occupation until he was killed by the Germans want to forget that play. He himself refuted all criticism with a few gay but arrogant words, addressed to those who had taken offence:

Shakespeare would easily hold his own.... That is what he told me, with an Englishman's polite smile, when we met last. For we do meet sometimes. I am a distant relative of his, whereas the others....

Kaj Munk was the last Danish writer to feel related to William Shakespeare, yet with some reason many wish they could manipulate a language rich as his.

This brief survey, including essentials only, is intended to prove that however limited the possibilities of the Danes may have been, they have always displayed a strong desire to understand and re-create.

INTERNATIONAL NEWS

A selection has here been made from the reports received from our correspondents, those which present material of a particularly interesting kind being printed wholly or largely in their entirety. It should be emphasized that the choice of countries to be thus represented has depended on the nature of the information presented in the reports, not upon either the importance of the countries concerned or upon the character of the reports themselves.

Austria: Shakespeare in the Villages

Not very much can be said on Shakespeare performances in Austria during the year 1948–9. The leading Vienna theatres had no new performances in the current year, although the Volkstheater brought out *Twelfth Night* and the Theater in der Josefstadt produced *The Winter's Tale*, both good average performances without any special distinction.

Graz opened its theatre season with two Shakespeare performances. The Städtisches Schauspielhaus opened with a lively performance of *Much Ado about Nothing*. More enterprising was the Landestheater with its open-air performance of *Twelfth Night* in the fine Renaissance Courtyard of the 'Landhaus'. Innsbruck also saw a fairly good *Othello* by the actors of the local 'Landestheater'.

The most enterprising Shakespearian performances, however, were the *Othello* and the *Midsummer Night's Dream* of the Theater für Vorarlberg—not so much because of the qualities of the performances as such, but because the plays were toured in the various small towns of the province and even to remote villages, where the stage was the dining and dance halls of inns. The versions they used were shortened ones, but they brought Shakespeare nearer to people many of whom probably had not heard of Shakespeare before.

KARL BRUNNER

Bulgaria: Accent on the Comedies

There has been a distinct increase in productions this year, though the accent still lies on the comedies. *Twelfth Night* and *As You Like It* have proved themselves popular successes once more at the National Theatre, the chief attraction being probably the rather farcical exaggeration of the low comedy, while in the provinces *The Merry Wives* and *The Comedy of Errors* have been given. The production of *Othello* at Russe

may, however, be the first sign of a return to a more balanced attitude.

Ognyanov has produced three further instalments of the Complete Works.

M. MINCOFF

Canada: Amateur Productions

After a comparatively rich year of Shakespeare productions by English and American professional companies, visiting the larger Canadian centres, the past twelve months have been in this respect a lean period. The only productions which come to mind are Margaret Webster's *Hamlet* and *Macbeth*. The credit for presenting Shakespeare in the theatre within the past year belongs almost wholly to Canadian companies, professional, semi-professional and amateur. And, judged by the plays seen and reports from responsible spectators, the best of these 'native' performances have less than might be expected to concede to the productions of some of the more highly publicized visitors. Staying in the eastern area alone, one might instance *The Tempest* and *Macbeth* given by The New Play Society of Toronto, *The Taming of the Shrew* produced by Robertson Davies at the Dominion Dramatic Festival, *As You Like It* staged at The Open-Air Playhouse by the Montreal company of Rosanna Seaborn, and *As You Like It*, *A Midsummer Night's Dream*, and *Twelfth Night*, simply and delightfully presented by The Earle Grey Players in the quadrangle of Trinity College, Toronto.

There have also been the Shakespearian productions of the various University Dramatic Societies, supervised by competent professional directors. Among them were the following: *Romeo and Juliet* at the University of Alberta; *As You Like It* at Queen's University, Kingston; *Macbeth* at Dalhousie, Halifax; *A Midsummer Night's Dream* at Saskatchewan; *Romeo and Juliet* and

Julius Caesar in the Hart House Theatre, the University of Toronto. If the other performances were like those in Toronto, which there is no reason to doubt, the general standard of undergraduate production and acting is high indeed.

On the air there has been an excellent series of broadcasts given by the Canadian Broadcasting Corporation and by the group called 'Stage 49': *Macbeth, The Winter's Tale, Richard II, Hamlet, Twelfth Night, Julius Caesar.*   R. S. KNOX

Germany: Shakespeare in the Theatre

The record of Shakespearian performances in Germany is, as is well known, a vast one: even during the war the plays kept their place well in the repertories, and now that the stages are making a certain recovery amid the ruins of so many cities the list of productions is once more growing in extent. During the year from May 1948 to May 1949 no less than thirty-three towns, from Aachen to Wuppertal witnessed a rich variety of Shakespeare's works—not only the popular *Hamlet, Othello* and *Lear*, or the equally popular *As You Like It, Midsummer Night's Dream* and *Twelfth Night*, but also such rarer dramas as *Timon of Athens, Measure for Measure* and *The Two Gentlemen of Verona.*

So outstanding and important is this German theatrical tradition that special welcome must be accorded to the handsome volume, *Shakespeare und das deutsche Theater*, which has recently been produced by Ernst Leopold Stahl (Stuttgart: Kohlhammer Verlag, 1947). This essays, in an ample seven hundred pages, to survey the fortunes of these dramas on the German stage from the first visits of the English comedians, through the tentative essays made by native seventeenth-century troupes, the diverse important endeavours undertaken in the eighteenth century and the great wave of enthusiastic effort in the nineteenth, on to the numerous experimental productions in our own era. Stahl has done his work well; both scholars and theatre-men could gain much from an examination of his pages. A notable feature of this volume is the series of illustrations gathered by Carl Niessen: this begins with a reproduction of the large map (which formed so decorative a wall-piece at the Magdeburg Theatre Exhibition) showing the wanderings of the English comedians, and it closes with a photograph of a modernistic puppet-show performance of *The Comedy of Errors.* Excellently selected, these illustrations add materially to the permanent value of an important contribution to the theatre library.

Hungary: A New Collected Shakespeare

The new Hungarian translation of Shakespeare's plays, announced in *Shakespeare Survey*, II, 127, appeared in four attractively presented volumes at the end of 1948. The most striking feature of this venture, launched by the Franklin Publishing Company in 1943, on the recommendation of András Péter and the late Gábor Halász, is the compromise solution it has reached between continuity of tradition and the dialogue technique of the modern stage. The Shakespearian vogue in nineteenth-century Hungary had produced a number of translations by the most outstanding poets of the period: Vörösmarty (*Lear, Julius Caesar*), Arany (*King John, Hamlet, Midsummer Night's Dream*), and Petőfi (*Coriolanus*). Quite apart from their intrinsic merits, these translations were too well known to be discarded. It was, therefore, decided to retain them—as well as the *Two Gentlemen* translated by Arany's son—and to have fresh translations of the other plays. Some of the leading writers of the pre-war period were enlisted; best known among them are Babits (*Tempest*) and Kosztolányi (*Romeo and Juliet, Winter's Tale*); in addition, a number of young translators of promise have been called upon to fill the gaps made by the late war. The heterogeneousness inherent in this stratification might have been reduced by a deliberate policy of stylistic archaism, or at least conservatism. In fact, however, the gap has been considerably widened by the free use of modern colloquialisms and slangy expressions, abbreviations, pet names and expletives, including some of the less reputable Germanisms of Budapest usage. In every other respect, the translators have set themselves very high standards of accuracy—in wording, rhythm, and stylistic flavour —and of artistic expressiveness. The scholarly qualities of the venture are enhanced by the excellent essays and notes on the various plays contributed by L. Orszägh, Professor of English in the University of Debrecen. There can be no doubt that the popularity of Shakespeare on the Hungarian stage, about which the previous volume of *Shakespeare Survey* (p. 128) gave some encouraging figures, will derive a considerable stimulus from this ambitious and congenial interpretation.

S. ULLMANN

Italy: Surrealistic 'Rosalinda'

Especially worthy of acclaim are the translations of several Sonnets by one of the foremost of Italian poets, Eugenio Montale (*Quaderno di traduzioni*, 1948). Here creative imagination meets creative imagination.

The text of Salvatore Quasimodo's version of *Romeo and Juliet* as produced at Verona last year (*Shakespeare*

Survey, II, 129) has now been published, as has that by Cesare Vico Lodovici of *Richard II* as presented at Milan (*Shakespeare Survey*, II, 129).

Among recent performances, Italy has had its first *Troilus and Cressida*, produced at the "Maggio musicale fiorentino", in 1949, with unparalleled magnificence of costume and circus-like pageantry (little, however, of the spirit of the play was preserved); but the most extraordinary of all the recent stagings of any of the plays is still the *Rosalinda* of 1948. *Rosalinda* is *As You Like It*, translated by Paola Ojetti, presented at Rome's Teatro Eliseo by the Luchino Visconti company with scenery and costumes by Salvador Dali (Plate VII B). In Dali's hands surrealism takes possession of Shakespeare's pastoral amid a rich riot of colour and wild imagination. In a note addressed to the public the artist declares that *As You Like It* appeals to him particularly because it is a work "typically anti-existentialist". His costume designs are inspired by eighteenth-century mode; he explains, however, that "they are not in fact ordinary eighteenth-century dresses but rather those dresses which were then on the point of reaching realization, of taking shape". Here is the Augustan age, modified by Renaissance pastoralism, interpreted by a modernist, surrealistic painter—one of the strangest performances of Shakespeare that the present age has seen.　MARIO PRAZ

Mexico: *Astrana Marín's Translations*

Astrana Marín, the *Survey*'s correspondent for Spain, has been providing both his native stage and that of Mexico with texts of Shakespeare's plays. Under the direction of Seki Sano, his *Taming of the Shrew* has been presented in Mexico City, where also was seen his *Romeo and Juliet*—reworked by Xavier Villaurrutia. The 'realistic' production of the latter play, however, was of no particular distinction.

RAFAEL HELIODORO VALLE

Norway: *'A Midsummer Night's Dream'*

There has been one notable Shakespeare production in Oslo—*A Midsummer Night's Dream* staged at The Norwegian Theatre on 31 August 1948.

Despite fears that this most delicate and capricious of the comedies might become rather heavy and clumsy in its handling, the producer, Sandro Malmquist, won complete success by his light, fantastic, gracious treatment of the action. In airy frolic he whirled his young actors across the stage; he made them call and fight and love at breath-taking pace: all the weird magic of the forest night came alive and invaded the action as elves

and fauns: a tree turned into a man, a shrub dissolved and was metamorphosed into human shape.... The thousand windings and arabesques of the benighted mystery, with the lovers who love and hate and love again, with the confusions and charms and elvish trickery, seemed to rush—a motley and festive chain—through the wood and across the tiny hillock in the midst, which, by means of a revolving stage, altered shape simply and naturally.

Sandro Malmquist found excellent collaborators. The scenery and the costumes, designed by Arne Walentin, were wholly in keeping with the idea of the production: the hill, the mottled fairy-tale forest, with its great-rooted trees, the elves' dresses sown with flowers, Oberon with enormous horns and Titania luminously veiled. In keeping, too, were the ballet movement lightly handled by Fernanda Smith and the merry, ear-catching music composed by Pauline Hall.

Altogether, a memorable performance.

LORENTZ ECKHOFF

Poland: *Diverse Performances*

After the great Shakespeare Festival last year, no new attempts were made to produce any of the plays in Warsaw itself, but the considerable interest in Shakespeare displayed by the provincial theatres may justifiably be regarded as a result of this Festival. *Othello* was presented at Łódź, *Twelfth Night* at Cracow, Swidnica, and Radom, *The Taming of the Shrew* at Lublin, *Much Ado* at Szczecin, *As You Like It* at Katowice, *Richard II* and *A Midsummer Night's Dream* at Poznań—a goodly and a variegated list.

Among the Shakespearian studies published during the year attention may be drawn to (1) Juliusz Krzyzan-owski's important survey of recent criticism in Europe and the U.S.A., covering with great thoroughness a field largely inaccessible to Continental scholars ("Szekspir-ologia wojenna i powojenna", *Nauka i sztuka*, January to March, 1948), and (2) a series of articles in *Łódź teatralna* (no. 8 (16)). These include an essay by W. Borowy warning against some pitfalls in the purely psychological approach to Shakespeare and an historical note by S. Dąbrowski on Ira Aldridge's stage career in Poland.　WITOLD CHWALEWIK

Portugal: *'Juliuş Caesar'*

The emeritus professor of the now extinct Faculty of Letters of the University of Oporto, Luiz Cardim, has published this year a revised and augmented second edition of his translation of *Julius Caesar*. Particularly noteworthy in this magnificent achievement are the stylistic correctness of the verse rendering, the sureness in interpretation, the skill with which exact equivalents have been found for the linguistic peculiarities of the original and the excellence of introduction and notes.

The same author has published in the review *Seara Nova* (Lisbon, nos. 1110–14) a series of five articles on the staging of *Hamlet*—*É o Hamlet representável?*—*A propósito do Hamlet-filme de Sir Laurence Olivier.*

PAULO QUINTELA

Switzerland: 'Measure for Measure' and 'All's Well'

Leaving out of account our University lecture-rooms and seminars where the study of Shakespeare's works and the discussion of Shakespearian problems have held their usual considerable place, the year that is coming to an end has been a rather barren one in our country so far as interesting performances of the plays, new translations and serious critical work are concerned. Which does not necessarily mean that Shakespeare is less of a living reality with us than in former years. His name, allusions to his characters, quotations from his poetry are of as frequent occurrence as ever under the pens of our writers and journalists.

King Lear, Hamlet and *All's Well that Ends Well* have been given in German, with the usual success, at the Zürich theatre. *Hamlet* appears to have been something of a new experience to the audience. The part of the King was taken by Siegfried Schürenberg and he made of Hamlet's uncle the powerful sovereign, fully worthy to be his nephew's antagonist, that I believe Shakespeare intended him to be taken for.

The Comedy of Errors was given at the Bâle municipal theatre at the beginning of last season and proved a great popular success, and the Berne municipal theatre gave last winter *Measure for Measure*. In both cases, unfortunately, the translation used was Hans Rothe's—which is more of an adaptation than a real translation, and is considered an offence to the poet's memory by his friends.

GEORGES BONNARD

A STRATFORD PRODUCTION: *HENRY VIII*

BY

MURIEL St CLARE BYRNE

This year a single production of a Shakespeare play has been selected by our reviewer for an extended description and critical analysis. It is hoped that this may prove of interest to readers who did not have the opportunity of seeing the performance itself, and that it may have some permanent value as an historical record.

I have selected the Stratford production of *Henry VIII* for a 'descriptive analysis' for various reasons, chief among them being the producer's evident desire to remain faithful to the author's intentions, his treatment of the text, and his utilization of a kind of stage which permitted him to secure effects impossible in an ordinary picture-frame set.

When the audience entered the theatre, instead of seeing a curtain, they had before their eyes a lighted permanent set which remained unchanged and unhidden until the end (see Plate VIII A). An excellent compromise between a platform and a picture-frame stage, it suggests a basic design which might well provide a happy and practicable solution to the problem of securing the effect of the Elizabethan stage within our modern theatres. Miss Tanya Moiseiwitsch is to be congratulated on the pleasing and dignified appearance as well as on the admirably functional qualities of this set, with its varied levels, its ample forestage, fifteen feet deep, and its well-thought-out modifications and rearrangements of the gallery and the inner-stage.

The text, though cut in places and abridged by one brief scene (v, ii), was so nearly the whole text in words, and so definitely the whole text in statement and intention, that it is probably the most complete and satisfactory version given in the commercial theatre since Shakespeare's time. In the average production *Henry VIII* is perhaps the most viciously and unintelligently cut play in the whole canon. The tradition is thoroughly bad, writing it off as no play at all, and treating it as a thing of pageantry with a few fine scenes and star opportunities.

The continuity was genuine, not fake. The average Shakespearian producer seems unable to realize that continuity is not the same thing as speed. Because he can manipulate his scenery or curtains in a matter of seconds instead of minutes it does not alter the fact that with his every black-out and every sliding, turning, dancing, flying or other ingenious scene-shift, continuity is destroyed. The flow of the Shakespearian action from scene to scene is a problem of bridge-and-break which must be done by words and movement. Tyrone Guthrie demonstrated this so successfully and used his property shifters with such tact that one was hardly aware how and when tables and stools had appeared or disappeared. The fluidity of movement and the power and pace thus given to the action were wholly admirable, and he caught the rapidly shifting emotional interest with a sureness we associate to-day with the films rather than with Shakespeare.

Yet another help to the continuity, in that it never called attention to itself, was the lighting, which had no colour and remained unaltered throughout, except when imperceptible light cues varied the emphasis. Set and lighting together gave a basic steadiness and reality which were a positive aid to concentration. One cannot avoid front-of-house lighting if a forestage is required, but there is no doubt that to the modern production-conscious audience its manipulation and its changes are a source of distraction. Everything here, however, combined to focus our whole attention on the actor, which is as it should be. Even the colour of the set helped, the woodwork being a natural light greyish oak in appearance, setting off the fine costumes admirably. It was a great pleasure to get rid of the usual theatrical reversal of colours, and to exchange century-darkened panelling and the wrong bright clothes for the genuine light background of Tudor life and the dark sober magnificence of its costumes. These were beautiful and congruous, and little details, such as the embroidered stockings worn by Henry in the Masque, showed how much loving delight in the authentic had gone into the designs. The reds and purples and the white and gold of the clerics provided a handsome contrast to the blacks and greys, yellows, russets, etc., of the noble personages.

The angling of the Elizabethan stage so that gallery and study are brought nearer to the audience is an excellent idea for a modern theatre. If the Elizabethan layout is faithfully preserved, depth must be sacrificed for the sake of lines-of-sight, and the space for movement which is thus lost is not compensated for by the upper-stage facilities gained. The set had no proscenium doors, but there was an ample downstage entrance (right), a fine large door entry, set at an angle, just above the dais, a large passage entry immediately above the study on the left, and an entry to the gallery. The orchestra pit was used for entrances and exits, the steps coming up from stage right and emerging just left of stage centre. The only touches of permanent colour decoration were Henry's state, and in the background and along the proscenium arch the banners with the Tudor badges—the Union rose, the red dragon, the fleur-de-lis of France, the Beaufort portcullis, etc.

It was of great advantage to the play to let us take in the set before the action started. Because one could register, for example, the impression made by the single pillar, two-thirds upstage right, with the red dragon banner of the Tudors to its left and a shaft of light striking across it diagonally and falling on the steps leading up to it, one was the more ready and receptive for the use made of that particular area and its symbolical value. The possible pace of a play must relate to the response of the audience, and there seemed a greater alertness than usual in this response, just because familiarity with the background before the stage was peopled had made us all better aware how and where to look without diverting any conscious attention from the players.

The Prologue was spoken by the Old Lady, Anne Bullen's friend (Wynne Clark)—a sound device to associate its serious and pertinent comment with the theme of the Tudor succession which is responsible for the structure of the whole play. Miss Clark was a perfect Holbein portrait to look at, and she seized her twofold opportunity firmly: the quality of life in her, the persuasive zest of her way of speaking and the authenticity of her appearance, all struck the dominant note of the entire production. The emphasis laid on the 'truth' of the play, 'our chosen truth', came over with full force as she drew us straight into a novel intimacy, speaking from the extreme front of the forestage (left). When she adjured us

> think ye see
> The very persons of our noble story
> As they were living,

upstage, right, the Dukes of Norfolk and Suffolk with three other nobles were seen for a moment in converse—a moment of breath-taking reality upon which the mind dwells with delight, especially when looking back over the production as a whole and realizing how skilfully their sober-suited group, caught in the shaft of light by the solitary pillar, drew the attention unconsciously to this significant feature which was afterwards to be related at important moments to the vital matter of the play. Then, as she began to speak her last line, what had held us as the timeless instant dissolved; and the play itself swept into action with the entry, right, of the Duke of Buckingham (Leon Quartermaine). The vigorous attack in this opening scene was remarkable. Norfolk (Michael Gwynne) and Buckingham held the attention by their obvious delight in the rhetorical force of speeches which are generally cut down by the theatre to a mere thirty or forty lines, and used less for their own sake than as a build-up for Wolsey's entry.

Wolsey's procession entered from the orchestra pit so that as it advanced upstage and across from the left the Cardinal encountered Buckingham almost centre, and with his back to the audience as he passed him. If we were waiting for a repetition of Irving's great moment we were to be disappointed, for we did not see Wolsey's face as "the Cardinal in his passage fixeth his eye on Buckingham, and Buckingham on him, both full of disdain": but it was perhaps judicious not to challenge this bright legend, and to let us see only Buckingham's expression, giving us instead, as the procession moved upstage, a magnificent and raised central position for Wolsey (Harry Andrews), where he could turn and face the audience and dominate the scene as he spoke the lines which prepare us for Buckingham's doom.

The only properties used throughout were long tables and joint stools, and the passage beneath the gallery, upstage of the study, was designed to give them easy and unobtrusive entry. The assembling of the furniture for the Council Chamber involved, consequently, no loss of time or continuity. A table and stools were set downstage centre for Wolsey and various officers and scriveners. As the King (Anthony Quayle) entered to take his seat on the dais it was clear that, although in costume and make-up this was recognizably the Henry of the Holbein portraits, the producer had taken his cue from historical fact rather than from theatre tradition and was presenting us not with the grossly corpulent figure of the later years of the reign but with the fine burly young man that was Henry in his prime. Queen Katharine (Diana Wynyard), though beautiful, was old in comparison with her hearty, ruddy, young husband.

This scene showed very clearly what magnificent opportunities for variety, grouping and dramatic movement the varied levels and the unusual layout of this semi-Elizabethan stage offer to a producer who understands how to use them. Pictorially and dramatically the first grouping of the three principals was very striking—Henry in his chair of estate, four steps up, facing three-quarters left, dominating the whole scene: Katharine, upstage of him, but a step lower, perfectly yet naturally placed for her spirited attack on Wolsey's oppression of the common people, and Wolsey below them and to their right on the forestage—the group admirably balanced by the mass of the crowd opposite and upstage left. For the examination of Buckingham's Surveyor, Wolsey moved across to the far end of the table opposite the King: the Surveyor stood above the table and spoke first to Wolsey and only turned afterwards to the King. Finally, as the excitement of his revelations mounted up, Henry came pounding down from the dais, thrust a clerk sprawling from a stool at the end of the table, and sat down and pushed the examination to its vigorous conclusion.

It was a strong, dramatic and highly significant move this bearing down of the King from the edge of the conflict into its heart. When the play opens Wolsey is at the height of his power, with Henry relying on him for everything. The pretended threat both to his own life and to the Tudor succession is what brings him into the arena to deal with his own affairs. His move took him nearly half-way across the stage, and we shall remember it when at the end of the trial-scene he comes down again from his throne and goes the whole way across to stage left and stands at last free of the great Cardinal.

As the Surveyor-scene ends, the next is already beginning, with the entry of the Lord Chamberlain and Lord Sands discussing the latest Court scandals. Though obscure and topical, only two short passages of detail (ll. 5–13 and 26–32) have been cut, and the scene is played with such vivacity, and the characters, especially Sands, are so quickly individualized, that it holds the interest and covers the preparations for Wolsey's banquet till it merges into the actual banquet-scene. Sands is a lively, raffish old gentleman, slightly red of nose and of lecherous inclination— a perfectly legitimate interpretation of the text. For the banquet two long tables are set more or less at right angles to the gallery, well over to stage left, while Wolsey's banners replace the King's. The display, however, is almost negligible: the banquet is successful as a scene because it is *acted*. The guests are lively, noisy and coarse; and, if their manners are perhaps more reminiscent of the city than the court, there is no infidelity to the text. Wolsey enters above in the gallery as the gaiety is at its height, immediately after Anne Bullen (Kathleen Michael) has been effectively established in a brisk passage with Lord Sands. This Anne Bullen looks very well and she is tremendously alive, outstanding even amongst this group of vigorous, assertive and attractive young women. The Masque is well done and the masquers in their Tudor green-and-white and their golden straw hats look as authentic as the spectators. What is more, the masquing costume gives us at precisely the right moment the best possible opportunity of realizing Henry as the *young* man in the prime of life: and if we take 1527 as the year which brought the declaration of his love for Anne Bullen, and this scene as its dramatization, then, by happy coincidence, the King and his impersonator are, in fact, precisely the same age. It is no derogation from Anthony Quayle's performance to allow that this has certainly contributed to its rightness.

The meeting between Anne and the King is excellent. She has jumped on a stool to see the masque over the heads of the crowd and suddenly Henry catches sight of her and stands trans-fixed—quite literally *caught*, vitality drawn to vitality, as she returns his gaze and meets its challenge. Miss Michael and Anthony Quayle play this moment for all it is worth: I have never seen it more strikingly and convincingly rendered, nor the value of the King's love for Anne more effectively established, and, as I believe, given precisely the stress which the author intended.

As the revel starts again and hurls itself off with the disappearing banquet tables, the walking-gentlemen scene, which precedes Buckingham's execution, begins. Here the producer has taken something of a liberty with the text by getting rid of the Second Gentleman and giving his part to Sands. As a device it seems reasonable: the cast is enormous, Sands' own part disappears at this juncture and it is theatrically a pity to lose a real character who has just registered effectively with the audience, while dramatically it aids both continuity and concentration to keep a known rather than to introduce a new minor personage. Of more interest, as a recurrent problem of Shakespearian production, is the treatment accorded to the scene. Not for the first time, Guthrie's theatrical inventiveness has drawn upon him some magisterial rebukes. It would be more to the purpose to recognize first his courage and correctness in keeping such scenes; an easy way out of the difficulty they present is to cut them altogether; or one can escape censure by letting them be as dull as most people find them. This is not Guthrie's way: he believes that the author has intention in what he writes and that it is our business to find out how to put a scene across to our own audience. In the present instance, having the right kind of stage at his command, he makes his walking-gentlemen *walk*—a genuine platform-stage device and therefore entirely legitimate. His next deduction is equally logical: they are walking through the streets of London to see the Duke going to execution, and he has no chorus to say to his audience "Work, work your thoughts" and *see* that walk; so instead he lets his actors mime the background of incident, of the *Gare l'eau* variety, which might reasonably be supposed to enliven their progress. It is novel and entertaining, and it makes the audience laugh. Is comic relief at this point destructive of the author's intention in the matter of the tragedy of Buckingham, or is it legitimate and Elizabethan? That Buckingham's beautifully spoken farewell was not spoilt for the audience by this little episode was made quite clear by rapt attention and two great bursts of applause. Of one thing we may be certain, walking-gentlemen scenes must have had more in them than we find to-day if they held the Elizabethan audience. Is this, Guthrie prompts us to ask, the kind of thing Elizabethan actors did with them?

At this point there was some cutting, and the action was altered so that Henry in his study overheard the talk which heralds his divorce; but it was interesting—and highly indicative of the producer's attitude—to find the passage between Campeius and Wolsey on the subject of Pace's death retained. Its matter is obscure Tudor politics and completely uninteresting to the average auditor, but it has its function, both dramatic and theatrical, confirming Wolsey's personal ambition at this crucial moment.

As they went off, with the business of the divorce resolved on, Anne Bullen and the Old Lady entered upstage, and came down to the forestage left, where they sat and wound wool as they talked. The intimate forestage playing, here as elsewhere, gave great scope for facial expression and made one realize for the hundredth time how much subtlety we lose when the actors retire into the picture-frame. One could *see* Anne experiencing the whole idea of what is to happen: it made her part much more vital and significant than it usually seems. The business of the Lord Chamberlain's message from the King was accompanied by the presentation of a small bouquet from which a pearl necklace dropped to the ground when Anne took the flowers, making an admirable silent moment for the three players and giving the Old Lady a delightful cough of comment. There is also a letter in the bouquet, and this Anne reads as she moves away from them, so that the Chamberlain's important comment on the succession theme (ll. 75–9) can be spoken to the Old Lady, which makes it more natural and effective than when it is taken as an aside.

In the Blackfriars Hall scene the bishops' procession, preceded by choristers, vergers and scribes, entered from the orchestra pit, their full canonicals and the banners of the Sees making a fine show. The procession of Wolsey and Campeius entered by the large doorway upstage right and advanced towards us, Campeius taking the seat at the right end of the table and Wolsey at the left. The gallery was crowded, Norfolk, Suffolk, Sands and the Old Lady being noticeable, and of course the First Gentleman. The anticipative susurration of "The King", was a genuine crowd whisper, but Henry did not enter, as expected, with the Guard: he came hurriedly in alone, upstage right, and went straight to his chair with the ruffled expression of the man who has missed his cue. The effect of this was to enhance the dignity of Katharine's entry, upstage left, with Griffith, Patience and two gentlewomen. She came straight down left, and sat at the extreme side of the forestage—a position which then gave her a magnificent move across to the King's state at the direction, "she goes about the Court".

In her appeal it was to the King alone that Katharine addressed herself, rejecting the authority of the Court from the opening line:

> Sir, I desire *you* do me right and justice.

I do not think this was the word-stress implied by Tudor English, but it gave great poignancy, intimacy and naturalness to what can easily become a set piece of rhetoric. Miss Wynyard made one feel as if it were being spoken for the first time. Henry played to it very well, deeply embarrassed, and moved as he had no wish to be. Then the intervention of the two Cardinals carries the action away from the personal plane at once, and baffled and silenced by the impersonal, impervious, irresistible process in which circumstance and the King's will have entangled her, she allowed Campeius to lead her to the bar of the Court, from which she delivered her attack on Wolsey with fine force, leaving it immediately after and moving upstage. Wolsey followed her to protest his good intentions, and she was thus perfectly placed, just above him, upstage centre, for her final refusal of the jurisdiction of the Court. She curtsied to the King while Campeius protested, turned to depart, and was stopped by Griffith at the gallery stairs. Having dealt with him she then swept on up the stairs and delivered her "I will not tarry" from the gallery, in a magnificent and commanding position. Throughout, as in the Surveyor-scene, she spoke with a clear purity and naturalness that delighted the ear.

The interest of this scene was held after Katharine's departure by the unusual method of trusting the author and playing the whole of his text simply and sincerely. It was the real test of the producer's understanding of his matter, and of his historical imagination, that he kept Henry's long speech (ll. 153–207) entire, save for some half-dozen lines. In most stage versions it is cut from l. 170 to l. 220; and this is the key passage in the play. Anthony Quayle rendered it with sincerity and conviction, beginning slowly as if thinking out this case of conscience, warming up as he went on to speak of the deaths of all his male heirs and of the danger to the Tudor succession and the realm, finally turning with vigorous appeal to the Bishop of Lincoln who stood downstage left and pulling him in as a witness, and then sweeping round the Court with eye and gesture and invoking the support of the Archbishop of Canterbury, standing upstage right by the pillar. It was a natural and yet vivid handling of a really difficult exposition.

It was a brilliant stroke of production to go all out for a naturalistic effect after Campeius had moved the adjournment of the Court; and to hold a total and overwhelming silence until the King chose to break it. The Bishops went into a marvellous ecclesiastical huddle of copes and mitres, oozing consternation and disapproval, and Henry strode angrily across to the far left of the forestage, and spoke his aside directly to the audience. Then, at

> My learn'd and well beloved servant Cranmer,
> Prithee, return:

with a commanding gesture he summoned the Archbishop of Canterbury forth from the crowd, upstage right. Cranmer's consequent move, down the steps centre, and across to the King, was a joy to watch, and has won critical notice as well as popular acclaim. It stressed the significance of Wolsey's isolated position, and made a striking conclusion to the first part of the play, but in point of fact it is plain both from the wording and from the references in the next scene (III, ii, 63–7, 402–4) that this apostrophe to the absent Cranmer is all part of Henry's aside. It is inconsistent to retain these later references and then amalgamate Cranmer and Canterbury for the trial; and to use Cranmer like this for its ending is to ignore the author's dramatic intentions. As he has planted Cranmer verbally at nine different points before he allows him to appear in person in Act V there is obvious intention behind this somewhat unusual procedure. Cranmer's dramatic function is to show the all-powerful and wise monarch in action and to prophesy the greatness of Elizabeth. It is *not* his function to replace Wolsey, and the point of the end of the trial-scene is to show that at last the lion knows his strength and that the King will stand alone. His strength when established, as it should be at this moment, is in his aloneness. Wolsey has failed him: the movement begun in the Surveyor-scene is now completed. It cries for visual realization. Cranmer's appearance at the trial and his magnificent move to the support of the King are, therefore, to me, functionally wrong—a sacrifice of the author's dramatic intention to theatrical effect.

For the scene of the Queen and the Cardinals, Katharine and her four maids seated themselves on joint stools and on the floor, downstage right. The Queen looked older, but with a strange added loveliness—a calm in her expression which spoke of ravaging strife of mind and spiritual agony, endured and survived. There was royal self-command in every movement and gesture: it was to the hands that one had to look for the signs of emotional strain; though this groundling will swear to it that when the Cardinals were announced her face sharpened as she braced herself for this new ordeal.

In the opening passage both sides were sparring quietly and warily for advantage; and the first round went to Katharine, as the author meant, when the warm, rich response of the whole audience came on "Good my Lord, no Latin". Then the battle begins in earnest, with the Cardinals one each side of her, Wolsey to the right, Campeius on the left. She listens with impressive stillness of demeanour until Campeius expatiates upon Wolsey's 'noble nature' and good intentions. This is too much: there is a little impatient tapping of the foot; she rises and walks away from them, gaining herself the necessary opening aside for her next speech: when the group re-forms Wolsey and Campeius are together on her left. Miss Wynyard's whole expression, and particularly the eyes, added greatly to the poignancy of "the last fit of my greatness"; and the touch of anger at "but little for my profit", and the tears in eyes and voice at "far hence, in my own country, lords", were all most affecting. Her stillness in these passages is especially noteworthy: the eyes alone move, until, with shrivelling scorn, she blazes momentarily into attack in the 'cardinal sins' speech. After this outburst and the deep, bitter, natural pathos of the description of her utter ruin and friendlessness which follows, again under rigid control she sits immobile while they make their final attempt at persuasion, and there is a grave and touching dignity in her

> Pray forgive me
> If I have used myself unmannerly.

As they rise to go Wolsey offers her his ring to kiss, and she looks at him, dismissing the gesture only with her eyes, every inch the Queen and descendant of the proudest royal line in Europe as she precedes them from the chamber.

So to Wolsey's doom. As the Cardinals and her maids follow the Queen out, the nobles,

Wolsey's enemies, enter to the attack. The opening of the scene is played for all it is worth, with steadily mounting force, Norfolk in particular establishing even more firmly his clear-cut and outstandingly Tudor portrait. The condescending huntin'-shootin'-fishin' intonation he gave to his approval of Cranmer, "a worthy fellah", was a pretty touch, and incidentally was not missed by the audience. A trifle, but indicative, as everything else, of the completeness and integrity of the producer's naturalistic conception.

This scene of the baiting of the great Cardinal is always effective, but on this fine spacious stage, with its varying levels, it was even more so than usual. The strength and significance which can be given to purposeful moves from upstage to downstage could not have been more excitingly demonstrated; and the mounting tension was fine as Henry came swooping down on his un-suspecting victim, with these power-greedy lords jackalling in after the lion. Norfolk delivered his last line with real Tudor insolence:

So fare you well, my little good Lord Cardinal.

Which brings us to the query—how good is this Wolsey? My own answer is, just as good as the author meant him to be. One must insist: this is not *The Downfall of Cardinal Wolsey*—that was another play belonging to the Henslowe repertoire, now lost. The author has not provided a hero, in the ordinary sense of the word, but a play for genuine teamwork, demanding a number of first-rate players, not rival stars and still less one "bright particular star". It is a realistic historical play, as the author insisted in the Prologue, not an historical adaptation with a strict eye to the main theatrical chance. It is a play about the Tudor succession, by an Elizabethan. It was the test of Harry Andrews' conception, I thought, that the nearer he came to the audience the better I liked his performance. I found him most real in his end, and just as the Queen's face seemed to sharpen with anxiety and distress in III, i, so here Wolsey's seemed to grow lined and stricken even as he was speaking.

As Wolsey made his exit by the orchestra pit, a silent scene was substituted for the coronation show. Anne herself came dancing on to the stage, and went proudly up the central steps and off as the bells began to ring out. It seemed to me a legitimate and imaginative touch, if we grant that Guthrie does well to cut the coronation procession which otherwise gives us our last glimpse of Anne Bullen. I was more moved by Miss Michael's brief moment, the gaiety and then the proud carriage of the slight figure and that thrown-back head, than I have ever been by the famous 'show'. It was more real, and therefore more congruous in this play, than the splendours of spectacle.

The coronation is given as seen through the eyes of the crowd, represented by the First Gentleman and Sands, who are joined at l. 55 by the Lord Chamberlain instead of the anonymous Third Gentleman of the text. It is the First Gentleman's big opportunity and George Rose takes it with both hands. He has the most engaging toothy grin which he flashes on and off like a child with an electric torch: to the life he is the pushful, eager procession hunter who will always elbow his way to the front row for the wedding or the funeral. He knows all about everybody who is anybody; he was the man who noticed how the Duke of Buckingham, when his judge-ment was pronounced, "sweat extremely": it is he who can tell us that Cranmer has pronounced the sentence of divorce and that Katharine lies sick at Kimbolton. He has the little mannerisms which mark the excitable utterance of the brisk gossip-hound: his 'Cin—*que* ports' and 'HWhitehall' win appreciative chuckles, and he finally bounces his way into the affection of us groundlings when at the climax of his excitement he matches the rhythm of his ecstatic "and all the rest are Countesses" with four excited little leaps. The effect was greatly helped by the excellent crowd noises off; but the text was, after all, the author's, and more than even the earlier example Guthrie's handling of this scene made me question just how far the lack of producer's imagination has damped down the force and vigour of walking-gentlemen scenes in general. What Guthrie and his actor have realized, in this instance, is that the whole passage is the grandmother and grandfather of all running commentaries. To look for the answer to the walking-gentlemen problem in acting, character work and the facilities of the Shakespearian stage is a solution that deserves something better than jibes about tricks.

Before the commentators had finished a chair had been brought on and set well downstage left for the scene at Kimbolton. Katharine was helped in, old and ill, and already remote from the world. Miss Wynyard looked and acted the dying Queen supremely well—that is to say, as written, on the realistic note. She hardly moved her head, only her eyes, and the little movement of her nerveless hand, up and down, on the arm of her chair, at "nothing," in "as he is now, *nothing*", was an infinitely pathetic and eloquent comment on the theme of ruined greatness. When Griffith—most sympathetically played, as a Welshman, by Robert Hardy—spoke Wolsey's praise she turned her head slightly, painfully, and smiled at him. She dropped asleep, and then, opening her eyes, saw the vision in the vacant air above our heads, playing the whole thing straight at us. It was finely and convincingly done; and the last speech to Capucius was beautifully spoken, with that momentary return of strength which flickers up before death which the author so obviously demands by providing this extremely moving farewell—a most skilful avoidance of anticlimax, after the exaltation of the vision, to bring us back to the realistic plane without any jolt.

Before Katharine has been led off the next scene has begun with the entry, upstage centre, of Gardiner, who appears to be as drunk as the King and Suffolk who come reeling in a moment later. The treatment of Gardiner, in this generally realistic production, runs true to the tradition of the theatre, where "the part of the bloody-minded Gardiner has always been given to the first comic actor". The picture comes back into realistic focus, however, as Henry sobers well and quickly, and the way in which he deals with Cranmer, the innocent, unworldly churchman, is excellent, jollying him along with practical advice and gracious encouragement. Of genuine structural importance, however, is the way in which, in these four speeches, Henry manoeuvres himself into the centre of the play. The dramatist is using his anticlimactic breathing space to work around to the triumph of the King which is the assertion of the theme, and the scene ends with the announcement of the birth of Elizabeth. The next scene, where the King and Dr Butts observe from above the Council's insolent treatment of Cranmer, was cut—the only instance here of the cutting of an entire scene. Most productions cut the entire episode (v, i–iii).

The council-chamber scene which follows showed once again the producer's mastery of movement. It was a pleasant little touch, hailed with delight by the audience, to let Cromwell, now risen in the world and Secretary to the Council, use his former master's slightly pompous trick of an admonitory or introductory 'a'hem'. That the audience was still alert to appreciate such niceties of production is eloquent testimony to the quality of life in the performance. But it was the amount and the interest of movement and the free use of so much of the stage that gave such life and such a lift to what in less skilled hands might have been a very static council-table scene. Henry had a fine entry upstage, which enabled him to bear down swiftly upon the table and take up a commanding position above it, centre. The councillors scattered right and left before his onslaught—a clever reversal, this, of the closing-in on Wolsey, in which four of the same gang had been concerned. As they circled nervously around, Henry sat and made Cranmer sit too, and then staged his carefully prepared scene of vigilant and active kingship which preludes the final assertion and triumph of the Tudor succession theme. It is the necessary dramatic complement to the Surveyor-scene and its implications. With a fine show of the famous Tudor rage he turns upon these other ministers who would also tyrannize and oppress, and rends them until the Lord Chancellor pours oily prelatical reasonableness upon the storm, and it subsides. With power thus vindicated by its defence of virtue Henry is ready enough to take the cue which the Chancellor so tactfully provides: in a moment he is bluff King Hal again, banging Cranmer on the back and jabbing him in the ribs over "You'll spare your spoons!", for now the matter in hand is reconciliation and the christening of Elizabeth, and the bells for the final scene have started before they are off the stage.

While the table and stools are being cleared away the porter and his man, in the orchestra pit, are repelling the crowds who are storming the doors. The porter staggers up, his face almost obliterated by a large dollop of whitewash—or was it genuine Tudor blanc-manger?—and while the crowd roars off-stage, he and his man sit on the step above the pit, drinking their ale and describing the tumult. Choristers in procession enter from the pit, followed by the nobility and gentry, while from upstage right the bishops enter, all in white and gold, and Cranmer appears above in the gallery. The pageantry and pattern of the mingling of the various crowds and of the white and gold pennons carried by the Guard seemed neither so skilful nor so purposeful as in the other massed scenes: I felt it belonged to another convention and was assailed by memories of the pantomime finale. The original stage-direction here deserved more sympathetic consideration.

The nobles marched up into the gallery and the infant princess was brought on in their midst in the arms of the old Duchess of Norfolk under a white and gold canopy. Cranmer came down from the gallery and took up his position by the pillar, the King went up into the gallery and stood there holding his child, and then Cranmer spoke his prophetic vision of the glory of the Elizabethan age, or, if one so prefers to phrase it, the dramatist pronounced his gravely beautiful valediction over the age that bred him. It should be recorded that the interruption of the Duchess's sneeze, which roused critical protest, was removed after the first night. Unfortunately, the passage about James I was cut (ll. 40–56). To concentrate on Elizabeth gives immediate theatrical effect, but to delete James destroys dramatic intention. The essential and final explicit statement of the theme is the triumph of the Tudor succession, which turns to failure if we end on the prophecy of the death of the Virgin Queen.

I was much impressed by the way the production made the oration balance the Prologue. (The Epilogue is, God bless us, a thing of naught; though while Miss Clark was speaking it she persuaded me for the moment that it really did mean something.) But as the speaking and staging of the Prologue coaxed us at once into a belief in the immediate reality of what we were about to see, so Cranmer's oration, just because it looked forward to what, for us, had been realized nearly four centuries ago, made the play itself retreat from us again, back into 'history'. For me, at any rate, it brought the wheel full circle.

THE YEAR'S CONTRIBUTIONS TO
SHAKESPEARIAN STUDY

1. CRITICAL STUDIES

reviewed by UNA ELLIS-FERMOR

This year's critical work shows some interesting developments in line with, but by no means repeating, those of the last two years. The tendency to give first place to the art and poetry of Shakespeare is confirmed and some searching and penetrating work in this field gives promise of a coming renascence in dramatic aesthetics. A new edition, by Napoleone Orsini, of Benedetto Croce's *Shakespeare* is symptomatic of the growing interest in the older criticism, as is also the constant reference back to Bradley, but one of the healthiest signs is the divergence of opinion on certain branches of Shakespeare's dramatic technique and the acute and close arguing which, in three or four volumes, accompanies the investigation of the functions and relations of these to the forms of specific plays and to the nature of dramatic art itself. Though many aspects of Shakespeare's work have here come in for their share—thought, structure, character, style and imagery—the treatment of character and its dramatic function has invited the widest range of critical judgements, from those of Henri Fluchère and of J. F. Danby, who, in different forms, deny psychological reality to character in drama (even in Shakespeare's drama), to those of H. B. Charlton and J. I. M. Stewart who stoutly maintain the fundamental truth of the character-drawing in the plays. Clearly the question of the relation of 'character' in drama to the basic nature of the art is disturbing some of our assumptions, and the problems that this uneasiness will ultimately disclose may tax to the full our powers of thought, even as those raised by the nature of dramatic imagery did some twenty years ago. Another tendency noticed last year, the detailed study of a single play in a volume of some length, also continues: last year's favourite play was *Hamlet*; this year's is *Lear*. But here again there is progression, not repetition; to devote a whole volume to a single play is itself a sign of simultaneous intensification and extension, but this year's work carries us a stage further, and special aspects of single plays—R. B. Heilman's study of the imagery of *Lear* and J. F. Danby's of its thought—mark new phases in modern criticism. There is some subtle and sympathetic analysis of the style of certain plays in Edith Sitwell's *Notebook* and technical examination of theatrical characteristics of the style in Richard Flatter's *Shakespeare's Producing Hand*.

Much of this criticism or analysis of special aspects of Shakespeare's art is, of course, contained also in books which are themselves surveys of the whole of his work or of particular sections. This year is peculiarly rich in these: H. B. Charlton's *Shakespearian Tragedy*, the new edition of Croce's *Shakespeare*, J. I. M. Stewart's *Character and Motive in Shakespeare*, E. M. W. Tillyard's *Shakespeare's Problem Plays*.[1] The study of Shakespeare in his setting as an Elizabethan dramatist falls more often, and naturally, to writers of other countries, and Henri Fluchère (*Shakespeare, dramaturge élisabéthain*) and Lorentz Eckhoff (*William Shakespeare*) treat this in widely differing

---

[1] This volume had not been published in England at the time of going to press and will be discussed in next year's *Survey*.

ways. Finally, this list is fittingly completed by Paul Van Tieghem's scholarly study of an early phase of Shakespearian criticism in *Le préromantisme....La découverte de Shakespeare sur le continent.*

"When", says H. B. Charlton, "...I read that *Hamlet* 'so far from being Shakespeare's masterpiece...is certainly an artistic failure', I feel that English is a language which I do not know." When we, on the other hand, read this sentence on the second page of his book,[1] we know exactly where we are. Charlton stands four-square in defence of the interpretation of Shakespeare's art in terms of human experience, human morals and human (or even, it may be, spiritual) wisdom. There is wit, pith and independence in this defence; independence (where need be) even of the great traditional criticism, from Dryden to Bradley, which he upholds. The book surveys Shakespeare's tragedy from its beginnings in *Titus*, tracing step by step through the earlier plays the causes of their breakdown as tragedies and the simultaneous growth of Shakespeare's tragic art. When he reaches the four great tragedies Charlton reveals, as he has promised in the introduction, yet another sequence of thought or of interpretation which is contained in them. For they embody "the depredations of the tragic fact at receding levels of human evolution, in different spiritual epochs; they seem like pictures of human life at great stages in the past history of its spiritual progress". To an analysis such as this the nature and function of character in drama is a question of first order and the concluding pages of his third chapter give a reasoned defence of the approach through characterization. This is illustrated in the next by his own analysis, in fearless detail, of the character of Hamlet, with a close study of the picture Shakespeare gives of that character before it is touched by knowledge of the murder. Throughout the book, whether he is treating character, structure or underlying tragic thought, Charlton relates the plays closely to their sources; progression from one kind of treatment to another is a significant index to the growth of his tragic form.

To turn from this to J. I. M. Stewart's book is to meet an extension, into other parts of Shakespeare's work, of certain ideas which, in somewhat different forms, had made part of Charlton's. Stewart limits himself to *Character and Motive in Shakespeare*,[2] but, as his sub-title suggests, this is in the first instance a survey of recent critical positions, most of them involving the "depreciating of Shakespearian character". The book is witty, shrewd, penetrating and for the most part clear-headed. As Stewart leads us an entertaining progress through the twentieth-century criticism in this field, he reveals his own position, and, like Charlton in this at least, declares himself of the old tradition which has of late become the new criticism. His attitude to the creative process is sound (even if he does, disturbingly, invoke Freud), for he acknowledges it as the touchstone to which all aesthetic theory must be brought. Perhaps the most important contribution he makes to the defence of character is the suggestion that Shakespeare's communication, whether with reader or audience, proceeds at a level of experience far below their conscious observation, in "recesses of human passion and emotion", "where the deeper mechanisms of dramatic illusion come into play". A presentation of character over whose validity there has been dispute may thus turn out to be "rather a handling, according to the laws of drama, of little recognized impulses and conflicts within our own minds" and the impact of such art "may be like that of the iceberg, most massive below the surface". Thus, while no

[1] H. B. Charlton, *Shakespearian Tragedy* (Cambridge University Press, 1948).
[2] *Character and Motive in Shakespeare. Some Recent Appraisals Examined* (Longmans, Green and Co., 1949).

ground is yielded to "facile historical extenuation", a theory is adumbrated which might resolve the honest doubts of the genuine historical critic.

The re-editing of Benedetto Croce's *Skakespeare*[1] is, as I have suggested, symptomatic of the growing determination to investigate anew and more strictly certain fundamental aesthetic assumptions. Napoleone Orsini has furnished it with an introduction explaining the rising interest in Shakespeare's work which has led to the separate publication of this essay without the companion studies of Ariosto and Corneille, tracing the development of Croce's theory of aesthetics up to its third and final phase, "quella dell' arte come intuizione cosmica" and examining briefly the position of Croce as a Shakespeare critic. The commentary and annotations at the end are designed to elucidate Croce's critical theories and to illustrate specific passages, primarily but not exclusively, for the Italian reader. It is now nearly thirty years since the first publication of *Ariosto, Shakespeare and Corneille* (1920), and Croce's views on historical criticism, on character and on "il sentimento shakespeariano" have a sudden, fresh relevance. Symptomatic also of the trend of criticism in England is a new edition, with three additional essays, of G. Wilson Knight's *The Wheel of Fire*.[2] This book was among the first modern subjective and imaginative studies of Shakespeare's imagery and its functional relation to his dramatic art. It differed in method from the work of Caroline Spurgeon on one hand, and, less markedly, from that of Wolfgang Clemen on the other, but there was no fundamental conflict between the three critics who in the 1930's established the study of Shakespeare's imagery as a significant branch of dramatic aesthetics. Certain of Knight's original suggestions in this volume—such as the distinction between the spatial and the temporal aspects of the structure of drama—are now commonplace of criticism.

Henri Fluchère's book[3] arrived in time only for brief notice last year and a word or two must now be added. To hear a voice from the Continent comment directly on the present state of Shakespeare studies and on the significance of the work done in England in the past twenty-five years is of great value. Fluchère associates himself with the historical school of criticism to this extent, that he insists upon a proper understanding in his French readers of those facts without which the essential Shakespeare and the human experience he transmits cannot justly be realized. They must, he explains, see Shakespeare as an Elizabethan, in terms of Elizabethan mood, thought and culture and in the setting of that Elizabethan drama and its theatre which was the centre of the community's life. This established, he passes to Shakespeare's technique and themes, analysing both with acute critical sense, but never losing sight of that background. He is of those critics who declare unhesitatingly that dramatic art is unrealistic in all aspects of its technique and he demonstrates this in terms of each in succession; structure, character, style are all shown, with acute and subtle reasoning, to be on the one hand utterly subsidiary to the poetry and the essential themes and on the other only a part of a vast apparatus of illusion which is yet the vehicle of essential truth. Those of us who disagree with his conclusions at some points cannot deny the validity of his inferences, though we might occasionally attack his premises. He, like Charlton, finds a sequence of thought, a progression of experience, in the tragedies, basing it on the Elizabethan conception of an ordered universe. The tragedies and indeed the whole series of Shake-

[1] Benedetto Croce, *Shakespeare*. Nuova edizione con introduzione e note di Napoleone Orsini (Bari: Laterza, 1948).

[2] Methuen, 1949.

[3] Henri Fluchère, *Shakespeare, dramaturge élisabéthain* (Cahiers du Sud, 1948).

speare's plays are written in terms of this conception: in the earlier this order is threatened, in the central tragic group it is overthrown and in the latest re-discovered and re-established.

Lorentz Eckhoff's *William Shakespeare*[1] is also written for a public which, whether it does or does not read English, cannot be assumed to have an English background and training; the numerous quotations are as a rule translated, necessary incidental aids to understanding are given and the attention paid to the views of Brandes, with which the author frequently disagrees, is greater than would perhaps be necessary outside Scandinavia. Eckhoff begins by extracting what he considers to be the essence of Shakespeare's thought and then proceeds to examine the plays in the light of this, grouping them, not chronologically, nor according to technique or kinds, but within the categories of Shakespeare's experience and its resultant thought. Thus each chapter follows from the findings of the preceding one: the study of Shakespeare's apprehension of the fact of evil leads the author to ask what are the characteristics which draw down suffering upon men and to conclude that, in Shakespeare's world, these are various forms of unbalanced passion. In contrast with such men stand the wise and the temperate, Horatio's kinsmen, who are in harmony with nature. Finally, he draws a picture of Shakespeare, himself in harmony with his age but not its slave, and a man in whom there is, besides, a strange and unknown territory, "den grenseløse vidden i hans forståelse".

Two books that approach Shakespeare from the artist's rather than from the scholar's or critic's point of view challenge and stimulate reflection, though they differ as widely from each other as from the usual critical surveys. The first is Edith Sitwell's *Notebook*,[2] a series of essays whose fruitful and illuminating thought serves to remind us (if we need reminder) how swift and sure is the poet's approach to the essence of another poet's art, how keen and how constructive her judgements. Poetic imagery has before now proved itself the clearest medium for thought in this domain and some of the finest passages in this book are themselves poetry in the form of criticism. Again and again we notice how the poet's instinct and the poet's medium lead not only to fine and illuminating description but to sound judgement, even in such matters as choice of disputed readings, scansions or lineations. Out of much that is good, perhaps the best are the passages on verbal music, the detailed analyses of the technique of metre; some of these are sustained through many pages, and here the work is both penetrating and profound. *Macbeth, Lear, Othello, Antony and Cleopatra, Cymbeline*—the list could be extended, but in these perhaps is to be found the fullest and the closest thought, culminating in a judgement such as that on the music of *Antony and Cleopatra*—"But the whole play is one of the greatest miracles of sound that has ever come into this world".

Frank O'Connor's[3] approach is that of a man of the theatre with a keen sense at once of the difference between Shakespeare's theatre and ours and of the enduring elements of his dramatic work. He finds in the chronological survey of the plays and the *Sonnets* evidence of Shakespeare's development from the subjective to the dramatic attitude, from egotism to abnegation; he shows us, that is to say, a poet becoming a dramatist. Looking on the plays with the eyes of a writer and a man of the theatre, he takes into account (in his own way) the work of certain modern scholars and the evidence of the sources; an artist himself, he knows to what use to put

[1] Oslo: Gyldendal Norsk Forlag, 1948.
[2] *A Notebook on William Shakespeare* (Macmillan, 1948).
[3] *The Road to Stratford* (Methuen, 1948).

this last. Whether they call forth agreement or disagreement, certain moments of critical insight arrest us; he diagnoses shrewdly what he suspects to be theatrical weakness. Some specific judgements are of special interest; he regards *Antony and Cleopatra* as the greatest of the plays, a view that many of us are sometimes tempted to take; he would include *Edward III* in the Shakespeare canon, a suggestion that holds out fewer temptations. But whether his conclusion is customary or unconventional, it is the result of his own experience, of the direct impact of the plays upon his imagination.

The long monographs, or full-length works, on individual plays are confined this year to *Lear*,[1] and, as has already been said, to particular aspects of its art or thought. Robert B. Heilman[2] examines at length the relation of imagery to structure. The strength of this book is in the design, clearly put before us in the first chapter, to study the relation of the imagery of a play, with its series of patterns, to the other aspects under which that play can be considered. Heilman's book is a genuine attempt to investigate fully the functions, superficial and fundamental, of imagery in drama. These functions and their relations to each other and to theme, subject and structure can best be demonstrated by analysis of an individual play, provided that play be, like *Lear*, rich enough in thought and art to use every function to the full. The analysis of one play along these lines should be enough for our guidance, and further development of this line of criticism will perhaps be in the direction of synthesis, of the definition of the principles revealed by this analysis and their organization in the form of an aesthetic of this branch of the subject.

Heilman's book helps to set criticism back on its right path also in that it approaches its subject with due reverence for the artistic process. In the mood of a sympathetic artist, he attempts to reveal a part of the poet's workmanship and, relating that part to the others, to demonstrate the homogeneity of their functions, the organic nature of the work of art itself. Such analysis, in the service of such synthesis, can give no offence.

The weakness of a book of this kind is generally found in the middle, where exemplification may become a little tedious and lead to repetition of generalizations which the reader has already grasped. There is moreover, in highly specialized work in this field, a temptation to quote and refer to recent criticism without taking account of that of the past, some of which has touched, at least by implication, the fields which have lately been more fully investigated. But experiments of the kind that we find in this and in the accompanying volume on *Lear* are well worth making.

John F. Danby's *Shakespeare's Doctrine of Nature*[3] is a penetrating piece of thinking which has the gravity of quiet, but genuine, originality and convinces the reader that it is the fruit of some years' consideration of its subject. Historical criticism of a peculiarly interesting kind, it makes a solid contribution to our understanding of the play, whether or not we accept the author's assumptions and conclusions. Some of them we must indeed accept: the careful distinctions drawn between the different conceptions of Nature contained in the play is masterly and so is the grouping of the characters in accordance with their acceptance either of the benignant nature of Bacon, Hooker and Lear himself or of the malignant nature, later defined by Hobbes, which is embodied in the attitude of Edmund, Goneril and Regan. These in their turn are related to the views, implicitly revealed or explicitly stated, of Shakespeare's contemporaries. Other themes,

---

[1] Roy Walker's study of *Macbeth* had not been received at the time of going to press.
[2] *This Great Stage. Image and Structure in 'King Lear'* (Louisiana State University Press, 1948).
[3] *Shakespeare's Doctrine of Nature. A Study of 'King Lear'* (Faber and Faber, 1949).

which accompany or arise from this, are also traced through the series of his plays and there is a careful analysis of his changing attitude to the killing of the king, finally elucidated in *Lear*. If we resist, from time to time, the theories of this unusual book, it is, as a rule, on some specific issue, which may in fact be the result of individual interpretation. The present writer disagrees, for instance, with parts of Danby's reading of the *Henry IV* plays and of the character of Henry V and with the emphasis upon 'allegory' at the beginning and 'symbol' towards the end of the book. But these differences arise from a difference in interpretations of the nature of drama and do not deny the logic of the inferences. This is not a book which can be overlooked or lightly set aside.

Richard Flatter's *Shakespeare's Producing Hand*[1] involves bibliographical assumptions the discussion of which belongs to another section of this survey. The central idea, that certain features of the texts can be made to reveal more than has hitherto been suspected of Shakespeare's intentions as a theatre-man, is a clear and stimulating challenge. "Whatever one examines, be it his punctuation, his way of dividing the lines, his policy of pauses, or any other aspect of dictation", will be found to add to the evidence. Whether or not this theory is sometimes pushed too far, whether or not *Macbeth* was, in view of its textual reputation, the best play to choose for extended analysis —these are questions that must be left to the relevant expert. All that can be ventured here is general agreement with some of the author's suggestions on the treatment of asides, entrances, pauses and simultaneous speech, with perhaps a slight doubt as to whether his ear is so well attuned to the music of some of the other Jacobean dramatists as it is to that of Shakespeare.

Two other works concerned even more directly with the production of Shakespeare may fitly be considered next. Herbert Farjeon's *The Shakespearean Scene*[2] is a collection of reviews extending over a quarter of a century. His clear judgement and taste, his consistent and principled advocacy of the type of production which puts Shakespeare first and the producer second, his firm but never ungenerous condemnation, when condemnation is necessary, give the book value as a record of the experiments that fall roughly between the two wars. His unerring sense for sound, unostentatious work leads him to pick out Atkin's season (1937) at the Blackfriars Ring and to give due honour to the unfailing purpose of the Old Vic productions. There are interesting things, too, on the experiments in modern dressing and on the Stratford Festival. His attitude may perhaps fitly be summed up in his own comment, "But in the beginning there was the word"—which 'word' itself might well be engraved on the proscenium arch of every English theatre that produces Shakespeare's plays.

Stanislavsky's notes for the production of *Othello*[3] make a remarkable and exciting book. His directions to the actors are documents in histrionic psychology which every actor and producer must enjoy. The technique he describes, with its fearless and effective introduction of pauses, its liberal use of mass groupings and miming, is foreign to English methods, but one cannot avoid the suspicion that Shakespeare would have enjoyed the resultant production. The little sketches of the characters' past lives which he introduces for the guidance of the players are not utterly unknown to our own professional stage (and it is here that his work most nearly reminds us of Granville-Barker's *Prefaces*), but many of them are remarkably persuasive. The imaginative

---

[1] Heinemann, 1948.
[2] Hutchinson, 1949.
[3] *Stanislavsky Produces 'Othello'* (Bles, 1948).

reconstruction of Iago's past relations with Othello, Cassio and Roderigo is a triumph of constructive fantasy which may well give not only the actor but the scholar a clue to motive that has been often sought in vain.

It is fitting that this survey of this year's volume in Shakespearian criticism should end with a note on one that is itself a survey of an early part of the field. Paul Van Tieghem's *Le préromantisme*[1] records and comments on that gradual discovery of Shakespeare on the Continent during the eighteenth century, which began with comments and references, went on to partial and complete translations, then to productions, and finally to the investigations of scholars. France and Germany were the leaders of this exploration throughout, though the influence of English taste in the Augustan period and of the English editors then and a little later was almost wholly accountable for the bent taken by Voltaire and his followers in the earlier part of the century. Van Tieghem's control of his material is admirable; he succeeds, while marshalling an array of detailed reference and quotation throughout the century, in giving us a clear picture both of the growth of knowledge and of the change in attitude. And this last is no mean task, for it involves tracing that revolution in taste which took place in the middle of the century. In 1745 the Abbé Le Blanc could say, representing fairly the taste of his own people: "Leur fameux Shakespeare est un exemple frappant du danger que l'on court en s'écartant des règles....Pas un d'eux [the plays] ne peut se lire du commencement à la fin." In or about 1770 we find in Germany what Van Tieghem briefly designates as "le début de cette shakespearolâtrie aveugle qui devait faire depuis, en maint pays, la belle carrière que l'on sait." It is a long journey, and one beset with vicissitudes, from *The Spectator* to *Wilhelm Meister* and we must record our respect for the guide who leads us so firmly through it.

Some twenty-five articles, some of considerable importance, have appeared this year in this field. Space does not admit of individual notices for each of these, but a rough classification may be made. As we might expect, the articles, taken apart from the longer studies, show a different range of interest; a close examination of the art, thought and poetry of Shakespeare cannot compress itself into an article, whereas a specific discovery or comparison or the elucidation of a particular problem finds its natural expression in that form. Thus, there are no full-length volumes on the relations of the sources to the plays (though Charlton's book, as has been said, lays emphasis upon this as a means to our understanding of the craftsmanship), but there are five articles: William Elton,[2] Hardin Craig,[3] and T. M. Parrott,[4] discuss particular sources of *Pericles*; J. M. Nosworthy,[5] the narrative sources of *The Tempest* and R. M. Sargent,[6] those of *Titus Andronicus*. There is one survey of the "Trend of Shakespeare Scholarship", that of Hardin Craig in *Shakespeare Survey*, II. Aspects of technique contribute four: M. M. Morozov's study[7] of imagery as a means of revealing character and Kenneth Severs's on dramatic

---

[1] *Le préromantisme. Études d'histoire littéraire européenne. La découverte de Shakespeare sur le continent* (Paris: Sfelt, 1947).

[2] "*Pericles*: A New Source or Analogue", *Journal of English and Germanic Philology*, XLVIII (January 1949), 138–9.

[3] "*Pericles* and the *Painfull Adventures*", *Studies in Philology*, XLV (October 1948), 600–5.

[4] "*Pericles*, the Play and the Novel", *Shakespeare Association Bulletin*, XXIII (July 1948), 105–13.

[5] "The Narrative Sources of *The Tempest*", *Review of English Studies*, XXIV (October 1948), 281–94.

[6] "The Source of *Titus Andronicus*", *Studies in Philology*, XLVI (April 1949), 167–83.

[7] "The Individualization of Shakespeare's Characters through Imagery", *Shakespeare Survey*, II (1949), 83–106.

imagery;[1] P. A. Jorgensen's study of "Vertical Patterns in *Richard II*",[2] as an aspect of structure, and R. M. Wiles's on the problem of relation.[3] Of the particular plays, *Hamlet* stands out again this year in the articles, despite the emphasis on *Lear* in the full-length monographs and in the general studies. There are five on various aspects of the thought, the art and the structure and one comparative study. Moody E. Prior writes on "The Thought of *Hamlet* and the Modern Temper",[4] Pearl Hogrefe on "Artistic Unity in *Hamlet*",[5] Richard Flatter on "The Dumb-Show in *Hamlet*",[6] and R. G. Gordon on "The Crux in *Hamlet*",[7] while Salvador de Madariaga adds a further study on the character of Hamlet and Don Quixote.[8]

The other plays are more evenly represented and the subjects of the articles fall within the fields of literary comparison, the study of the art and thought of a given play and its relation to the background of its times. J. Dover Wilson, in *Shakespeare Survey*, II, makes a study of Ben Jonson's comments on and references to *Julius Caesar*[9] and Kenneth Muir initiates a discussion on "*Macbeth and Sophonisba*",[10] *Lear* is treated by O. J. Campbell,[11] *Love's Labour's Lost* by J. W. Draper,[12] the background of *Measure for Measure* by Elizabeth M. Pope,[13] *Othello* by C. S. Lewis,[14] a character in *Troilus and Cressida* by W. Elton[15] and an aspect of the structure of *Timon* by J. W. Draper.[16]

It is not easy to see in what direction this branch of Shakespeare studies will move in the next few years, nor is it perhaps entirely profitable to attempt it. But the contributions of the last three make two things clear: first that the stream of general studies is setting steadily in the direction of interpretation and that Lascelles Abercrombie's 'plea' for that 'liberty' has been heard, and second that the increasing tendency (at the time of writing) is to a close and, when necessary, an abstract habit of thought which, nevertheless, acknowledges the fundamentally unabstract nature of dramatic art. Taken in conjunction, these two facts would seem to point one way. We have developed the instruments and the skills necessary for the sustained practice of the logic of aesthetics and we have accumulated in the laboratory the records of a succession of fine analyses. The time is perhaps hardly yet ripe for analysis to give place again to synthesis, but when this happens we may begin to look for that major work in dramatic aesthetics which should be one of the achievements of our generation.

[1] "Imagery and Drama", *Durham University Journal*, x (December 1948), 24–33.
[2] *Shakespeare Association Bulletin*, XXIII (July 1948), 119–34.
[3] "'In My Mind's Eye, Horatio'", *University of Toronto Quarterly*, XVIII (October 1948), 57–67.
[4] *ELH* xv (December 1948), 261–85.
[5] *Studies in Philology*, XLVI (April 1949), 184–95.
[6] *Shakespeare Quarterly*, I, 26–49.
[7] *Times Literary Supplement*, 11 December 1948.
[8] *Shakespeare Quarterly*, I (Summer 1948), 22–5.
[9] "Ben Jonson and *Julius Caesar*", *Shakespeare Survey*, II (1949), 36–43.
[10] *Times Literary Supplement*, 9 October 1948 *et seq.*
[11] "The Salvation of Lear", *ELH* xv (June 1948), 93–109.
[12] "Tempo in *Love's Labour's Lost*", *English Studies*, XXIX (October 1948), 129–37.
[13] "The Renaissance Background of *Measure for Measure*", *Shakespeare Survey*, II (1949), 66–82.
[14] *Times Literary Supplement*, 19 June 1948.
[15] "Shakespeare's portrait of Ajax in *Troilus and Cressida*", *PMLA* LXIII (June 1948), 744–8.
[16] "Patterns of Tempo in Shakespeare's *Timon*", *Shakespeare Association Bulletin*, XXIII (October 1948), 188–94.

2. SHAKESPEARE'S LIFE AND TIMES

reviewed by CLIFFORD LEECH

Nine years ago we knew that Alan Keen had discovered a copy of Hall's *Chronicle* with numerous marginalia believed to have some connexion with Shakespeare's second historical tetralogy. Now Moray McLaren has produced a book[1] in which the marginalia are claimed to be in Shakespeare's hand. He usefully gives an appendix in which the notes relating to the subject-matter of *Richard II* are set out, along with the passages from Hall that they annotate and the corresponding lines from the play. It might indeed have been better at this stage to have devoted the book to a reproduction of all the 406 notes: a basis for judgement would have been more securely provided in this way than by McLaren's rather impulsive pleadings. Space is given, for example, to the arguments that the annotator was 'poetically minded' because he writes the words "Prisoners pitifully slayne", and that he was not unfamiliar with the theatre because, like the author of *Thomas of Woodstock*, he used the name 'Woodstock' for Gloucester. Certainly there are interesting points of contact between some of the marginalia and passages in Shakespeare; there is, too, the sketch of a large-nosed face against Hall's account of the soldier hanged for stealing the pyx; but many other parallels adduced by McLaren are altogether nugatory. Nor is it helpful to read that, if Shakespeare was a schoolmaster, he would have had to use Hall as a text-book for the teaching of English history. Nowhere is it sufficiently recognized that the marginalia could be the work of a man who enjoyed annotation for its own sake, and perhaps of one who had already seen or read the relevant Shakespeare plays. But no decision can be reached until the annotations as a whole have been given to the public.

Alfred Günther[2] and Ivor Brown[3] have produced imaginative essays in Shakespeare biography. Günther's account of the years 1587–94 is highly and conventionally coloured, providing much unsubstantiated detail concerning the relationships of Shakespeare, Marlowe, Chapman, Southampton and the Dark Lady: he tells us that Shakespeare himself played the roles of Henry VI, Theseus, and Marcus in *Titus Andronicus*, that he wrote *Love's Labour's Lost* and *Lucrece* while staying with Southampton at Titchfield, that the affair of the Dark Lady was over by 1594. This kind of fancy spinning would be the better for accuracy in such details as one can check: Günther describes Zenocrate as the daughter of Bajazeth, says that Marlowe's *Dido* is based on the first book of the *Aeneid*, implies that the Painter-scene in *The Spanish Tragedy* is Kyd's, and suggests that Chapman's *Iliad* was completed by 1588.

Ivor Brown has been more ambitious and more diligent. He, too, hazards guesses, suggesting that the first draft of *Love's Labour's Lost* came from Southampton's pen, that the alleged gift of £1000 may have been an official recognition of Shakespeare's service to the Crown in his second tetralogy (a remarkable reward for plays which seem to have caused censorship problems), that Hamlet's advice to the players could not have been spoken in performance (disregarding, I think, the sturdy self-respect of the First Player's reply: "I hope we have reformed that indifferently

---

[1] '*By Me...*' *a report upon the apparent discovery of some working notes of William Shakespeare in a sixteenth-century book* (John Redington, 1949).

[2] *Der junge Shakespeare. Sieben unbekannte Jahre* (Stuttgart: Deutsche Verlags-Anstalt, 1947).

[3] *Shakespeare* (Collins, 1949).

with us").[1] He believes almost fervently in the existence of Anne Whateley, and he finds traces of the Dark Lady in the Rosalines of Romeo and Berowne and in many another woman-character up to Cleopatra herself—who is, he thinks, treated more sympathetically than her predecessors because the Lady herself was then dead or remote from Shakespeare's world. The desire to trace Shakespeare's emotional history leads on occasion to strained interpretation. In *Troilus and Cressida* the Greeks, we are told, represent the privileged courtier class while the Trojans—Paris, Hector and Pandarus included—are the simple country folk. *Antony and Cleopatra* is a tale of love triumphant over death, in which at the end the lovers have our unqualified sympathy—though the man runs from battle in pursuit of a woman wrinkled deep in time, and the woman promises herself an after-life of love, anxious only lest Iras may get Antony's first Elysian embrace.

The book is engagingly written and, though it is not likely to strengthen a reader's grasp of the plays, it presents a vigorous account of the late sixteenth-century setting. A few details need amendment in a second edition: for the matter of John Shakespeare's recusancy reference should be made to J. H. de Groot's *The Shakespeares and 'The Old Faith'*;[2] the word 'sympathize' in the passage from *Henry V*, quoted on p. 112, means 'show a like disposition'; 'Mystery Plays', on p. 119, should be 'Morality Plays'; 'Scholasticism', on p. 121, should be 'Humanism'. The assertion that the Elizabethans were not highly sex-conscious does not suggest a wide reading in the drama of Shakespeare's contemporaries. The 'common-sense philosophy of moderation' attributed to Shakespeare in the concluding chapter is hardly consonant with the picture of a tormented poet which Brown has drawn in many earlier pages of his book. Occasionally the writing becomes a little arch, as when, in the manner of the Higher Anglican verse-drama, we are told that Shakespeare "could hardly have lived sane in a community of form-filling, inquisitions, and controls". But the book will serve its public, and assist in the diffusion of useful knowledge.

In "Shakespeare's Rival Poet"[3] Henry David Gray has argued that Spenser was Shakespeare's rival for Southampton's favour. The "affable familiar ghost" of Sonnet 86 is Ariosto. Book VII of *The Faerie Queene* was to have had for its central figure a knight modelled on Southampton, but the project was abandoned when Southampton fell from court favour: only the 'Mutability' Cantos were saved for future publication. The words in Sonnet 85—"While comments of your praise, richly compiled, Reserve their character"—have reference to the oblique form of the praise given to Southampton in Spenser's allegory. It is ingeniously argued, but has to depend on a shrugging aside of "compeers by night" and "nightly gulls him" in Sonnet 86.

Other essays in identification are made by William Elton in "Shakespeare's Portrait of Ajax in *Troilus and Cressida*"[4] and by Arthur W. Secord in "I. M. of the First Folio Shakespeare and

---

[1] Brown is also doubtful whether Cleopatra's fear of the squeaking boy-player could be safely expressed on the stage. But Marston's *Antonio's Revenge*, acted by Paul's Boys *c.* 1599, contains this:

> "Why, all this while I ha but plaid a part,
> Like to some boy, that actes a Tragedie,
> Speakes burly words, and raves out passion:
> But, when he thinks upon his infant weaknesse,
> He droopes his eye."   (IV, v)

[2] Noticed in *Shakespeare Survey*, I (1948).
[3] *The Journal of English and Germanic Philology*, XLVII (October 1948), 365-73.
[4] *PMLA*, LXIII (June 1948), 744-8.

Other Mabbe Problems".[1] Elton revives Fleay's suggestion that Ajax is a portrait of Jonson which served as the "purge that made him beray his credit", referred to in 2 *Return from Parnassus*. The case depends chiefly on the date of *Troilus and Cressida*, which could have been written just before 2 *Return*, on the use of 'beray' in the sense of 'befoul' in the *Parnassus* plays and the consequent pun on 'Ajax', and on the attack on the Chamberlain's Men made by Jonson in *Poetaster* a few months before. Secord's identification of 'I. M.' as James Mabbe is based on Mabbe's association with Jonson, Blount and Digges, all of whom were in some way concerned with both the First Folio and Mabbe's *The Rogue*. Of the other chief claimants, Marston had retired to his Hampshire cure of souls, Mayne was only nineteen.

In each of these three articles the case argued is reasonable, in none is it compelling.

H. S. Bennett has followed his British Academy lecture of 1944, "Shakespeare's Audience",[2] with an article on "Shakespeare's Stage and Audience"[3] in which he argues that the Elizabethan stage-structure made things in a sense too easy for the playwright, enabling him to assemble his plays haphazardly, with no thought for the *liaison des scènes* which was cultivated later. Certainly compactness is the last virtue one would attribute to most Elizabethan tragedies and comedies, but a free-ranging employment of time and space, a deliberate diversity of content as in *Hamlet*, can be a source of strength. Bennett has chosen useful examples to demonstrate the way in which the action was localized by the dialogue, though one might quarrel with the use of the 'Dover cliff' speech as an illustration of the capacity of Shakespeare's language to render scenic display unnecessary: in this instance the dependence on language holds good on whatever stage the scene is played. The Academy lecture concludes strongly with the plea that, though we may gain *more* from a private reading, it must not be *other* than we would get in the theatre. This is a useful generalization, though Shakespeare's plays may appear to us very differently in the theatre if we have given close study to the text.

In "Conventions of Medieval Art in Shakespearian Staging",[4] John H. McDowell has related the episodic structure of Elizabethan drama to the medieval multiple setting. He sees the outer-stage as a *platea*, with the rear-stage, the upper-stage or a special structure introduced on the outer-stage (e.g. a tent) functioning as a medieval 'house'. The spectator's eye moves from one locality to another as on the Valenciennes stage, the only difference being that a section of the stage may change its identity during the performance, doing duty for several 'houses' in turn. McDowell shows how in medieval painting it was usual for a house or temple or cave to be indicated in skeleton or abbreviated form, so that, for example, figures outside a building would be imagined as being within it. He has also some useful evidence for the use of scene-labels in medieval paintings and tapestries. This article throws further light on some of the theories advanced by George F. Reynolds in his work on the Red Bull plays.

If McDowell is right in arguing for the basically medieval character of the Elizabethan stage, we should expect that the upper-stage would function freely as an acting-area which could be

[1] *The Journal of English and Germanic Philology*, XLVII (October 1948), 374–81. Cf. Howard Parsons, "The Identity of I. M.", *Notes and Queries*, CXCIV (22 January 1949), 38, in which James Mervyn, prologue-writer for Shirley's *The Royal Master*, is put forward as a possibility.

[2] *Proceedings of the British Academy*, 1944 (Cumberlege, 1948), pp. 73–86.

[3] *Neophilologus*, XXXI (January 1949), 40–51.

[4] *The Journal of English and Germanic Philology*, XLVII (July 1948), 215–29.

localized as a 'house'. But this is doubtful. Richard Flatter, in "The Dumb-Show in *Hamlet*",[1] believes that the Dumb-show preceding *The Murder of Gonzago* was given on the upper-stage with Claudius and Gertrude seated on the rear-stage immediately below. This would solve the problem why Claudius shows no sign of being disturbed by the Dumb-show. Flatter dismisses Dover Wilson's view that Claudius, Gertrude and Polonius were deep in conversation while it was being acted: he points out that such a conversation would disturb the theatre audience from grasping the significance of the Dumb-show and that more than Dover Wilson's 'few moments' would be required for the performance. This is ingenious, but we may still wonder at an arrangement which makes the players, acting in front of the King, give their Dumb-show in such a way that the King could not see it. The problem in *Hamlet* remains, but Flatter's speculations once again focus attention on the possible uses of the upper-stage. In the Stratford production of *Much Ado* in 1949, III, iv showed Margaret and Hero on a raised structure with Beatrice below: this could conceivably be an Elizabethan arrangement, but evidence there is of course none.[2]

The year has produced several short studies in which the plays are interpreted in the light of Elizabethan thought. Nevill Coghill has uttered a warning against extracting a 'meaning' from a play: "it becomes", he says, "abstract, fixed, and dead".[3] Nevertheless, he argues that a producer should look for a 'governing idea' and try to bring that out in performance: in *The Merchant of Venice* this is the New Testament resolution of Justice and Mercy, which is demonstrated when Antonio bestows half Shylock's fortune on Jessica and forces Christianity upon him. Similarly, Irving Ribner, in "Bolingbroke, A True Machiavellian",[4] suggests that the character of Bolingbroke illustrates not the pseudo-Machiavellianism of Gentillet but the genuine doctrine of *The Prince*. In both these cases we may feel that the idea, if brought into sharp focus, will distort the total effect of the play. In *The Merchant of Venice* there are satiric overtones, there is the fooling of Act V, there are the unpleasing aspects of Jessica's elopement, and all these seem to have little to do with Justice or Mercy. In *Richard II*, Ribner has to admit that "there are a few incidents where Bolingbroke does not follow Machiavelli to the letter". Moreover, if Shakespeare is here illustrating the Machiavellian doctrine, he is doing so critically: Bolingbroke does not cease to be other than a usurper, a man whose guilt prepares the scene for civil strife. He is also, in *Henry IV*, remorseful in a way that Machiavelli could not approve, for we can hardly follow Ribner in thinking that the projected Crusade was only a means of creating a good impression. In both these instances it may well be that, at certain points in the play, Shakespeare had in his mind the idea suggested, but the total 'meaning', as Coghill has put it, "is the meaning that it takes a whole play to say". Even 'governing ideas' are dangerous merchandise, for critics or producers.[5]

[1] *Shakespeare Quarterly*, I (Summer 1948), 26–49.

[2] T. S. R. Boase, "Illustrations of Shakespeare's Plays in the Seventeenth and Eighteenth Centuries", *Journal of the Warburg and Courtauld Institutes*, X (1947), 83-108, draws attention to the woodcut facing the title-page of *Arden of Feversham*, 1633: it shows the murder of Arden and, as Boase points out, very possibly came from a ballad or broadsheet on the subject: it could be only hazardously used as evidence of staging.

[3] "The Governing Idea. Essays in Stage-Interpretation of Shakespeare. I. *The Merchant of Venice*", *Shakespeare Quarterly*, I (Summer 1948), 9–17.

[4] *Modern Language Quarterly*, IX (June 1948), 177–84.

[5] These comments are also, I think, applicable to Miss Elizabeth Marie Pope's "The Renaissance Background of *Measure for Measure*", *Shakespeare Survey*, II (1949), 66–82, and to John F. Danby's *Shakespeare's Doctrine of Nature. A Study of 'King Lear'* (Faber and Faber, 1949), which is referred to in the preceding section.

Edwin Muir[1] and Douglas Hewitt,[2] on the other hand, have attempted to consider certain contemporary aspects of *King Lear* without implying that the total 'meaning' is thus revealed. In Muir's view, *Lear* illustrates a clash between two ideas of society, between "a civilization of legendary antiquity" and "a perfectly up-to-date gang of Renaissance adventurers". Though there are odd statements here, such as that Lear could not make elementary mistakes in judging human beings, Muir illustrates the local significance of the tragic struggle without doing violence to the play. Hewitt's suggestion is that in Elizabethan drama there are not only vestiges of folk-lore but surviving folk-attitudes. He notes that the Puritan pamphleteers linked plays and folk-games in their denunciations, and that Paris Garden was used for folk-festivals as well as for plays and bear-baiting. Lear driven out into the storm, he says, has something of the character of the scapegoat and the divine victim: his railing comments on society thus express a view "from outside" and "acquire a more objective validity". Put in this condensed way, Hewitt's case is hardly convincing, for Lear's madness and loss of kingship are enough to constitute him a man 'outside'. But the survival of folk-myth into the Elizabethan age may certainly have come together with orthodox belief to provide a cosmic frame for the tragic action: in association they would help to make possible that ambivalent attitude to the universe that Elizabethan and Jacobean tragedies persistently imply.

In her British Academy lecture, *Shakespeare the Dramatist*,[3] Miss U. Ellis-Fermor has continued to explore the nature of drama and the marks of its greatness. Characteristic of the drama, she says, is the playwright's wide-ranging and evenly distributed sympathy; dramatic genius manifests itself through passion, thought and poetic imagination. The scope of the lecture does not always allow her to indicate the limits of her generalizations, as when she comments on Shakespeare's avoidance of 'explicit commentary' for the re-expression of the thought implicit in his plays: one is bound to think of speeches from the Bastard in *King John*, from Ulysses, Enobarbus, the Duke in *Measure for Measure*. She puts a special stress on characterization as a determinant of dramatic writing, perhaps going a little further than comedy will always allow and perhaps not doing full justice to the novelist's scope: we may feel on more intimate terms with Lambert Strether than with Sir Epicure Mammon, and we get in a few lines as powerful an impression of the French Lieutenant in *Lord Jim* as we get of the two Murderers in *Macbeth* whom Miss Ellis-Fermor chooses to illustrate Shakespeare's imaginative sympathy. And perhaps her final claim that in Shakespeare "there is no prepossession, no prejudice, no theory" does not remain on Jonson's side of idolatry. But, though one may hesitate over this detail or that, this is critical writing of an exceptional order.

[1] *The Politics of King Lear*. The Seventh W. P. Ker Memorial Lecture delivered in the University of Glasgow 23 April 1946 (Glasgow: Jackson, 1947).

[2] "The Very Pompes of the Divell—Popular and Folk Elements in Elizabethan and Jacobean Drama", *The Review of English Studies*, xxv (January 1949), 10–23.

[3] *Shakespeare the Dramatist*. Annual Shakespeare Lecture of the British Academy, 1948 (Cumberlege, 1948).

3. TEXTUAL STUDIES

reviewed by JAMES G. McMANAWAY

A survey of recent textual work in Shakespeare may begin appropriately with companion essays [1] by colleagues at the University of Pennsylvania, one the editor of the Variorum 2 *Henry IV* and the other the prospective editor of the Variorum *Richard II*. Rarely does one find the problems of an editor more delightfully explained. M. A. Shaaber notes the deficiencies of current editions of Shakespeare and describes the potential benefits of several types of edition not now in existence. "It is a strange anomaly," he points out, "that, while the standard editions of most Elizabethan authors print the spelling of the contemporary books and manuscripts from which it is derived, there has never been a complete edition of Shakespeare in the old spelling....Indeed I think there is room for an edition which would reproduce the most authoritative text of each play with no editing at all except to correct undoubted mistakes and make good undoubted omissions. This would serve chiefly as a convenient substitute for facsimiles. Just so it would be welcome, since there is no complete set of reliable facsimiles of the Quartos and all facsimiles are expensive." Shaaber is confident that "in the future we can make better texts of Shakespeare than we have to-day", and he illustrates the possibility by showing how little attention has been paid to the editorial policies and practices of the first Folio by the citation of passage after passage in the fifth Quarto text of 1 *Henry IV* that has been altered in the Folio. Pollard's judgement about the absence of 'editorial meddling' in the latter has been reversed by Greg, who is of the opinion that the plays "underwent a good deal of modernization, and general tidying up in spelling, punctuation, grammar, metre, and so on". "But what has never been done", concludes Shaaber, "is to go beyond general statements or illustrations drawn from a single play and to define the editorial work done on the Folio on a broad scale."

M. W. Black concerns himself with *explication du texte*. "The interpreters of Shakespeare... have as a body been myriad-minded in the worst sense of the word: they have never, as a body, agreed on which meaning they should seek; and I think it could be demonstrated that not one of those who have been large-minded enough to set up a principle has succeeded in adhering to it in every instance....Yet ever and anon the best of them, at their best, have struck out a comment or a paraphrase so manifestly, convincingly right that we say instinctively, 'That is what Shakespeare meant'." How difficult it may be to discover Shakespeare's intention, Black's charming essay illustrates in a penetrating discussion of the images, rhetoric, and the operation of Shakespeare's memory and mind in certain passages of *Richard II*.

The preoccupation of H. T. Price with his forthcoming Variorum edition of *Titus Andronicus* and the publication of Dover Wilson's volume of the play in the New Cambridge edition [2] have combined to focus attention as never before upon this early play, which some admirers of Shakespeare would gladly exclude from the canon. The positions of the two editors are antipodal. Price, who has as yet published only fragmentary reports of his studies, accepts *Titus Andronicus*

[1] Matthias A. Shaaber, "Problems in the Editing of Shakespeare: Text", *English Institute Essays*, 1947 (New York: Columbia University Press; London: Geoffrey Cumberlege, 1948), pp. 97–116. Matthew W. Black, "Problems in the Editing of Shakespeare: Interpretation" (*op. cit.*), pp. 117–36.

[2] The New Shakespeare, *Titus Andronicus* (Cambridge University Press, 1948).

as the exclusive work of Shakespeare, but gives no hint of his regard for it as poetry or play. Distaste is clearly manifested in Wilson's introduction, the first purpose of which is to deny to Shakespeare more than a reviser's share, as other commentators have done ever since Ravenscroft in 1687 called the play a "heap of Rubbish" to which Shakespeare had given "only...some master touches to one or two of the principal parts or characters"; the second purpose of the introduction being to assert, with Symons, Robertson and Mark Van Doren, that many of the Shakespearian passages, filled with 'tawdry rant' or 'bleating pathos', are 'burlesque and melodramatic travesty".

The external evidence is all in favour of those who hold with Price, for Meres ascribed the play to Shakespeare in 1598 and Heminges and Condell included it in the first Folio and, moreover, inserted an admittedly Shakespearian scene (III, i) which was available only in manuscript. In support of his case, Price [1] argues that throughout the text of the first Quarto (1594) are to be found the same spellings, and particularly the elided and clipped forms, which Shakespeare habitually used to guide the pronunciation of the actors in the reading of his lines. Using the two narrative poems, *Venus and Adonis* and *Lucrece*, which must have been printed from holograph copy, and also the 'good' quarto texts of seven early plays for purposes of comparison, he examines metrical spellings, as 'grac'd', 'facde', 'sentst' (but 'beleevest'), 'tirde', 'thou'st'; and phonetic spellings, as 'batchiler', 'semitars', 'cote' (quote), 'Iubiter'; and his tentative conclusion is that "we find the same general pattern [in the poems] as in *Titus* and the Quartos. No text is altogether consistent with itself nor does any text resemble the general pattern in every detail. But there is enough general likeness to support the theory that these Quartos all belong to one family. The ground for their resemblance to one another which makes them a family is that they are printed from the same kind of copy, which was a manuscript written by Shakespeare himself. To this family of texts we have every right to add *Titus Andronicus*".

For the sake of argument it might be granted that the first Quarto of *Titus* was printed from a manuscript in Shakespeare's hand without admitting more than that in the process of revising or enlarging the play Shakespeare had done more than recopy it from beginning to end with the insertion of a few passages. The spellings might be his, but only portions of the verse. On the other hand, one may inquire whether Price has analysed the spelling in each of his chosen texts and made due allowance for the fact that a given quarto may be the work of two or more compositors, each of whom may be expected to have modified the copy spellings according to his own preferences and habits—or the need to justify a line. Can one be sure that each compositor whose work is preserved in the texts under discussion followed his copy with equal fidelity? To what extent does the age or the dialect of the compositor alter the copy spelling? Were there no changes in orthographical styles in the decade after 1594? How many of the spelling habits now attributed to Shakespeare are shared equally by other writers of the time? Price is aware of some of these difficulties, but I am doubtful that he has taken them sufficiently into account. (The misspelling *Epeon* for *Hyperion* at V, ii, 56 which suggests to Price that the manuscript was hard to read and the compositor ignorant of classical words probably appeared in the manuscript in the phonetic form *Epion* = Eperion.)

Price is on surer ground in his discussion of "Mirror-Scenes in Shakespeare",[2] in which he

---

[1] "The First Quarto of *Titus Andronicus*", *English Institute Essays*, 1947, pp. 137–68.

[2] In *Joseph Quincy Adams: Memorial Studies* (Washington: The Folger Shakespeare Library, 1948), pp. 101–12.

reveals how it was Shakespeare's practice to halt the action of a play to permit the introduction of an episodic scene that contributes nothing to the plot but serves by its symbolism or its emotional tension to reflect or epitomize the theme of the entire play. Such a scene is III, ii, the Fly Episode. Price points out incidentally that in this scene of the killing of the fly Titus speaks of wresting an alphabet from Lavinia's actions and refers to II, i, in which Titus and Marcus "construct an alphabet by means of which her story is spelled out" and v, i, where Aaron boasts, "I have done a thousand dreadful things, as willingly as one would kill a flie"; he is persuaded "that III, ii was in the play from the first", but that it was marked for omission on the stage and unintentionally omitted from the quarto. This interesting hypothesis receives indirect support from Wilson, who in this as in many other matters follows T. M. Parrott's early study of the play. It contains the implication that the 1594 prompt-book, though inaccessible to the printers of the second and third Quartos, remained continuously available to Shakespeare's company and that Heminges and Condell needed only to turn to it for a transcript of the text of III, ii when a copy of the third Quarto was given to Jaggard at the printing of the first Folio.

Few of Shakespeare's plays present as many puzzles to the editor as *Titus Andronicus*, which was published, and probably had been written, at a time when the London theatrical world was in a state of flux, with companies springing up overnight and disintegrating just as rapidly. Amalgamations and interchanges of personnel and of play-books seem to have been the order of the day. According to the title-page of *Titus Andronicus*, for example, this play was acted more or less contemporaneously by the servants of the Earls of Derby, Pembroke and Sussex. And one of Wilson's problems is to piece together a history that will provide acting versions for three companies and at the same time meet his own requirement that Shakespeare shall be only a reviser.

His solution is to postulate a short play by George Peele for the use of Strange's men in the provinces in 1593, a transcript of which passed into the hands of Pembroke's, apparently an offshoot of Strange's; but Pembroke's were back in London by September, bankrupt; and by December Sussex's had acquired acting rights in one or the other versions for use in what proved to be a short season at the Rose (from 26 December to 6 February). Since a full-length play would have been needed for London performances, Peele was assigned the task of augmenting his own play, and he complied with such inserted episodes as those of Alarbus and Mutius in Act I. For some reason, possibly Peele's dilatoriness, the manuscript was taken from him and given to Shakespeare, and the revised play was acted as "ne" (new) at the Rose on 23 January 1594. On the date of the third performance, 6 February, the theatres were closed again by the plague, and Sussex's company, being bankrupt, paid Shakespeare with the prompt-book and Peele with the foul sheets of the revised play, which he sold at once to John Danter, the publisher. (Wilson's chronology is hazy at this point. Danter must surely have secured his manuscript before the closing of the theatres, for he entered it in the Registers of the Stationers' Company on the very day acting was suspended. Does this fact necessitate a revision of Wilson's explanation?) The prompt-book delivered to Shakespeare was used by his fellow-actors at Newington Butts in June 1594.

This is a pretty, if complicated, story. It utilizes the parallels between *Titus* and Peele's *Honour of the Garter* and between the play and Shakespeare's two narrative poems, particularly *Lucrece*, which was in process of composition at this very time. And it offers an explanation, not perceived by Wilson or by Parrott,[1] of the omission of III, ii from the first Quarto: if Peele received the foul sheets, they may have failed to include Shakespeare's manuscript of this scene, either as a result of carelessness or because it was not composed until after Peele had been paid off. Plausible though Wilson's hypothesis may be, it is open to certain objections, as Parrott points out. The word 'palliament' is used accurately at *Titus*, I, i, 182 but improperly at *Garter*, 92; so the poem must borrow from the play. But *Garter* may be exactly dated in June 1593. What then becomes of Wilson's chronology? Parrott suggests that Peele probably composed the original play before 1593 and borrowed from it in the poem hastily written for his patron who was created Knight of the Garter on 26 June 1593; his additions to the play may probably be limited to the two incidents in Act I; and his manuscripts must have been turned over to Shakespeare, who gave the text its present form.

I can but admire the confidence with which Wilson assigns segments of the play to its supposed authors. His distaste for the tragedy is shared by Parrott, who prefers Raleigh's word, 'bravado', to Wilson's 'burlesque' to describe Shakespeare's attitude towards his additions, and who suggests that sometime after 1594 Shakespeare's company "induced [him] to write a new scene (III, ii) which for rant and false sentiment yields to no other in the play". In this connexion it is well to keep in mind Hardin Craig's wise comment—not the only wise one in the book—on the subject of Shakespearian authorship:[2] "The case...externally considered, is nevertheless a very good one.... Nor is the case, internally considered, a bad one. It is yet to be shown that the Elizabethans looked upon the play with horror and revulsion; it is not the only violent tragedy of the time, nor the only case of blood and horror in Shakespeare himself.... In other words *Titus Andronicus* is theoretically—in intent and structure—a very great tragedy. Practically it is not so.... In spite of Shakespeare's masterly motivation in his rearrangement of scenes and in spite of excellent invention and noble rhetoric, *Titus Andronicus* remains a relatively unpleasing work. We may say that the subject is impossible, unsuited to Shakespeare's wise and gentle genius, and these things are true; but it is the change in our race and its *mores* which is to be blamed, or it may be congratulated, that *Titus Andronicus* has lost its charm.... The modern objection...is not mere squeamishness. The play is indeed horrible with a horror that nobody but Shakespeare could have given it."

The Longleat illustration of *Titus* continues to be the centre of controversy. In *Shakespeare Survey*, I, Dover Wilson took up the subject where Chambers and Adams had left it and offered three important suggestions. Taking up the cudgels, John Munro[3] argues that instead of being a picture of what was seen on the stage the drawing is an illustration of the continuous variety in which a figure may be represented as participating in two or more entirely distinct incidents. Though he cites Adams' facsimile of the first Quarto, Munro speculates that since at V, i, 137 the manuscript alters the order of words, "evidently an early text was followed, perhaps Q I (1594)", thus betraying the fact that he has not read the quarto text in Adams' volume. He ignores the suggestion of Adams, which Wilson echoes, that the figure now called Aaron

---

[1] T. M. Parrott, review of Wilson's edition in *Shakespeare Association Bulletin*, XXIV (April 1949); see also pp. 191–7 of Parrott's *Shakespearean Comedy* (New York: Oxford University Press, 1949).

[2] *An Interpretation of Shakespeare* (New York: The Dryden Press, 1948), pp. 38–41.

[3] "*Titus Andronicus*", *Times Literary Supplement* (10 June 1949).

was originally the executioner and that the colouring was added after the completion of the first draft.

By way of rejoinder, Wilson[1] repeats his previously stated opinions and reminds Munro that if Aaron is represented as he is in v, i he should have a noose about his neck, thus forcing Munro[2] to take refuge in the explanation that Aaron is not represented in the precise circumstances of v, i but as the kind of man his speech at this point reveals him to be. A new turn is given the discussion by Arthur J. Perrett,[3] who finds additional evidence for the belief that the sketch is a pictorial conflation, but who insists that Heminges and Condell had every reason to know what happened in performance and that "exit with Alarbus" means just that.

We pass directly from Shakespeare's least admired and poorest tragedy to his grandest, *King Lear*, edited by Ian Duthie.[4] The play survives in two substantive texts, the version in the 'Pide Bull' quarto of 1608 and that of the first Folio. It is Duthie's purpose, after establishing the genetic relationship between the two, to produce a text that will be the closest possible approximation to what Shakespeare wrote—hence his title, *Shakespeare's 'King Lear'*—and in the compilation and presentation of the evidence he makes strenuous demands, both on himself and on his readers.

Though entered normally in the Stationers' Register, the 'Pide Bull' quarto provides a text that is obviously inferior to that of such 'good' quartos as *Much Ado* and *Merchant* but is definitely superior to that of such 'bad' quartos as the first editions of *Romeo* and *Hamlet*. It is intermediate, like that of *Richard III*, with which Duthie finds it has much in common.

He agrees with Alexander Schmidt and W. W. Greg that the first Quarto of *Lear* is a reported text, but he rejects shorthand as the means by which the text was reported. There being no role or combination of roles which is consistently better than the rest, Duthie concludes, as did Patrick in the case of *Richard III*, that no one actor or small group of actors produced the text but that the whole company joined in a communal effort, dictating their lines as accurately as might be, while a scribe recorded them, probably in the form of prose, with a minimum of punctuation. "The actors thus virtually gave a performance of the play, and upon this 'performance' the Q text entirely depends. The actors made such mistakes as they doubtless habitually made in performances in the theatre—anticipation and recollection, inversion, the introduction of gratuitous exclamations, vocatives, connectives, etc., synonym-substitution, vulgarization, metrical breakdown, omission, patching." The scribe's report would have been unsuited for regulating a performance, and so it is necessary for Duthie to suppose that a transcript was prepared for use as a prompt-book; cursorily edited, however, and placed in the hands of a compositor, the first draft could readily become the sort of text we find in the 'Pide Bull' quarto. All this is conjectured to have taken place while the King's men were on tour, probably in 1605–6. The patience and skill with which Duthie presents his evidence are calculated to win assent.

Curiously enough, however, the editor has nothing to say about how the scribe's first draft was released to the publisher, or by whom; and there is little speculation about why this rough

---

[1] *Ibid.* (24 June 1949).
[2] *Ibid.* (1 July 1949).
[3] *Ibid.* (1 July 1949).
[4] *Shakespeare's 'King Lear'. A Critical Edition* (Oxford: Basil Blackwell, 1949).

manuscript (the equivalent of an author's foul papers) was sold, rather than the prompt-copy conjectured to have been derived from it. Nathaniel Butter's entry of his copy in the Stationers' Register suggests that there was nothing surreptitious in his acquisition of his copy, yet an experienced printer should have recognized the difference between such a manuscript as has been described and a normal book of the play or even a set of author's foul sheets. It remains to be discovered who was the agent that sold the manuscript of *Lear* to its publisher.

The origin of the Folio text has long been known—a copy of the first Quarto in which one or more sheets were in the uncorrected state (see Greg's monograph, *The Variants in the First Quarto of 'King Lear'*) was corrected by reference to a playhouse manuscript that had suffered certain deletions. Duthie works relentlessly through the two substantive texts in order to record all differences between the texts, accepting Greg's paradox that the authenticity of the text is least assured when the two agree.

The resultant text is avowedly eclectic. The Folio is accepted as copy-text, but the Quarto always lies open upon the table. Responsibility for every departure from the Folio is accepted by the editor, and he would be the first to recognize that not every student of *Lear* will concur in all of his decisions. In so far as the variants in the Quarto are concerned, and in particular the variants that result from stop-press corrections, there is not likely to be much or violent disagreement. Greg's analysis of the variants in the twelve extant copies of the first Quarto is used to good advantage (Duthie does not concern himself with the strictly bibliographical problems as elucidated by Greg in his monograph or more recently by F. T. Bowers), though Duthie and he do not always agree on the authoritative reading.

The weakness in Duthie's attempt to produce a definitive text of *Lear* with the Folio version used as copy-text is in his neglect of the Folio itself. Nowhere does he name the particular copy of the Folio (or the facsimile, as the case may be) which he made his copy-text. He does not take into account the fact that, if in the twelve surviving copies of the first Quarto eight out of the twenty formes present textual variants, variants resulting from proof-reading and press corrections may surely be expected in the seventeen formes of the Folio text as preserved in more than two hundred extant copies. I happen to know that a minute collation of the text of another play in more than fifty copies of the first Folio has led to the discovery of variants in half of the formes, and when the nature of the printer's copy for the Folio text of *Lear* is recalled, it becomes incredible that proof-reading should not have resulted in the introduction of variants quite as noteworthy as those in the first Quarto which have been so meticulously evaluated. Not that Duthie may reasonably be expected to collate two hundred odd copies of the Folio before making his text. The task is at present physically and financially impossible. But it should be recognized once and for all that until all the Folios have been collated, it is not possible to speak or write of *the* Folio reading. Let one example suffice. At v, iii, 170, the first Quarto reads:

> My name is *Edgar*, and thy fathers sonne,

Duthie reads, without comment;

> My name is Edgar and thy Fathers Sonne,

Now this last is the reading in certain copies of the Folio and also in the Methuen facsimile; in other copies, however, and in the Lee facsimile, there is a comma after *Edgar*, as in the first

Quarto. The difference is not, as might be supposed, a case of press correction but simply a matter of inking. In certain copies, the comma was too lightly inked to print.[1] This variant is inconsequential,[2] but collation of as few as a dozen copies might bring to light substantive variants in the Folio of the sort which were introduced by Duthie's 'Scribe E' when he corrected a copy of the Quarto for the printer—in a word, such collation may be expected to recapture authentic Shakespearian readings now unknown.

In a detailed study[3] Harry A. Hoppe solves many of the puzzles in the first Quarto of *Romeo and Juliet*. The records of John Danter's brief and troubled career as a printer and publisher supply details that Hoppe integrates with the facts known about Lord Hunsdon's men and enable him to date the publication of this play, for which there is no entry in the Stationers' Register, within narrow limits. Danter appears to have begun work between 9 February and 17 March 1597 but to have been compelled by the seizure of his types and presses after only quires A to D had been completed to turn the job over to another man, possibly Edward Allde, who printed quires E to K in a different measure with types of a smaller size. Hoppe's account of the bibliographical peculiarities of the Quarto supersedes previous studies.

The stigmata of memorial reconstruction are so manifest and numerous that Hoppe disposes readily of earlier hypotheses that the first Quarto represents a preliminary draft or that it is the result of shorthand reporting. Instead, he believes that this Quarto is a reported text that derives ultimately from performances of a version like that preserved in the second Quarto. His analyses of the evidence are enriched by a clear statement of the difficulties an Elizabethan actor had in becoming letter perfect in a role (he never did) and by voluminous parallels from other 'bad' quartos.

The widely variant versions of II, vi and part of v, iii in the two Quartos are accounted for by the supposition that the actors who reconstituted the text had recently participated in the performance of an abbreviated text from which these lines had been largely or entirely omitted and that they were compelled to reconstruct the passages in question from their vague recollections of earlier performances of the complete text.

The first Quarto seems to Hoppe to require only about twelve actors and no musicians, as against the twenty players required for a performance of the second, which introduces instrumental music, and he cites numerous textual modifications to meet the needs of the smaller troupe. He notes, however, as did Greg before him, the presence of echoes of passages in the uncut version. At least one of the reporters could produce tolerable blank verse at a need, and this he did with greatest success when he was least trammelled by remembered phrases of the authentic text. The paucity of unmistakable mishearings suggests that oral dictation, in which one person acts as scribe while the others dictate their parts, did not play an important part in the transmission of the text; rather, the scribe was one of the actor-reporters, whose familiarity with the play and whose poetic skill enabled him to correct obvious errors.

[1] I am indebted to Charlton Hinman for calling this variant to my attention.

[2] Omission of the comma in all copies of the Folio might have been the result of the choice of the compositor or of deliberate alteration by Duthie's 'Scribe E'. Its presence in some copies and absence in others as a result of press correction would have to be explained as a deliberate insertion or removal of type, depending on the direction of the change.

[3] *The Bad Quarto of 'Romeo and Juliet'. A Bibliographical and Textual Study.* Cornell Studies in English, XXXVI (Ithaca: Cornell University Press; London: Geoffrey Cumberlege, 1948).

The actors whose lines are most accurately reproduced played Romeo and Paris, one or the other being present in all but seven scenes. Of these seven, six are badly reported; the exception is I, iii, which, with portions of I, ii, is partly set in the second Quarto from the corresponding pages of the first Quarto. The average of good lines in the episodes in which Romeo or Paris appears is generally 50 per cent or higher; in other episodes it seldom rises above 35 per cent. This is important, for it clears the book-keeper of the guilt that has sometimes been imputed to him in the theft of texts from Shakespeare's company.

Hoppe suggests diffidently that Gabriel Spencer and William Bird, who early in 1597 transferred from some London company (possibly the Chamberlain's) to the newly reorganized Pembroke's, may well have been the actor-reporters. The Chamberlain's men, who were in a shaky position following the death of the first Lord Hunsdon in July 1596, may, he thinks, have dropped some of their hired men before going on tour, including Spencer and Bird. (It may be objected, however, that *Romeo* is most likely to have been given in abbreviated form only while the company was in the provinces and that this touring version is probably the one chiefly represented in the first Quarto—if so, the defecting actors must have accompanied the travelling company on at least part of its journey before being dropped.) Chettle is named as a third potential reporter of this first Quarto.

If all of Hoppe's points have not been proved with equal finality, for the necessary data are sometimes wanting, he is always careful to point out the difficulties. He seems not quite decided whether the copy for the first Quarto was prepared originally for use as a prompt-book or for sale to a publisher, or for both purposes, and there are typographical links between the two Quartos that are not yet adequately discussed. But the book is a valuable contribution to Shakespeare scholarship.

"The Bibliographical Links Between the First Two Quartos of *Romeo and Juliet*" is the title of an article[1] in which Sidney Thomas argues cogently that the bibliographical dependence of the second on the first Quarto is more extensive than generally admitted and that this dependence is directly upon the printed page, unedited by a corrector. Thomas makes a further contribution to the discussion of mooted points by adducing contributory evidence[2] that *A Shrew* is not a corrupt rendering of *The Shrew* but derives from an earlier version. While Grumio of *The Shrew* is an unusually short person, Sander of *A Shrew* is at least average in height, and part of the comedy in the latter play, but not in the former, consists of railing scenes between a small page and a tall clown. "It is easy to believe", Thomas concludes, "that an actor or reporter, reconstructing the text of a play from memory or incomplete notes, could garble lines and confuse scenes, but it is rather more difficult to assume that he could forget the physical characteristics of the principal clown in the piece, or the low-comedy business."

There is nothing so stimulating as seeing Shakespeare's plays in performance. The presentation of *Pericles* at the Stratford Memorial Theatre in 1947 afforded many people their first experience of the theatrical effectiveness of this much maligned play, and two valuable articles may be traced directly to this revival. T. M. Parrott's review[3] of the whole matter of the origin and

[1] *Review of English Studies*, XXV (April 1949), 110–14.

[2] "A Note on *The Taming of the Shrew*", *Modern Language Notes*, LXIV (February 1949), 94–6.

[3] "*Pericles*: The Play and the Novel", *Shakespeare Association Bulletin*, XXIII (July 1948), 105–13. See also his *Shakespearean Comedy*, pp. 366–75.

publication of the play confesses the source of its inspiration, and Hardin Craig[1] was among the fortunate who sat comfortably in the theatre by the Avon and applauded the performance. Assuming that the "booke called the booke of Pericles prynce of Tyre" which Edward Blount entered in the Stationers' Register on 10 May 1608 was an original or a transcribed prompt-book of a play, Parrott briefly presents his reasons for believing that this was an early version by Heywood or another; that Shakespeare was commissioned to revise or improve it, his handiwork being everywhere traceable after the close of Act II; that Henry Gosson procured and printed a stenographic or memorial report of the theatrical performances of this revision; and that George Wilkins and his publisher, Nathaniel Butter, attempted to cash in on the popularity of the play by publishing a novelized version, *The Painfull Adventures of Pericles Prince of Tyre* (1608). He deplores the influence on Heminges and Condell of Ben Jonson, who "seems to have [had] very special aversion" for this "mouldy tale" (the phrase is Jonson's), and whom Parrott blames for the exclusion of *Pericles* from the first Folio. The King's men, he reminds us, performed the play at Court on 20 May 1619 and he thinks Jonson's aversion has deprived us of the knowledge of the prompt-book used in that performance, a prompt-book that "contained a fuller and clearer text than the thing of rags and patches which has come down to us to puzzle and distract the modern editor".

A detailed comparison of Wilkins' novel with the play confirms Craig in the belief that the former is primarily an account of a theatrical performance, "in telling [which] Wilkins introduces gestures and actions he had presumably seen on the stage", supplemented by long passages lifted from Twine's *Pattern of Painfull Adventures*. Few discrepancies exist between play and novel in Acts I, II and III, except that the more detailed account of the starving city of Tarsus in Wilkins may indicate that at this point a scene has been cut from the play.[2] The major discrepancies in Acts IV and V are, in Craig's opinion, the result of what may be called a post-Wilkins revision by Shakespeare. These discrepancies occur in precisely the passages in which Shakespeare's hand is most readily traced; and so Craig appears to suggest that Shakespeare's part in the play may be limited to a revision late in 1608. This is indeed startling. What, may one ask, is to be done about Pericles' apostrophe to the new-born Marina, "Poore inch of Nature", which occurs in the novel and of which Chambers writes, "surely in its setting it is Shakespearean"? The character of Lysimachus and the moral tone of the incidents in which he participates are so different in Shakespeare—and so consonant with the character of the Duke and the moral tone of *Measure for Measure*—that Craig asserts they originate in a post-Wilkins revision.

Pericles, Craig thinks, is not a 'bad' quarto, "but from the points of view of adequacy and completeness appears to be a good quarto, the result of painstaking revision.... What has made the text seem worse than it is is the fact that no quarto, except possibly the 1608 version of *King Lear*, has so much verse printed as prose". This is "no casual matter", he continues, "to be accounted for as a marginal revision. One is obliged to conclude that the reviser wrote a great deal of his verse in the form of prose, a practice not without parallel in Elizabethan manuscripts, of which there are other cases in Shakespearean texts, the 'Pide Bull' quarto of *King Lear* being the most conspicuous". And since he finds no signs of a prompt-hand in the first Quarto, Craig

---

[1] "*Pericles* and *The Painfull Adventures*", *Studies in Philology*, XLV (October 1948), 600–5.

[2] If so, Craig observes, T. S. Graves may have been correct in advocating that a performance of *Pericles* was given as early as 1606. In that case, of course, the reprint of Twine in 1607 may have been caused by the play's popularity.

believes that the play was printed from a manuscript consisting of a transcript of an *Ur-Pericles* with interpolated pages on which in Shakespeare's hand are the passages attributed to him, written in the form of unlined blank verse.

This thesis should be tested in every possible way. Are there Shakespearian spellings in the revisionary passages? Or did Shakespeare transcribe the whole play? Is there any external evidence that Shakespeare ever wrote unlined verse? The additions to the play of *Sir Thomas More* afford no support to the proposition. Nor will Craig find comfort in the statement of Heminges and Condell that Shakespeare's "mind and hand went together: And what he thought, he vttered with that easinesse, that wee haue scarse receiued from him a blot in his papers". It would be most remarkable that the compositors of the second Quarto of *Hamlet*, for example, could line Shakespeare's verse with such success if the foul papers they received as copy consisted of unlined poetry.

But to dwell on this point is to miss the main purpose of the article. I find the suggestion of a post-Wilkins revision attractive (i.e. a revision made after the publication of Wilkins' novel; the possibility that Wilkins had a hand in the play is ignored); but if Ben Jonson disliked *Pericles* so much and criticized it so harshly, is it not possible that the pre-Wilkins *Pericles* contained at least a considerable amount of Shakespeare? Or to put it more directly, may there not be two stages of Shakespearian revision in *Pericles* as we have it, a revision before Wilkins wrote his novel and a second revision between that time and the publication of the play? And may not the second revision have been made as a result of Jonson's criticism, as Dover Wilson thinks the text of *Julius Caesar* was modified to meet Jonson's objections? (See *Shakespeare Survey*, II, 36–43.)

The initial volume of *The Papers of the Bibliographical Society of the University of Virginia* contains two articles of direct Shakespearian interest. Philip Williams adds one more bit of information about the 'Pide Bull' quarto of *Lear* in a neat demonstration[1] that the text was set by one compositor. And Giles E. Dawson continues his investigation[2] of eighteenth-century editions of Shakespeare's plays and of the printing-house practices that frequently appear to have been followed on the shady side of the law. As Shakespeare was the most pirated playwright in his own day, so he seems to have continued to be in the eighteenth century. It is a thing to be wondered at that the works of a century-dead playwright should have been the focal point in the battle which upset the old concepts of copyright and helped establish new ones.

In another paper[3] Dawson relates some of the practices of the seventeenth-century publishers and states his belief that the system "worked fairly well.... A copyright could change hands quite smoothly and quite securely without any entry being made in the Register....And the members of the Stationers' Company were undoubtedly well satisfied with a system of copyright which relied to a large degree upon common gossip, verbal agreements not recorded, and informal notes not preserved."

---

[1] "The Composition of the 'Pied Bull' *Lear*", *Papers of the Bibliographical Society of the University of Virginia*, I, (ed. F. T. Bowers; Charlottesville, Virginia, 1948), 59–68.

[2] "Three Shakespeare Piracies in the Eighteenth Century", *loc. cit.* pp. 47–58.

[3] "Copyright of Plays in the Early Seventeenth Century", *English Institute Essays*, 1947, pp. 169–92.

BOOKS RECEIVED

BROOKE, C. F. TUCKER. *Essays on Shakespeare and Other Elizabethans* (Oxford University Press, 1948).

BROWN, IVOR. *Shakespeare* (London: Collins, 1949).

BRUNNER, KARL (ed.). *William Shakespeare, Romeo und Julia. Englischer Text mit deutscher Übersetzung nach August Wilhelm Schlegel.* Textrevision, Einleitung und Anmerkungen von Dr Karl Brunner (Britisch-Amerikanische Bibliothek. Linz: Österreichischer Verlag für Belletristik und Wissenchaft, 1947).

CHARLTON, H. B. *Shakespearian Tragedy* (Cambridge University Press, 1948).

CROCE, BENEDETTO. *Shakespeare.* Nuova edizione con introduzione e note di NAPOLEONE ORSINI (Biblioteca di cultura moderna, n. 129. Bari: Laterza, 1948).

DANBY, JOHN F. *Shakespeare's Doctrine of Nature. A Study of 'King Lear'* (London: Faber and Faber, 1949).

DUTHIE, GEORGE IAN. *Shakespeare's 'King Lear'. A Critical Edition* (Oxford: Blackwell, 1949).

ELLIS-FERMOR, UNA. *Shakespeare the Dramatist.* Annual Shakespeare Lecture of the British Academy, 1948. From the *Proceedings of the British Academy*, vol. XXXIV (London: Cumberlege).

English Institute Essays, 1947 (New York: Columbia University Press, 1948).

FARJEON, HERBERT. *The Shakespearean Scene. Dramatic Criticisms* (London: Hutchinson, [1949]).

FLATTER, RICHARD. *Hamlet's Father* (London: Heinemann, 1949).

FLATTER, RICHARD. *Shakespeare's Producing Hand. A Study of his Marks of Expression to be found in the First Folio* (London: Heinemann, 1948).

GÜNTHER, ALFRED. *Der junge Shakespeare. Sieben unbekannte Jahre* (Stuttgart: Deutsche Verlags-Anstalt, 1947).

HEILMAN, ROBERT B. *This Great Stage. Image and Structure in 'King Lear'* (Louisiana State University Press, 1948).

HOGAN, J. J. (ed.). *The Tragedy of Hamlet Prince of Denmark.* The Malone Shakespeare (Dublin: Browne and Nolan, n.d.).

HOPPE, HARRY R. *The Bad Quarto of 'Romeo and Juliet'. A Bibliographical and Textual Study.* Cornell Studies in English, vol. XXXVI (Cornell University Press; London: Cumberlege, 1948).

KNIGHT, G. WILSON. *The Wheel of Fire. Interpretations of Shakespearian Tragedy with Three New Essays.* Fourth edition, revised and enlarged (London: Methuen, 1949).

LAFINUR, LUIS MELIÁN. *Las Mujeres de Shakespeare.* Con un prólogo de Alvaro Melián Lafinur (Montevideo: Claudio Garcia, 1942).

O'CONNOR, FRANK. *The Road to Stratford* (London: Methuen, 1948).

OPPEL, HORST. *Das Shakespeare-Bild Goethes* (Mainz: Kirchheim, 1949).

Proceedings of the British Academy, vol. XXX, 1944 (London: Published for the British Academy by Geoffrey Cumberlege).

SCHÜCKING, LEVIN L. *Shakespeare und der Tragödienstil seiner Zeit* (Berne: Francke, 1947).

SEDGEWICK, G. G. *Of Irony, Especially in Drama* (University of Toronto Press, 1948).

Shakespeare Association Bulletin, The, vol. XXIII, 1948.

Shakespeare Összes Drámai Müvei (Franklin-Társulat Kiadása, 4 vols. n.d.).

SITWELL, EDITH. *A Notebook on William Shakespeare* (London: Macmillan, 1948).

STAHL, ERNST LEOPOLD. *Shakespeare und das Deutsche Theater. Wanderung und Wandelung seines Werkes in dreiundeinhalb Jahrhunderten.* Mit Bilddokumenten zusammengestellt von Carl Niessen (Stuttgart: Kohlhammer, 1947).

Stanislavsky Produces 'Othello'. Translated from the Russian by Dr Helen Nowak (London: Bles, 1948).

STEWART, J. I. M. *Character and Motive in Shakespeare. Some Recent Appraisals Examined* (London: Longmans, Green and Co., 1949).

VAN TIEGHEM, PAUL. *Le préromantisme. Études d'histoire littéraire européenne. La découverte de Shakespeare sur le continent* (Paris: Sfelt, 1947).

WALKER, ROY. *The Time is Free: A Study of 'Macbeth'* (London: Dakers, 1949).

WILLIAMSON, AUDREY. *Old Vic Drama: A Twelve Years' Study of Plays and Players.* Foreword by Dame Sybil Thorndike (London: Rockliff, 1948).

WILSON, J. DOVER. *Alfred William Pollard, 1859–1944.* From the *Proceedings of the British Academy,* vol. XXXI (London: Cumberlege).

WILSON, J. DOVER (ed.). *Titus Andronicus.* The New Shakespeare (Cambridge University Press, 1948).

Year's Work in English Studies, The, vol. XXVII, 1946. Edited for the English Association by F. S. BOAS (Oxford University Press, 1948).

INDEX

INDEX

INDEX

INDEX

INDEX

Napoleon, 99, 100
Nashe, Thomas, 25, 45
   Pierce Pennilesse, 54
Neale, J. E., *Queen Elizabeth*, 7
Neilson, W. A., 31
Neveux, Georges, translation of *Othello*, 104–5
Newcastle, William Cavendish, Duke of, *The Country Captain*, 52
Newington Butts, *see* Theatre, Elizabethan: Playhouses
New York Public Library, 48
Nielsen, Carl, 114
Nielsen, Hans Jacob, 114
Niessen, Carl, 117
Noble, Richmond, 28
North, Sir Thomas, translation of Plutarch, 6, 18, 54
Northamptonshire, 34
Northumberland, Earl of, *see* Percy
Norway, report on Shakespeare in, 118

O'Connor, Frank, *The Road to Stratford* reviewed, 133–4
Ognanyov, L., 116
Ojetti, Paola, 118
Old Vic Company, 114, 135
Olivier, Sir Laurence, 113, 114
   film of *Hamlet*, 119
O'Loughlin, S., *The Voyage to Illyria*, 9
Olympic Games, 1936, 96
Onions, C. T., 6
Open-air theatres, German, 95–7
Orságh, L., 117
Orsini, Napoleone, edition of Croce's *Shakespeare* reviewed, 130, 132
Österberg, Valdemar, 110
   translations of Shakespeare, 111–12
Othello (*see also under* Shakespeare), history of, on French stage:
   Aicard's version, 103
   de Vigny's version, 102–3
   early translations, 99
   English tours, 100–2
   necessary approach, 105–6
   operatic versions, 100
   popularity, 98
   recent productions, 104–6
   Sarment's version, 104
   Voltaire's *Zaïre*, 98
Ottosen, Ingeman, *Shakespeare under Elizabeth*, 111
Ovid, 14, 19
   Metamorphoses, 4, 6
Oxford, Edward de Vere, Earl of, 11
Oxford University, 74

Painter, William, *Palace of Pleasure*, 54
Parabosco, *Il Pellegrino*, 90
Paris Garden, *see* London
Parrott, T. M., 24, 136, 145, 146
   "*Pericles*: The Play and the Novel" reviewed, 150–1
Pasta, Mme G., 100
Patrick, D. L., 23
Paul, H. N., 27, 29, 30
Peacham, Henry, illustration of *Titus Andronicus*, 146–7
Peele, George, 24, 45, 145
   Anglorum Feriae, Englandes Hollydayes, 52
   Honour of the Garter, 24, 145
Pembroke's Men, *see* Theatre, Elizabethan: Companies
Penley, S., and family, 100
Percy, Henry, Earl of Northumberland, 10, 25
Pericles (*see also under* Shakespeare), problems of text and authorship, 150–2
Perrett, A. J., 147
Perrett, Wilfrid, 18
Péter, András, 117
Petőfi, Sándor 117
Petrarch, Francis, 15
Piachaud, René-Louis, translation of *Othello*, 105
Place, P. A. de la, 98
Plato, 6
Plautus, 15
   Menaechmi, 53
Playford, John:
   Dancing Master, 56
   Select Ayres, 56
Plimpton, E. A., *The Education of Shakespeare*, 5
Plots of Elizabethan Plays, 51, 52
Plutarch, 6, 17, 36–9, 54
Poel, William, 74
Poland, report on Shakespeare in, 118
Politeuphuia, Wit's Commonwealth, 19
Pollard, A. W., 3, 28, 29, 31, 44, 45, 47, 50, 57, 143
Pope, Alexander, 1, 26, 49
Pope, E. M., "Renaissance Background of *Measure for Measure*", 66–73, 137, 141 n.
Porto, Luigi da, 54, 55
Portugal, report on Shakespeare in, 118–19
Pouch, Captain, 35, 41 n.
Poulsen, Johannes, 113, 114
Poulsen, Olaf, 112
Poynet, John, *Politic Power*, 20
Price, H. T.:
   "The First Quarto of *Titus Andronicus*" reviewed, 143–4
   "Mirror-Scenes in Shakespeare" reviewed, 144–5
Pride of Life, The, 20

INDEX

Date Due